# KU KLUX KLAN

America's First Terrorists

EXPOSED

The Rebirth of
the Strange Society of
Blood and Death

Published by
Idea Men Productions

*We do not fear censorship, for we have no wish to offend with improprieties or obscenities, but we do demand, as a right, the liberty to show the dark side of wrong, that we may illuminate the bright side of virtue ...*

- from the opening sequence of D. W. Griffith's
**THE BIRTH OF THE NATION** (1915)

Dedicated to the memory of Sheriff Robert "Bob" Buchanan of Lorena, Texas, for having the courage and conviction to hold the line.

Acknowledgments

Idea Men Productions would to thank:

Matt Jacobsen of OLDMAGAZINEARTICLES.com, a virtual treasure trove for researchers, and David Seitz of the New York Times.

Cover illustration by W. C. Nicolson

## IMP
presents

# KU KLUX KLAN
### AMERICA'S FIRST TERRORISTS EXPOSED

edited and
designed
by Patrick
O'Donnell

researched
by Edward
Robinson
& William
McCauley

Copyright 2006 © by Idea Men Productions
634 Eagle Rock Avenue, P. O. Box 354
West Orange, New Jersey 07052
ideamen@aol.com
www.ideamenproductions.com

All Rights Reserved.

ISBN:1-4196-4978-7

# Table of Contents

Publisher's Note..................................................................................IX
Introduction ......................................................................................XI

# I
## The Official Overview

Historical Background of the Ku Klux Klan ..........................................4
The Ku Klux Klan Act of April 30,1871................................................14
The Klan During and After World War I...............................................18

# II
## The Ku Klux Klan in Popular Culture, Politics, and Their Own Words

### Popular Culture

The Ku Klux Klan of 1866 - Its Origin, Growth, and Disbandment........36
New Light on The Ku Klux Klan..........................................................68
Facts about the Lynchings of 1914......................................................72
Last Year's Lynchings.........................................................................74
K. K. K. - The Strangest Secret Society on Earth..................................76
The Klan as a National Problem..........................................................90
New York's Anti-Klan Outburst............................................................94
Protestants Disowning the Ku Klux....................................................100
When the Klan Rules - The Giant in the White Hood..........................102
The Giant Clears for Action...............................................................112

### Politics

The Ku Klux and Politics...................................................................122
Klan Victories in Oregon and Texas...................................................126
The Ku Klux in Politics......................................................................130
Governor Allen on The Ku Klux Klan..................................................132
Invisible Government.......................................................................134
Night-Riding Reformers....................................................................136
The Klan Shows Its Hand in Indiana..................................................146

### Their Own Words

Symbolism of The Klan.....................................................................158
The Klan's Fight for Americanism .....................................................164

## III
### The K. K. K. Exposed! by Erza A. Cook

The Old Ku Klux Klan..........................................................................198
The New Ku Klux Klan..........................................................................214
How the Ku Klux Klan Was Organized....................................................218
Oath of the Ku Klux Klan......................................................................222
Modern Kleagles Pledge of Loyalty........................................................226
How the Dollars Roll In........................................................................234
The Ku Klux Klan and the Jews.............................................................238
The Ku Klux Klan and the Catholics......................................................242
The Ku Klux Klan and the Masons........................................................252
The Ku Klux Klan and the Negroes........................................................256
The Ku Klux Klan and Women..............................................................260
Atrocities Committed in the Name of the Order....................................262

### Is the Ku Klux Klan Constructive or Destructive?
A Debate Between Imperial Wizard Evans, Israel Zangwill and Others

Creed of the Klansman and Those Who Debate It.................................272
Mr. Zangwill Criticizes the Klan............................................................284
Terre Haute Mayor Talks......................................................................295
Prominent Klansman's Views...............................................................300
For the Colored Race...........................................................................305

Afterword...........................................................................................312

# WARNING

The Ku Klux Klan's reach in the 1920s was national. With it came an ongoing debate, pro, con, or studiedly neutral about the Hooded Society, its methods, motives and ultimate goals. The controversy was played out in the popular press -- the widely circulated newspapers and magazines of the day.

This book consists of primary source documents and articles, reprinted complete and unabridged. Readers are strongly cautioned that much of this text contains racial slurs, ethnic stereotyping, and other ugly and offensive material. This is the way and the terms in which the national dialogue on the Klan and other racial topics was conducted in that time.

To censor or suppress the texts would be to distort their true meaning and intent, and do a disservice to both the general reader and the historian of today.

Also, please note that the articles and documents reprinted here come from a multiplicity of sources, such as books, government documents, newspapers and magazines; each of which had its own editorial variations on spelling, punctuation and capitalization. Rather than standardize them, they have been presented here as they first appeared, to better convey the flavor and authenticity of the original texts.

THE BLACK MASK, a popular pulp mystery magazine, dedicated an entire issue on the subject of the Klan in 1923. Copyright 1923 Pro-Distributor Publishing Co., Inc.

# KU KLUX KLAN - AMERICA'S FIRST TERRORISTS EXPOSED

Publisher's Note by DAVID JACOBS

On Thanksgiving night, 1915, on Stone Mountain outside Atlanta, Georgia, a fiery cross blazed into being, signaling the rebirth of the Ku Klux Klan.

The original Klan came to being in the aftermath of the Civil War as an insurgency of former Confederate rebels against occupying Federal troops. It ended in the early 1870s primarily due to two reasons:

1. President U.S. Grant had cracked down hard on the KKK, directing Federals to arrest and neutralize its most egregious elements; and,

2. Whites throughout Dixie had succeeded in their aim of preserving their power base by thwarting Reconstruction and segregating by law their Black population into second-class status.

The 1915 revival of the Klan took place in a radically different world, one marked by rapid industrialization and technological innovation, and the dramatic social change and upheaval these had brought about.

This reborn Klan expanded its anti-Black bias to encompass Jews, Catholics and the foreign-born. In some ways, it sprang from the same impulse which had brought about the Prohibition acts and the national banning of alcoholic beverages (a program which the Klan, at least officially, endorsed): a nativist revolt against the perceived "immorality" (and rising power) of the big cities, with their "fast" ways and "foreign hordes."

By 1925, with a membership of about four million, the Klan was established throughout the United States. Its numbers were greater in northern states such as Indiana and Ohio than they were in the southern states. Its influence extended to countless city and country governments, including more than a few statehouses and not all of them in the South, either.

The Klan played no small role in the Presidential elections of 1928, which was contested by Republican candidate Herbert Hoover and Democratic candidate Al Smith. Smith's Catholicism was anathema to the KKK, which came out strongly against him. Crosses were burned in the hills of Long Island, outside Smith's New York City hometown, another ugly incident in what experts reckon as one of America's all-time dirtiest political campaigns (no mean feat, that).

Hoover won the election. A year later, the stock market crashed, sending the nation lurching into economic ruin. President Hoover's do-nothing policies helped balloon the slump into a catastrophe that would become known as the Great Depression.

At the same time, the Klan ceased to be a power in the land. With banks gone bust, businesses bankrupted, millions of people with their life savings wiped out and millions more unemployed, the KKK ceased to be a player on the national stage.

It had been brought low by its nemesis, the ultimate foe the Klan had set itself against: the complexities of the modern world.

[David Jacobs has authored more than twenty books, including THE BEST OF COURT TV: TO YOUNG TO DIE, THE SHIELD- NOTES FROM THE BARN: THE ELITE STRIKE TEAM FILES, and THE MAFIA'S GREATEST HITS.]

Reprinted from ONLY YESTERDAY: AN INFORMAL HISTORY OF THE 1920'S published in 1931, Harper & Row

Introduction by FREDERICK LEWIS ALLEN

Illustration by Art Young

Intolerance during the 1920s took many forms. Almost inevitably it took the form of an ugly flare-up of feeling against the Negro, the Jew, and the Roman Catholic. The emotions of group loyalty and of hatred, expanded during war-time and then suddenly denied their intended expression, found a perverted release in the persecution not only of supposed radicals, but also of other elements which to the dominant American group--the white Protestants--seemed alien or "un-American."

Negroes had migrated during the war by the hundreds of thousands into the industrial North, drawn thither by high wages and by the openings in mill and factory occasioned by the draft. Wherever their numbers increased they had no choice but to move into districts previously reserved for the whites, there to jostle with the whites in street cars and public places, and in a hundred other ways to upset the delicate equilibrium of racial adjustment. In the South as well as in the North the Negroes had felt the stirrings of a new sense of independence; had they not been called to the colors just as the whites had been, and had they not been fighting for democracy and oppressed minorities? When peace came, and they found they were to be put in their place once more, some of them showed their resentment; and in the uneasy atmosphere of the day this was enough to kindle the violent racial passions which smolder under the surface of human nature. Bolshevism was bad enough, thought the whites, but if the niggers ever got beyond control . . .

One sultry afternoon in the summer of 1919 a seventeen-year-old colored boy was swimming in Lake Michigan by a Chicago bathing-beach. Part of the shore had been set aside by mutual understanding for the use of the whites, another part for the Negroes. The boy took hold of a railroad tie floating in the water and drifted across the invisible line. Stones were thrown at him; a white boy started to swim toward him. The colored boy let go of the railroad tie, swam a few strokes, and sank. He was drowned. Whether he had been hit by any of the stones was uncertain, but the Negroes on the shore accused the whites of stoning him to death, and a fight began. This small incident struck the match that set off a bonfire of race hatred. The Negro population of Chicago had doubled in a decade, the blacks had crowded into white neighborhoods, and nerves were raw. The disorder spread to other parts of the city--and the final result was that for nearly a week Chicago was virtually in a state of civil war; there were mobbings of Negroes, beatings, stabbings, gang raids through the Negro district, shootings by Negroes in defense, and wanton destruction of houses and property; when order was finally restored it was found that fifteen whites and twenty-three Negroes had been killed, five hundred and thirty-seven people had been injured, and a thousand had been left homeless and destitute.

Less than a year later there was another riot of major proportions in Tulsa. Wherever the colored population had spread, there was a new tension in the relations between the races. It was not alleviated by the gospel of white supremacy preached by speakers and writers such as Lothrop Stoddard, whose Rising Tide of Color proclaimed that the dark-skinned races constituted a worse threat to Western civilization than the Germans or the Bolsheviks.

## INTRODUCTION

The Jews, too, fell under the suspicion of a majority bent upon an undiluted Americanism. Here was a group of inevitably divided loyalty, many of whose members were undeniably prominent among the Bolsheviki in Russia and among the radical immigrants in America. Henry Ford discovered the menace of the "International Jew," and his Dearborn Independent accused the unhappy race of plotting the subjugation of the whole world and (for good measure) of being the source of almost every American affliction, including high rents, the shortage of farm labor, jazz, gambling, drunkenness, loose morals, and even short skirts. The Ford attack, absurd as it was, was merely an exaggerated manifestation of a widespread anti-Semitism. Prejudice became as pervasive as the air. Landlords grew less disposed to rent to Jewish tenants, and schools to admit Jewish boys and girls; there was a public scandal at Annapolis over the hazing of a Jewish boy; Harvard College seriously debated limiting the number of Jewish students; and all over the country Jews felt that a barrier had fallen between them and the Gentiles. Nor did the Roman Catholics escape censure in the regions in which they were in a minority. Did not the members of this Church take their orders from a foreign pope, and did not the pope claim temporal power, and did not Catholics insist upon teaching their children in their own way rather than in the American public schools, and was not all this un-American and treasonable?

It was in such an atmosphere that the Ku Klux Klan blossomed into power.

The Klan had been founded as far back as 1915 by a Georgian named Colonel William Joseph Simmons, but its first five years had been lean. When 1920 arrived, Colonel Simmons had only a few hundred members in his amiable patriotic and fraternal order, which drew its inspiration from the Ku Klux Klan of Reconstruction days and stood for white supremacy and sentimental Southern idealism in general. But in 1920 Simmons put the task of organizing the Order into the hands of one Edward Y. Clarke of the Southern Publicity Association. Clarke's gifts of salesmanship, hitherto expended on such blameless causes as the

Roosevelt Memorial Association and the Near East Relief, were prodigious. The time was ripe for the Klan, and he knew it. Not only could it be represented to potential members as the defender of the white against the black, of Gentile against Jew, and of Protestant against Catholic, and thus trade on all the newly inflamed fears of the credulous small-towner, but its white robe and hood, its flaming cross, its secrecy, and the preposterous vocabulary of its ritual could be made the vehicle for all that infantile love of hocus-pocus and mummery, that lust for secret adventure, which survives in the adult whose lot is cast in drab places. Here was a chance to dress up the village bigot and let him be a Knight of the Invisible Empire. The formula was perfect. And there was another inviting fact to be borne in mind. Well organized, such an Order could be made a paying proposition.

The salesmen of memberships were given the entrancing title of Kleagles; the country was divided into Realms headed by King Kleagles, and the Realms into Domains headed by Grand Goblins; Clarke himself, as chief organizer, became Imperial Kleagle, and the art of nomenclature reached its fantastic pinnacle in the title bestowed upon Colonel Simmons: he became the Imperial Wizard. A membership cost ten dollars; and as four of this went into the pocket of the Kleagle who made the sale, it was soon apparent that a diligent Kleagle need not fear the wolf at the door. Kleagling became one of the profitable industries of the decade. The King Kleagle of the Realm and Grand Goblin of the Domain took a small rake-off from the remaining six dollars of the membership fee, and the balance poured into the Imperial Treasury at Atlanta.

An inconvenient congressional investigation in 1921--brought about largely by sundry reports of tarrings and featherings and floggings, and by the disclosure of many of the Klan's secrets by the New York World--led ultimately to the banishment of Imperial Kleagle Clarke, and Colonel Simmons was succeeded as Imperial Wizard by a Texas dentist named Hiram Wesley Evans, who referred to himself, perhaps with some justice, as "the most average man in America"; but a humming sales organization had been built up and the Klan continued to grow. It grew, in fact, with such inordinate rapidity that early in 1924 its membership had reached according to the careful estimates of Stanley Frost--the staggering figure of nearly four and a half million. It came to wield great political power, dominating for a time the seven states of Oregon, Oklahoma, Texas, Arkansas, Indiana, Ohio, and California. Its chief strongholds were the New South, the Middle West, and the Pacific coast, but it had invaded almost every part of the country and had even reached the gates of that stronghold of Jewry, Catholicism, and sophistication, New York City. So far had Clarke's genius and the hospitable temper of the times carried it.

The objects of the Order as stated in its Constitution were "to unite white male persons, native-born Gentile citizens of the United States of America, who owe no allegiance of any nature to any foreign government, nation, institution, sect, ruler, person, or people; whose morals are good, whose reputations and vocations are exemplary . . . to cultivate and promote patriotism toward our Civil Government; to practice an honorable Klanishness toward each other; to exemplify a practical benevolence; to shield the sanctity of the home and the chastity of womanhood; to maintain forever white supremacy, to reach and faithfully inculcate a high spiritual philosophy through an exalted ritualism, and by a practical devotion to conserve, protect, and maintain the distinctive institutions, rights, privileges, principles, traditions and ideals of a pure Americanism."

Thus the theory. In practice the "pure Americanism" varied with the locality. At first, in the South, white supremacy was the Klan's chief objective, but as time went on and the organization grew and spread, opposition to the Jew and above all to the Catholic proved the best talking point for Kleagles in most localities. Nor did the methods of the local Klan organizations usually suggest the possession of a "high spiritual philosophy." These local organizations were largely autonomous and beyond control from Atlanta. They were drawn, as a rule, mostly from the less educated and less disciplined elements of the white Protestant community. ("You think the influential men belong here?" commented an outspoken observer in an Indiana city. "Then look at their shoes when they march in parade. The sheet doesn't cover the shoes.") Though Imperial

Wizard Evans inveighed against lawlessness, the members of the local Klans were not always content with voting against allowing children to attend parochial schools, or voting against Catholic candidates for office, or burning fiery crosses on the hilltop back of the town to show the niggers that the whites meant business. The secrecy of the Klan was an invitation to more direct action.

If a white girl reported that a colored man had made improper advances to her--even if the charge were unsupported and based on nothing more than a neurotic imagination--a white-sheeted band might spirit the Negro off to the woods and "teach him a lesson" with tar and feathers or with the whip. If a white man stood up for a Negro in a race quarrel, he might be kidnapped and beaten up. If a colored woman refused to sell her land at an arbitrary price which she considered too low, and a Klansman wanted the land, she might receive the K. K. K. ultimatum--sell or be thrown out. Klan members would boycott Jewish merchants, refuse to hire Catholic boys, refuse to rent their houses to Catholics. A hideous tragedy in Louisiana, where five men were kidnapped and later found bound with wire and drowned in a lake, was laid to Klansmen. R. A. Patton, writing in Current History, reported a grim series of brutalities from Alabama: "A lad whipped with branches until his back was ribboned flesh; a Negress beaten and left helpless to contract pneumonia from exposure and die; a white girl, divorcée, beaten into unconsciousness in her own home; a naturalized foreigner flogged until his back was a pulp because he married an American woman; a Negro lashed until he sold his land to a white man for a fraction of its value."

Even where there were no such outrages, there was at least the threat of them. The white-robed army paraded, the burning cross glowed across the valley, people whispered to one another in the darkness and wondered "who they were after this time," and fear and suspicion ran from house to house. Furthermore, criminals and gangs of hoodlums quickly learned to take advantage of the Klan's existence: if they wanted to burn someone's barn or raid the slums beyond the railroad tracks, they could do

INTRODUCTION

it with impunity now: would not the Klan be held responsible? Anyone could chalk the letters K. K. K. on a fence and be sure that the sheriff would move warily. Thus, as in the case of the Red hysteria, a movement conceived in fear perpetuated fear and brought with it all manner of cruelties and crimes.

Slowly, as the years passed and the war-time emotions ebbed, the power of the Klan waned, until in many districts it was dead and in others it had become merely a political faction dominated by spoilsmen, but not until it had become a thing of terror to millions of men and women.

FREDERICK LEWIS ALLEN

Scarsdale, New York June, 1931

[During his literary career, Frederick Lewis Allen worked for such magazines as ATLANTIC MONTHLY, CENTURY and HARPER'S. He is most remembered as a notable American Historian focusing on the events of the first half of the twentieth century. His books include, ONLY YESTERDAY: AN INFORMAL HISTORY OF THE 1920'S IN AMERICA ,SINCE YESTERDAY: THE 1930'S IN AMERICA and THE BIG CHANGE: AMERICA TRANSFORMS ITSELF, 1900-1950.]

# I

The

Official

Overview

Illustration by Arthur I. Keller from Thomas Dixon's THE CLANSMAN (1905)

HISTORICAL BACKGROUND ON THE KU KLUX KLAN is from THE PRESENT-DAY KU KLUX KLAN MOVEMENT, December 11, 1967 report by the Committee on Un-American Activities, House of Representatives, Ninetieth Congress, First Session - Edwin E. Willis, Chairman.

[COMMITTEE PRINT]

# THE PRESENT-DAY KU KLUX KLAN MOVEMENT

## REPORT

BY THE

### COMMITTEE ON UN-AMERICAN ACTIVITIES
HOUSE OF REPRESENTATIVES
NINETIETH CONGRESS
FIRST SESSION

Prepared and released by the Committee on Un-American Activities

## HISTORICAL BACKGROUND

Present-day klan organizations customarily dedicate themselves to commemorating the achievements of the Ku Klux Klan of the Reconstruction era and to perpetuating the principles of the first phalanx of nightriders to appear on the American scene.

Modern klans furthermore promise to save the Nation just as their forerunners allegedly saved the Nation following the Civil War.

Some reference to historical antecedents is therefore essential to understand the activities of klansmen in the 20th century.

## THE RECONSTRUCTION KLAN

The six Confederate Army veterans credited with originating the Ku Klux Klan on Christmas Eve of 1865 in Pulaski, Tenn., are not memorialized in current klan literature. These young men had adapted the Greek word for circle (kuklos) in christening their new organization. They had devised mystical titles and a ritual for a membership sworn to secrecy. And they were responsible for converting bed linen into a means of disguise. Their purpose, however, was reputedly pure amusement.

The organization to which modern klansmen pay homage was the Ku Klux Klan headed by Nathan Bedford Forrest, which officially operated in at least nine Southern States from 1867 to 1869 and unofficially for some years thereafter.

The conversion of klan purposes from amusement to terrorism had already been demonstrated by the time representatives of various local klan "dens" held a unifying convention in Nashville, Tenn., in 1867 and elected former Confederate Army General Forrest as their grand wizard. Stimulative of the klan's new purposes were a series of laws enacted by the

U.S. Congress beginning in 1866 which sought to bestow civil rights on the recently freed slaves, and the Reconstruction Act of March 1867 which substituted military governments for the locally created governments in most of the former secessionist States.

"Maintenance of the supremacy of the white race" was selected as the "main and fundamental objective" of the Ku Klux Klan led by General Forrest. Membership was restricted to those who would oppose not only Negro "social and political equality" but also the Radicals then dominant in the U.S. Congress who were to be defeated in order to "restore State sovereignty." A set of outwardly laudable aims adopted by the organization called for support of the U.S. Constitution, assistance in execution of all constitutional laws, protection of the weak and innocent, relief of the injured and oppressed, and succoring of the unfortunate, especially widows and orphans. (The same objectives have been repeated almost word for word by succeeding klan organizations up to the present time; the exception being that Radical is spelled with a small "r" in the contemporary situation.

By the autumn of 1868, General Forrest estimated klan membership at 550,000. Although he claimed to have disbanded the organization early the following year on the grounds that it was no longer needed for "self-protection," Ku Klux Klan terrorism continued to mount over the next few years to such a degree that the President and Members of Congress demanded action to remedy the "insecurity of life and property" in some of the Southern States.

The Congress acted against racial violence in three civil rights laws, loosely known as the Ku Klux Klan Acts. Section 6 of an act of May 31, 1870, provided criminal penalties for persons who conspire or who go in disguise on the public highways or on the premises of another with intent to deprive him of rights and privileges granted by the Constitution or laws of the United States. The voting safeguards set forth in other sections of this act were amended and supplemented by an act of February 28, 1871. Finally, on April 20, 1871, Congress approved an act enforcing the provisions of the 14th amendment which included, among other things, Presidential authority to use military force to prevent interference with court civil rights orders. (1)

As the President signed the third act directed against the Ku Klux Klan, a joint congressional committee of 7 Senators and 14 Representatives was organized to investigate the secret order. Formally known as the Joint Select Committee on the Condition of Affairs in the Late Insurrectionary States, this investigating committee held 57 days of hearings in Washington, D.C., in addition to sending subcommittees to take testimony in the States of South Carolina, Georgia, Florida, Alabama, and Mississippi. Although Grand Wizard Forrest refused to cooperate with the committee- even refusing to admit membership in or firsthand knowledge of a Ku Klux Klan- testimony taken by the committee provided a grisly record of violence engaged in by the masked bands.

## A RECORD OF VIOLENCE

Killings and floggings of Negroes and whites, the burning of schools and churches, and the hounding of individuals from their communities are among the outrages recorded in 12 printed volumes of the committee's hearings. A majority report issued by the committee on February 19 1872, described the Ku Klux Klan as "a fearful conspiracy against society, committing atrocities and crimes that richly deserve punishment." The report also accused the Klan of demoralizing society and holding men silent by the terror of its acts and its powers for evil. Continuance of the special powers granted to the President by the Ku Klux Klan Act of April 30, 1871, was recommended. A minority report, which took; issue with the majority as to the causes, purpose, and scope of klan activity, nevertheless declared:

---

1 These are the only laws specifically directed against the ku klux klan ever enacted by Congress. Little remains of this Reconstruction era legislation. Among the few survivors is the section dealing with private racial violence which is now contained in title 18. United States Code, at section 241. Recent Federal prosecution of a number of klansmen under this section of the code is discussed in Chapter VIII.

...we do not intend to deny that bodies of disguised men have, in several of the States of the South, been guilty of the most flagrant crimes, crimes which we neither seek to palliate nor excuse ...

Historians have suggested a combination of reasons for the eventual decline of the Ku Klux Klan of the Reconstruction period: (1) growth of public sentiment in the South against activities of masked terrorists; (2) State, and even more particularly Federal legislation, under which, martial law was declared and hundreds of alleged klansmen arrested in one State; and (3) so-called changed historical conditions which included the gradual restoration of segregation oriented State governments. The last factor was one of the bases for klan claims in later years that the post-Civil War Klan had achieved its objectives and "saved the South" (or the entire "Nation" as modern klan leaders prefer to put it.)

## KNIGHTS OF THE KU KLUX KLAN

In 1915 the Klan was exhumed by "Colonel" William Joseph Simmons, a native of Alabama who had previously been engaged in soliciting members for fraternal organizations for a fee.

The spirit of fraternalism was so shrewdly exploited by the new klan organization that millions of members were enrolled in almost every State of the Union before it declined and eventually dissolved in 1944.

As Simmons explained to the House Committee on Rules inquiring into the revived klan, his decision to launch an organization known as the Knights of the Ku Klux Klan was put into effect in October 1915 at a meeting (in Atlanta, Ga.) attended by 34 residents of the State of Georgia. A charter signed by the secretary of state of Georgia was issued in December, and another charter was granted by the Superior Court of Fulton County, Ga., on July 1, 1916, for what purported to be a purely benevolent and charitable operation.

After "resurrecting" the klan, Simmons admittedly proceeded to "reconstruct" and "remodel" the organization. (2)

The organizational structure of the new Knights-involving an autocratic hierarchy of officials on national, State, "province" and local levels-was borrowed from the Reconstruction klan. "The government of this order shall ever be military in character, especially in its executive management and control," asserted the constitution of Simmons' klan. Simmons' authority as the imperial wizard, he told congressional investigators, could be compared with that of a general in an army.

Simmons did, however, select new titles for most of the klan officialdom. He also prescribed rules for the functioning of the organization on its various levels and an elaborate ritual to be followed at local klan meetings and initiations. These were published and protected by copyright. These rules and ritual, together with a lengthy new oath swearing klansmen to obedience and secrecy, are being used today with only minor modifications by such organizations as the United Klans of America, Inc., and the National Knights of the Ku Klux Klan, Inc. (3)

The first klan organization of the 20th century vowed that it would commemorate the "service" and "achievement" of the Ku Klux Klan of the Reconstruction period and perpetuate its ideals. A booklet, "Ideals of the Knights of the Ku Klux Klan," spelled out the racial ideals which were inherited:

This is a White Man's organization, exalting the Caucasian Race and teaching the doctrine of White Supremacy. All of Christian Civilization depends upon the preservation and upbuilding of the White Race.

Any effort to permit "blacks or any other color" to share in the control of this "White Man's Republic" would constitute "an invasion of our

---

2 The changes were reflected In "Constitution and Laws of the Knights of the Ku Klux Klan (Incorporated)." copyright 1921 by the Knights of the KKK. Inc . Atlanta, Ga.
3 One of the exceptions is the White Knights of the Ku Klux Klan of Mississippi whose operations will be discussed In subsequent sections of this report.

sacred constitutional prerogatives and a violation of divinely established laws," the booklet further declared.

## PATRIOTISM AND PROFIT

A number of additional objectives were introduced by the Simmons' klan in an effort to broaden the klan's appeal. Thus, the klan's constitution and laws listed as its No.1 purpose the cultivation and promotion of patriotism. Recruiting literature issued by the organization in 1917 described the klan's "paramount feature" as "active, pure patriotism," and declared it was proud to carry on the traditions of its 19th century forebears because the latter were "paragons of patriotism." Simmons gave secondary emphasis to the charity allegedly dispensed by the klan; in third spot was its provision for "real fraternity" in which "mystery and action" would be combined with "wholesome mirth." (4)

The so-called patriotism of the klan was allegedly expressed by its uncompromising defense of "a pure Americanism, untrammeled by alien influences." Alien influences from which the Republic was to be protected were expanded by the revived klan to include not only the "inferior colored races" but also the Roman Catholic, Jewish, and foreign-born minorities within the United States.

Another new feature of the Knights of the Ku Klux Klan was its commercialism. Simmons advertised his Knights as an organization "founded and operated by consecrated business brains." His office of

---

4 "The ABC of the Knights of the Ku Klux Klan," leaflet copyrighted 1917 by W. J. Simmons, Atlanta, Ga. The same three purposes-patriotism. benevolence and fraternity are listed In the same order of priority In recruiting literature currently being circulated by the largest of the exls,ting klan organizations, the United Klans of America, Inc. See "An Introduction to the Knights of the Ku Klux Klan," a leaflet with the Imprint of the United Klans of America, Inc., Suite 401, Alston Bldg., Tuscaloosa, Ala.

imperial wizard was guaranteed revenue from a percentage of initiation fees (klectokons); a monthly per capita tax on the membership (imperial tax); and profits from the sale of robes and other regalia, jewelry, stationery, etc. Initiation fees, were described as "donations" and not reportable as taxable income in the event anyone questioned the right of the klan to tax exemption as a fraternal and charitable organization.

The services of professional publicists, Edward Young Clarke and Elizabeth Tyler, in the period 1920-23 reputedly helped propel the Knights into a nationwide role. High-powered publicity represented the klan as having an answer to both real and imaginary problems of society, as teams of professional organizers fanned out into Northern and Western States as well as the South. (Clarke's organizing department was rewarded with 80 percent of each $10 initiation fee.) Simmons told the House Committee on Rules that within 16 months after he enlisted the services of Clarke and Tyler, klan membership increased from 5,000 to almost 100,000.

The House committee questioned the imperial wizard during 3 days of public hearings on the Ku Klux Klan in October 1921. The committee lacked authority to administer oaths and its hearings predated by several years the peak of klan strength in the United States. In addition to hearing Members of Congress who had introduced resolutions against the KKK, the committee received an account of investigations conducted by staff members of the N.Y. World, and by a U.S. postal inspector, and heard contradictory accounts of the klan purposes from Imperial Wizard Simmons and one of his kleagles (organizers) who had defected. Charges by the other witnesses that the klan was making "millions" out of spreading racial and religious hatred and being credited with acts of violence in many States were blandly denied by the imperial wizard.

# HISTORICAL BACKGROUND ON THE KU KLUX KLAN

## THE KLAN AS A NATIONAL OPERATION

By 1924, the Knights activity had extended to the four corners of the Nation. States such as Maine, Oregon, and California housed units of the hooded order, which attained an overall membership of between 3 million and 5 million. While historians differ on total membership, they agree that the klan rolls were larger in certain Northern States (Indiana and Ohio for example) than in any State south of the Mason-Dixon line.

Activities of the Knights varied from State to State, and within various counties of the same State. Murders committed by hooded bands were reported in some areas in the early 1920's, while in other areas the klan's public image was confined to ceremonial parades and rallies with the distinctive burning of a wooden cross, and intense "politicking." Dynamiting and bombings were also reported, but the most common form of violence attributed to the modern klan was kidnaping of persons who were then flogged and/or tarred and feathered.

Although victims did include Negroes attempting to register other Negroes to vote, historians have observed that many of the persons singled out for punishment by the hooded order were men and women of white Protestant stock allegedly guilt of violating some "moral" law. Repeated incidents are cited of the flogging of persons because they allegedly gambled, dealt in liquor, peddled dope, or deserted a spouse.

Among the more "refined" forms of intimidation practiced by the modern klan were boycotts of businesses owned by Catholics or Jews, and campaigns to oust Roman Catholic public school teachers and persons of Catholic or Jewish faiths holding elected positions. Meanwhile, klansmen entered politics and used the labels of both major political parties to put klansmen in local sheriff and police departments, courts, and State legislatures. Klansmen allegedly served as Governors in three States, as attorney general for another State, in addition to obtaining seats in the U.S.

Senate and House of Representatives before the klan's fortunes declined in the last half of the 1920's.

In the mid-1920's, a number of States had adopted anti-mask laws in an effort to curb klan violence; one State also introduced laws making even threats by a masked person a felony, and requiring a registration of klan membership. Convictions for vigilante activity became more frequent than acquittals in some areas. Meanwhile, klan leadership was engaged internal struggles over power and division of rich financial rewards (Colonel Simmons himself had been ousted from the wizardship by a Texan, Hiram Wesley Evans, in a power play in November 1922). The publicity given to the venality and immorality of certain klan leaders was costly in terms of membership. By 1928, the invisible empire was estimated to have shrunk to 200,000 or 300,000 members.

The Ku Klux Klan Act was authored by Benjamin Franklin Butler, a Republican Member of the U.S. House of Representatives.

# THE KU KLUX KLAN ACT OF 1871

Be it enacted..., That any person who, under color of any law, statute, ordinance, regulation, custom, or usage of any State, shall subject, or cause to be subjected any person within the jurisdiction of the United States to the deprivation of any rights, privileges, or immunities secured by the Constitution of the United States, shall, any such law, statute, ordinance, regulation, custom or usage of the State to the contrary notwithstanding, be liable to the party injured in any action at law, suit in equity, or other proper proceeding for redress; such proceeding to be prosecuted in the several district or circuit courts of the United States, with and subject to the same rights of appeal, review upon error, and other remedies provided in like cases in such courts, under the provisions of the [Civil Right Act of 1866], and the other remedial laws of the United States which are in their nature applicable in such cases.

SEC. 2. That if two or more persons within any State or Territory of the United States shall conspire together to overthrow, or to put down, or to destroy by force the government of the United States, or to levy war against the United States, or to oppose by force the authority of the government of the United States, or by force, intimidation, or threat to prevent, hinder, or delay the execution of any law of the United States, or by force to seize, take, or possess any property of the United States contrary to the authority thereof, or by force, intimidation, or threat to prevent any person from accepting or holding any office or trust or place of confidence under the United States, or from discharging the duties thereof, or by force, intimidation, or threat to induce any officer of the United States to leave any State, district, or place where his duties as such office might lawfully be performed, or to injure him in his person or property on account of his lawful discharge of the duties of his office, or to injure his person while engaged in the lawful discharge of the duties of his office, or to injure his property so as to molest, interrupt, hinder, or impede him in the discharge of his official duty, or by force, intimidation, or threat to deter any party or witness in any court of the United States from attending such court, or from testifying in any matter pending in such court fully, freely, and truthfully, or to injure any such party or witness in his person or property on account of his having so attended or testified, or by force, intimidation, or threat to influence the verdict, presentment, or indictment, of any juror or grand juror in any court of the United States, or to injure such juror in his person or property on account of any verdict, presentment, or indictment lawfully assented to by him, or on account of his being or having been such juror, or shall conspire together, or go in disguise upon the public highway or upon the premises of another for the purpose, either directly or indirectly, of depriving any person or any class of persons of the equal protection of the laws, or of equal privileges or immunities under the laws, or for the purpose of preventing or hindering the constituted authorities of any State from giving or securing to all persons within such State the equal protection of the laws, or shall conspire together for the purpose in any manner impeding, hindering, obstructing or defeating the due course of justice in an State or Territory, with intent to deny to any citizen of the United States the due and equal protection of the laws, or to injury any person in his person or his property for lawfully enforcing the right of any person or class of persons to the equal protection of the laws, or by force, intimidation, or threat to prevent any citizen of the United States lawfully entitled to vote from giving his support or advocacy in a lawful manner towards or in favor of the election of any lawfully qualified person as an elector of President or Vice-President of the United States, or as a member of the Congress of the United States, or to injure any such citizen in his person or property on account of such support or advocacy, each and every person so offending shall be deemed guilty of a high crime, and upon conviction thereof in any district or circuit court of the United States or district or supreme court of any Territory of the United States having jurisdiction of similar offences, shall be punished by a fine not less than five hundred nor more than five thousand dollars, or by imprisonment, with or without hard labor, as the court my determine, for a period of not less than six months nor more than six years, as the court may determine, or by both such fine and imprisonment as the court shall determine...

SEC. 3. That in all cases where insurrection, domestic violence, unlawful combinations, or conspiracies in any State shall so obstruct or hinder the execution of the laws thereof, and of the United States, as to deprive any portion or class of the people of such State of any of the rights, privileges, or immunities, or protection, named in the constitution and secured by this act, and the constituted authorities of such State shall either be unable to protect, or shall, from any cause, fail in or refuse protection of the people in such rights, such facts shall be deemed a denial by such State of the equal protection of the laws to which they are entitled under the constitution of the United States: and in all such cases ...it shall be lawful for the President, and it shall be his duty to take such measures, by the employment of the militia or the land and naval forces of the United States, or of either, or by other means, as he may deem necessary for the suppressions of such insurrection, domestic violence, or combinations...

SEC. 4. That whenever in any State or part of a State the unlawful combinations named in the preceding section of this act shall be organized and armed, and so numerous and powerful as to be able, by violence, to either overthrow or set at defiance the constituted authorities of such State, and of the United States within such State, or when the constituted authorities are in complicity with, or shall connive at the unlawful purposes of, such powerful and armed combinations; and whenever, by reason of either or all of the causes aforesaid, the conviction of such offenders and the preservation of the public safety shall become in such district impracticable, in every such case such combinations shall be deemed a rebellion against the government of the United States and during the continuance of such rebellion, and within the limits of the district which shall be so under the sway thereof, such limits to be prescribed by proclamation, it shall be lawful for the President of the United States, when in his judgment the public safety shall require it, to suspend the privileges of the writ of habeas corpus, to the end that such rebellion may be overthrown: Provided, that all the provisions of the second section of [the Habeas Corpus Act of March 3, 1863], which relate to the discharge of prisoners other than prisoners of war, and to the penalty for refusing to obey the order of the court, shall be in full force so far as the same are applicable to the provisions of this section: Provided further, that the President shall first have made proclamation, as now provided by law, commanding such insurgents to disperse: And provided also, that the provisions of this section shall not be in force after the end of the next regular session of Congress.

SEC. 5. That no person shall be a grand or petit juror in any court of the United States upon any inquiry, hearing, or trial of any suit, proceeding, or prosecution based upon or arising under the provisions of this act who shall, in the judgment of the court, be in complicity with any such combination or conspiracy; and every such juror shall, before entering upon any such inquiry, hearing, or trial, take and subscribe an oath in open court that he has never, directly or indirectly, counseled, advised, or voluntarily aided any such combination or conspiracy.

SEC. 6. That any person or persons, having knowledge that any of the wrongs conspired to be done and mentioned in the second section of this act are about to be committed, and having power to prevent or aid in preventing the same, shall neglect or refuse to do so, and such wrongful act shall be committed, such person or persons shall be liable to the person injured…for all damages caused by any such wrongful act which such first-named person or persons by reasonable diligence, could have prevented.

THE KLAN DURING AND AFTER WWI is from THE KU KLUX KLAN SECTION I 1865 – 1944 was compiled in July, 1957 by the Federal Bureau of Investigation, United States Department of Justice, John Edgar Hoover, Director.

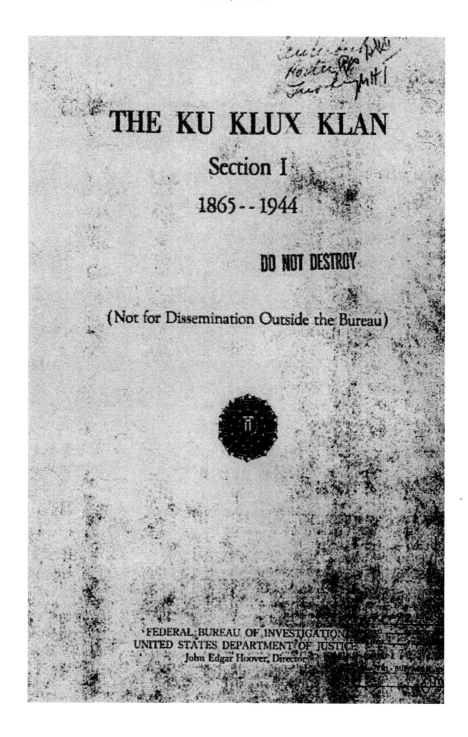

# THE KLAN DURING AND AFTER WORLD WAR I

## KLAN REVIVAL LINKED TO OTHER INTOLERANT MOVEMENTS

Chaotic conditions in the South after the Civil War largely explained the rise of the original Klan. This explanation is not valid for the revival of the Klan during and after World War I. It flourished, not as a result of relative social chaos, but as a commercial, promotional scheme directed by unscrupulous promoters who capitalized on various hatreds, prejudices, intolerance, and the postwar relaxation of ethics and morals in this country to create an invisible empire based on fear, violence, and secrecy. There was money to be made in this type of social racketeering.

The spirit of nativism which spawned the Know-Nothing movement of the 1850's and the American Protective Association forty years later was part of the postwar hysteria which made the Klan revival possible and profitable. A review of these and other examples of expressions of racial and religious prejudice through the years is set forth below to show the historical background of intolerance upon which the revived Klan was based.

### THE KNOW-NOTHING MOVEMENT

The Know-Nothing movement grew out of the nativism engendered by the increasing rate of immigration to this country in the mid-1800s. Although it was intolerant of all immigrants, it was predominantly an anti-Roman Catholic movement. Such intolerance was branded by Abraham Lincoln in these words:

"...How can anyone who abhors the oppression of negroes, be in favor of degrading classes of white people? .... As a nation, we began by declaring that all men are created equal. We now practically read it all men are created equal, except negroes. When the Know-Nothings get control, it will read all men are created equal, except negroes, and foreigners, and catholics..."

Local societies were formed to combat "foreign" influences and to uphold the "American" view. Efforts were directed toward electing only native Americans to office and requiring a 25-year residence for citizenship. Attempts to question supposed leaders concerning the movement were met with statements to the effect that they knew nothing -- hence, the name Know-Nothing arose. Although there was never a political organization bearing this name, the movement grew so rapidly that by 1855 it openly assumed the name American Party. This party was hopelessly split over the issue of slavery, and the strength of the movement was soon broken.

## THE AMERICAN PROTECTIVE ASSOCIATION

The American Protective Association was an anti-Catholic organization formed in Clinton, Iowa, on March 13, 1887, by a group of led by Henry F. Bowers, who sought to curb the number of Catholics in this country by restricting immigration and to preserve the public schools from what they viewed as the Catholic purpose to subvert them. As the organization developed, it seized every opportunity to create a fear of imminent Catholic control of the United States, utilizing lurid anti-Catholic propaganda without regard for truth or decency. In its campaign to restrict immigration, the American Protective Association called for prohibition of the importation of pauper labor; restriction of immigration to those proving their qualifications for citizenship; and a change in the laws so that no aliens would be naturalized or allowed to vote unless they spoke the English language and had lived for seven continuous years in this country.

By capitalizing on racial and religious intolerance, the American Protective Association grew rapidly. It reached its peak in 1895-96, when it claimed a membership of 2,500,000 persons. No accurate figures are available; however, it is doubtful if actual membership was ever much more than 1,000,000.

The American Protective Association declined steadily after 1896. The Presidential candidates in 1896 were William McKinley and William J. Bryan, and Bryan's proposal for the free and unlimited coinage of silver became the dominant political issue of the day. The leadership of the American Protective Association had refused to support McKinley's nomination because some of his intimate friends and backers were Catholics. This caused a split in the organization, one faction endorsing McKinley's nomination while another faction condemned such action. Public attention became focused on other issues, particularly after the outbreak of the Spanish-American War in 1898. Little was heard of the American Protective Association after 1900, although it existed, at least in name, until about 1911.

## THE RISING TIDE OF IMMIGRATION

Intolerance of persons of foreign birth was one of the fundamental precepts of the revived Ku Klux Klan. As has been noted previously, this same intolerance played a part in the activities of the Know-Nothings and the American Protective Association.

Between 1790 and 1840, fewer than a million immigrants entered the United States. In the next ten years, however, 1, 713, 251 immigrants arrived, most of them from Germany and Ireland. After the Civil War, the United States entered into a period of industrial expansion. Cheap, unskilled labor was in demand. Immigrants came to this country in great numbers to fill this demand, but after 1880 the trend of immigration changed. The bulk of "the old immigration" had come from northern and western Europe, but by 1896 more than half of all immigrants were coming from southern and eastern Europe. By 1910, "the new immigration" accounted for four fifths of the immigrants to the United States.

The new immigrants tended to settle in language groups and to retain their Old World customs. Social conflicts arose. The competition of cheap labor brought demands from labor groups that immigration be restricted. European immigration continued with few restrictions, however, during the early 1900s. After World War I, European immigrants came to the United States in great numbers, but industry could no longer absorb them and the feeling against immigration became very strong.

A law which refused admittance to immigrants who could not read or write in at least one language was passed over President Wilson's veto in 1917. The quota system of immigration was first established in 1921, and made more restrictive in 1924. The "national origins" law went into effect in 1929, limiting the number of quota immigrants to 150,000, and basing the quota for individual countries on the number of people of those origins living in the United States in 1920.

## THOMAS E. WATSON

During the years before World War I, there were always those to fan the flames of intolerance, to agitate against the foreign born, the Catholics, and the Jews. One of the most notorious was Thomas E. Watson, Populist Party candidate from Georgia for Vice President in 1896 and for President in 1904. His publication, Watson's Magazine, scurrilously attacked Catholics and Jews from 1910 until it was excluded from the mails after the entry of the United States into World War I in 1917. His book, The Roman Catholic Hierarchy, published in 1910, was a virulent attack on Catholicism. He was indicted three times for the publication of this book, but was never convicted. In fact, he was elected United States Senator from Georgia in 1920 and served from 1921 until his death in 1922.

## THE MENACE

The anti-Catholic publication, The Menace, was established at Aurora, Missouri, in November, 1911. By its own statement, "The Menace was launched in the belief that the Roman Catholic Political Machine, in its political intrigues and its interference with established American institutions, is the deadliest enemy to our civilization and liberties." It continued publication until 1925, and built a vast circulation on the most inflammatory agitation against the Catholic religion."

## WILLIAM JOSEPH SIMMONS REVIVES THE KLAN IN 1915

In 1915, another organization appeared -- Knights of the Ku Klux Klan. It was the brain child of William Joseph Simmons, a fraternal organizer who has been described variously as a "dreamer and idealist" and as a "cunning, shrewd adventurer."  Knights of the Ku Klux Klan was chartered by the State of Georgia on December 4, 1915, and by the Superior Court of Fulton County, Georgia, on July 1, 1916, as "a purely benevolent and eleemosynary society" for the purpose of conducting a patriotic, secret, social, benevolent order.  Simmons borrowed the name, the regalia, and some of the nomenclature of the original Klan, but the organization and purposes of the two Klans were entirely different.

## PROGRAM OF "PURE AMERICANISM"
## BASED ON RACIAL AND RELIGIOUS PREJUDICE

Ostensibly, the Klan stood for "love of country and a pure Americanism." Actually, it capitalized on racial and religious prejudices, with a fourfold program of antagonism toward Catholics, Jews, Negroes, and the foreign born. Klan rituals and official documents were couched in high-sounding, patriotic, sentimental language which gave little indication of the basic intolerance of the organization, and could be interpreted as the occasion required. For example, the oath taken by prospective Klansmen contained this masterpiece of literary double talk:

"I swear that I will most zealously and valiantly shield and preserve by any and all justifiable means and methods the sacred constitutional rights and privileges of free public schools, free speech, free press, separation of church and state, liberty, white supremacy, just laws, and the pursuit of happiness against any encroachment of any nature by any person or persons, political party or parties, religious sect or people, native, naturalized, or foreign of any race, color, creed, lineage, or tongue whatsoever."

In the case of the Reconstruction Klan, it was in the questions to be satisfactorily answered by prospective members that the true purposes of the organization became clearer. This is also true of the "Qualifying Interrogatories" composed by Simmons for candidates for "citizenship" in the "Invisible Empire," as set forth below:

"SIRS: The Knights of the Ku-Klux Klan, as a great and essentially a patriotic, fraternal, benevolent order, does not discriminate against a man on account of his religious or political creed, when same does not conflict with or antagonize the sacred rights and privileges guaranteed by our civil government and Christian ideals and institutions."

Therefore, to avoid any misunderstanding and as evidence that we do not seek to impose unjustly the requirements of this order upon anyone who can not, on account of his religious or political scruples, voluntarily meet our requirements and faithfully practice our principles, and as proof that we respect all honest men in their sacred convictions, whether same are agreeable with our requirements or not, we require as an absolute necessity on the part of each of you an affirmative answer to each of the following questions:

"Each of the following questions must be answered by (each of) you with an emphatic - Yes."

"First. Is the motive prompting your ambition to be a klalsman serious and unselfish?"

"Second. Are you a native-born white, Gentile American citizen?"

"Third. Are you absolutely opposed to and free of any allegiance of any nature to any cause, Government, people, sect, or ruler that is foreign to the United States of America?"

"Fourth. Do you believe in the tenets of the Christian religion?"

"Fifth. Do you esteem the United States of America and its institutions above any other Government, civil, political, or ecclesiastical, in the whole world?"

"Sixth. Will you, without mental reservation, take a solemn oath to defend, preserve, and enforce same?"

"Seventh. Do you believe in clannishness and will you faithfully practice same towards klansmen?"

"Eighth. Do you believe in and will you faithfully strive for the eternal maintenance of white supremacy?"

"Ninth. Will you faithfully obey our constitution and laws, and conform willingly to all our usages, requirements, and regulations?"

"Tenth. Can you be always depended on?"

## KLORAN OUTLINES GOVERNMENT OF KLAN

Simmons composed the Klan's rituals and published them in a book called the Kloran. The following statement from the Kloran outlines the administrative machinery of the Klan:

"THE GOVERNMENT of the Invisible Empire is vested with the Imperial Wizard, the Emperor, assisted by his fifteen Genii - - the Imperial Officers constituting his official family; The government of a Realm is vested with a Grand Dragon, assisted by his nine Hydras -- the Grand Officers; the government of a Province is vested with a Great Titan, assisted by his twelve Furies -- the Great Officers, and a Klan is governed by an Exalted Cyclops, assisted by his twelve Terrors -- the elective officers of a Klan."

Officers of individual Klans were listed as follows:

| | |
|---|---|
| Exalted Cyclops | - President |
| Klaliff | - Vice-President |
| Klokard | - Lecturer |
| Kludd | - Chaplain |
| Kligrapp | - Secretary |
| Klabee | - Treasurer |
| Kladd | - Conductor |
| Klarogo | - Inner Guard |
| Klexter | - Outer Guard |
| Klokan (singular) | - Investigator |
| Klokann (plural) | - Board of Investigators |
| Night-Hawk | - Charge of Candidates |

## PROFESSIONAL PROMOTERS TAKE OVER THE KLAN

Whatever else he may have been, Simmons was not a successful promoter, for the Knights of the Ku Klux Klan made little progress from 1915 to 1920. Simmons has claimed that one of his trusted employees embezzled all of the Klan's funds in 1916, but that, in spite of this, he steadfastly refused the offers of those who would commercialize the Klan, even though they would have made him rich.

Subsequent events belie Simmons' sincerity. On June 7, 1920, Simmons, as Imperial Wizard of the Knights of the Ku Klux Klan, entered into a contract with Edward Young Clarke whereby Clarke was appointed Imperial Kleagle of the Klan in full charge of the solicitation of new members. Clarke was a professional fund raiser. With Mrs. Elizabeth Tyler, whom he brought with him into the Klan work, Clarke had operated the Southern Publicity Association in Atlanta, Georgia, specializing in fund-raising campaigns for various groups, such as the Salvation Army, the Anti-Saloon League, et cetera.

Clarke set up a Propagation Department in the Klan to organize Klan units throughout the country. A high-pressure, well organized campaign was launched for members. The country was divided into various sales territories, or Domains, each supervised by a sales manager known as a Grand Goblin. Domains were further broken down into Realms, under the supervision of King Kleagles, who were the salesmen who actually solicited memberships. Each new member made a contribution (klectoken) of $10.00 to the Klan. Clarke's contract with Simmons gave to Clarke $8.00 of each $10.00 collected. Out of this $8.00 Clarke reimbursed his solicitors. In practice, the Keagle who sold the membership kept $4.00; the King Kleagle, $1.00; the Grand Goblin, 50 cents; and the Imperial Kleagle (Clarke), $2.50. Two dollars went to the treasury of the Imperial Palace.

Under the professional leadership of Clarke and Tyler, membership in the Klan increased rapidly. Although accurate records are not available, best estimates are that the membership approximated 2,500 when Clarke signed his contract with Simmons in June, 1920. During the next 15 months, some 90,000 "aliens" were "naturalized into the Invisible Empire."

## ACTS OF TERRORISM LEAD
## TO CONGRESSIONAL INVESTIGATION

Simmons and his Klan have been described as "more or less historical accidents." High-pressure salesmanship applied during a period of postwar hysteria capitalized on all the old intolerance against Catholics, Jews, Negroes, and the foreign born. "Pure Americanism" was the slogan. Secret rituals and passwords combined with mysterious language and strange attire gave the whole operation an air of fraternal importance. But what the Klan lacked was a legitimate reason for existence. True, the Kloran did state:

" ... The prime purpose of this great Order is to develop character, practice clanishness, to protect the home and the chastity of womanhood, and to exemplify a pure patriotism towards our glorious country."

Such language was not much help to the membership in defining specific objectives, even when interpreted in the light of the portion of the Klan oath mentioned previously. One Kleagle, seeking advice as to what new Klans should do upon receiving their charters, was told by his King Kleagle, "Tell them to clean up their towns." It is not surprising that acts of terrorism began to take place. Klansmen, or those purporting to be Klansmen, took it upon themselves to punish persons who had, in their opinion, violated some law, legal or moral. Warnings, floggings, kidnapings, and murders became so widespread by the summer of 1921 that the House Committee on Rules, in October, 1921, held hearings on Klan activities.

Simmons proved to be an evasive witness before the Committee. He denied that the Klan was responsible for acts of violence, but in the few instances where Klan involvement could be definitely shown, he quickly noted that the charters of the Klans involved had been cancelled. His testimony consisted largely of self-serving declarations on behalf of himself and the Klan, which he maintained was an innocent, fraternal organization.

## DISSENSION ARISES- WITHIN THE KLAN

No action was taken against the Klan as a result of the Committee's hearings, and the leaders of the Klan utilized this as an implied approval of Klan activities. Membership increased rapidly under the promotional direction of Clarke, but the enormous possibilities for profit and power soon brought about a struggle for control. By June, 1922, Clarke was issuing orders as the Imperial Wizard and was the active head of the Klan until November, 1922. Simmons had been shunted into the background, allegedly because of illness. In the meantime, Dr. Hiram Wesley Evans, a dentist from Dallas, Texas, who had formerly acted as Exalted Cyclops and as Great Titan of the Klan in Dallas, came to Atlanta to assume the position of Imperial Kligrapp (Secretary).

On December 28, 1921, a petition, signed by 197 insurgent Klansmen, had been filed in Superior Court, Fulton County, Georgia, against the Knights of the Ku Klux Klan, asking that a receiver be appointed for the Klan and that Clarke and Mrs. Tyler be enjoined and restrained from any further connection with the organization. It developed that Clarke and Mrs. Tyler, guiding lights in this organization of supposedly high principles, had been arrested in Mrs. Tyler's house in Atlanta on October 15, 1919, and fined for disorderly conduct.

## HIRAM WESLEY EVANS GAINS CONTROL

The struggle for control of the Klan turned into a battle between Clarke, supported by Simmons, and Evans. Evans prevailed and, on November 28, 1922, he was elected Imperial Wizard to succeed Simmons, who was given the title of Emperor.

By February, 1923, Evans had forced Clarke out of the Klan. It is worthy of note that on February 28, 1923, Clarke was indicted at Houston, Texas, for a violation of the White Slave Traffic Act allegedly taking place in February, 1921. On March 10, 1924, Clarke entered a plea of guilty and paid a fine of $5,000. Clarke apparently continued his promotional activities, for on January 26, 1933, he was indicted at Jacksonville, Florida, for using the mails to defraud in connection with the promotion of The Esskaye, Incorporated, an organization which had been advertised as a "super-klan" and as a "universal brotherhood to further prosperity and mutual love."

Evans faced a problem in disposing of Simmons, for it developed that Simmons had copyrighted in his own name the Klan ritual, constitution, et cetera, and had filed copies of these supposedly secret documents with the Library of Congress. As a result, Evans was forced to make a settlement with Simmons. Simmons later said that he accepted $90,000 in lieu of continued payments of $1,000 per month for life, and that he lost this $90,000 in a futile attempt to start a new order, the Knights of the Flaming Sword.

It was under the leadership of Evans that the Klan reached its peak. By the mid-1920s, its membership was estimated at from 4,000,000 to 5,000,000, although the actual figure was probably much smaller. The Klan claimed to be nonpolitical, but it controlled politics in many communities and was an active force in the elections of 1922, 1924, and 1926. Texas, Oklahoma, Indiana, Oregon, and Maine were particularly under its influence. The Klan's influence was also felt to some extent in the Presidential campaign of 1928, when Alfred E. Smith, a Catholic, was a candidate.

## EXCESSES IN INDIANA CONTRIBUTE
## TO DOWNFALL OF KLAN

The story of the Klan in Indiana is especially sordid. Shortly after World War I, David C. Stephenson arrived in Evansville, Indiana, and set about organizing war veterans. When his first efforts to enter politics were unsuccessful, he joined the Klan, taking his war veterans with him.

In 1922, Evans gave Stephenson the job of organizing the Klan in Indiana. Stephenson hired full-time organizers and found Indiana to be a fertile field for the Klan's traditional program directed against Catholics, Jews, Negroes, and foreigners, which he extended to include communists, bootleggers, pacifists, evolutionists, and all persons whom the Klan considered immoral. On July 4, 1923, Stephenson assumed the office of Grand Dragon of the Realm of Indiana. Stephenson's political ambitions continued and he used the Klan to further them. In 1923, when the Governor of Indiana was convicted of using the mails to defraud, Stephenson seized the opportunity to point out that it was the duty of the Klan to purify and purge Indiana politics. His duplicity will soon become apparent.

Stephenson took the Klan into the Indiana political campaigns of 1924. Klan candidates were successful, including the candidate for governor, and Stephenson became a political power in Indiana.

In the meantime, Stephenson had incurred the enmity of Evans. On April 17, 1924, or, in Klan language, "on the Deadly Day of the Weeping Week of the Appalling Month of the Year of the Klan LVII," Evans signed an Imperial Edict ordering the Klan in Evansville, Indiana, to try Stephenson on charges of conduct "unbecoming a Klansman," addressing the order to "All Genii, Grand Dragons and Hydras, Great Titans and Furies, Giants, King Kleagles and Kleagles, Exalted Cyclops and Terrors, and to all Citizens of the Invisible Empire, in the name of the valiant and venerated dead."

Stephenson fought back, seeking to separate the Indiana Klan from the "domination" of Evans and attacking the "money-mad" individuals seeking to selfishly exploit Klan power.

Stephenson charged, among other things, that Klan leaders in Atlanta were trying to frame him on a morals charge. In this connection, it is interesting to note that on May 24, 1924, a special investigator for Imperial Wizard Evans appeared at the office of the United States Attorney in Nashville, Tennessee, accompanied by a woman who said that in June, 1923, she and another girl had accompanied Stephenson and one of his henchmen on a trip from Cincinnati, Ohio, to Atlanta, Georgia, Nashville, Tennessee, and Louisville, Kentucky. Her story may well have been true, but when, on the night of May 28, 1924, Evans' investigator and the alleged victim were ejected from their hotel in Nashville for immoral activities, prosecution of Stephenson under the White Slave Traffic Act was declined.

It appeared that the sole motive behind the complaint was to use the Department of Justice for the purpose of enabling the Klan to get rid of Stephenson.

In the end, it was Stephenson who brought about his own downfall. On April 2, 1925, he was arrested for the murder of Madge Oberholtzer in March, 1925. Due to the prominence of Stephenson and the political implications involved, the case was a controversial one, but on November 14, 1925, Stephenson was found guilty of second degree murder. Two days later he was sentenced to life imprisonment.

Stephenson later said, "I should have been put in jail for my political activities but I am not guilty of murder." He fully expected that Governor Jackson, whom he had put into office, would pardon him. When no pardon was forthcoming, Stephenson began to divulge a story of graft and corruption in Indiana politics. In Indianapolis, the mayor was indicted and convicted for corrupt practices, and six members of the city council paid fines and resigned after being indicted for receiving bribes. The Governor was indicted, but invoked the statute of limitations. Numerous lesser officials were involved.

The heyday of the Klan was past. Saner voices began to prevail. True, these same voices had always spoken out against the Klan and all it stood for, but the spirit of the times had caused their warnings to fallen deaf ears. After 1928, relatively little was heard of the Klan until the appointment to public office of a former Klansman called forth criticism.

(Not for Dissemination Outside the Bureau)

Federal Bureau of Investigation
United States Department of Justice
John Edgar Hoover, Director

# II

The Ku Klux Klan

in Popular Culture,

Politics, and Their

Own Words.

Illustration by Arthur I. Keller from Thomas Dixon's THE CLANSMAN (1905)

# THE KU KLUX KLAN OF 1866

ITS ORIGIN, GROWTH, AND DISBANDMENT

by D. L. Wilson and J. C. Lester, a founding member of the Klan

No chapter in American history is more strange than the one which bears for a title: "Ku Klux Klan." The secret history of the Invisible Empire, as the Klan was also called, has never been written. The Klan disappeared from Southern life as it came into it, shrouded in deepest mystery. Its members would not disclose its secrets; others could not. Even the investigating committee appointed by Congress, after tedious and diligent inquiry, was baffled. The voluminous reports containing the results of the committee's labors do not tell when and where and how the Ku Klux Klan originated.

But the time has now arrived when the history of the origin, growth, and disbandment of "The Invisible Empire" may be given to the public. Circumstances, which need not be detailed here, have put it in the power of the writer to compile such a history. For obvious reasons the names of individuals are withheld. But the reader may feel assured that this narrative is drawn from sources which are accurate and authentic. The writer does not profess to be able to reveal the secret signs, grips, and pass-words of the order. These have never been disclosed, and probably never will be. But we claim to narrate those facts relating to the order which have a historic and philosophic value. It is due to the truth of history, to the student of human nature, and to the statesman, that such facts connected with this remarkable episode in our nation's history he frankly and fairly told.

A wave of excitement, spreading contagion till the minds of a whole people are in a ferment, is an event of frequent occurrence. The Ku Klux movement was peculiar by reason of the causes which produced and fed the excitement. It illustrates the weird and irresistible power of the unknown and mysterious over the minds of men of all classes and conditions in life;

and it illustrates how men by circumstances and conditions, in part of their own creation, may be carried away from their moorings and drifted along in a course against which reason and judgment protest.

The popular idea supposes the Ku Klux movement to have been conceived in malice, and nursed by prejudice and hate, for lawlessness, rapine, and murder. The circumstances which brought the Klan into notice and notoriety were of a character to favor such a conclusion. No other seemed possible. The report of the Congressional Investigating Committee confirmed it. But granting the truthfulness of that report, it is a fragmentary truth; it does not tell the whole story; and it leaves the impression that the Ku Klux Klan was conceived and carried out in pure and unmixed deviltry. Whether this conclusion is just and true, the reader who follows this narrative to its end will decide.

The Ku Klux Klan was the outgrowth of peculiar conditions, social, civil, and political, which prevailed at the South from 1865 to 1869. It was as much a product of those conditions as malaria is of a swamp and sun-heat. Its birthplace was Pulaski, the capital of Giles, one of the southern tier of counties in Middle Tennessee. Pulaski is a town of two thousand five hundred to three thousand inhabitants. Previous to the war the people possessed wealth and culture. The first was lost in the general wreck. Now the most intimate association with them fails to disclose a trace of the diabolism which, according to the popular idea, one would expect to find characterizing the people among whom the Ku Klux Klan originated. A male college and a female seminary are located at Pulaski, and receive liberal patronage. It is a town of churches.

There, in 1866, the name Ku Klux first fell from human lips. There began a movement which in a short time spread as far north as Virginia and as far south as Texas, and which for a period convulsed the country. Proclamations were fulminated against the Klan by the President and by the Governors of States; and hostile statutes were enacted both by State and national legislatures, for there had become associated with the name of Ku Klux Klan gross mistakes and lawless deeds of violence.

During the entire period of the Klan's organized existence Pulaski continued to be its central seat of authority, and some of its highest officers resided there. This narrative, therefore, will relate principally to the growth of the Klan and the measures taken to suppress it in Tennessee. It is necessary to a clear understanding of the movement to observe that the history of the Klan is marked by two distinct and well-defined periods. The first period covers the time from its organization in 1866 to the summer of 1867. This period of its history, though less interesting, should be described somewhat minutely, because of its bearing on subsequent events.

When the war ended in 1865 the young men of Pulaski who escaped death on the battlefield returned home and passed through a period of enforced inactivity. In some respects it was more trying than the ordeal of war which lay behind them. The reaction which followed the excitement of army scenes and service was intense. There was nothing to relieve it. They could not engage in active business or professional pursuits. Their business habits were broken up, no one had capital with which to conduct agricultural pursuits or to engage in mercantile enterprises, and this restlessness was made more intense by the total lack of the amusements and social diversions which prevail wherever society is in a normal condition. One evening in June, 1866, a few of these young men met in the office of one of the most prominent members of the Pulaski bar. In the course of the conversation one of the number said: "Boys, let us get up a club or a society of some description."

The suggestion was discussed with enthusiasm. Before they separated it was agreed to invite a few others whose names were mentioned to join them, and to meet again the next evening at the same place. At the appointed time eight or ten young men had assembled. The club was organized by the election of a chairman and a secretary. There was entire unanimity among the members in regard to the end in view, which was diversion and amusement. The evening was spent discussing the best means of attaining the object in view. Two committees were appointed, one to select a name, the other to prepare a set of rules for the government of the society, and a ritual for the initiation of new members. Then the club adjourned, to meet the following week to hear and act upon the reports of these committees. Before the arrival of the appointed time for the next meeting one of the wealthiest and most prominent citizens of Pulaski went on a business trip to Columbus, Miss., taking his family with him. Before leaving he invited one of the leading spirits of the new society to take charge of and sleep at his house in his absence. This young man invited his comrades to join him there; so the place of meeting was changed from the law office to this residence. The owner of the house outlived the Ku Klux Klan, and died ignorant of the fact that his house was the place which its organization was fully effected. This residence afterward came into the possession of Judge H. M. Spofford, of Spofford - Kellogg fame. It was his home at the time of his death, and is still owned by his widow.

The committee appointed to select a name reported that they had found the task difficult, and had not made a selection. They explained that they had been trying to discover or invent a name which would be in some degree suggestive of the character and objects of the society. They mentioned several names which they had been considering. In this number was the name "Kukloi" from the Greek word kuklos, meaning a band or circle. At mention of this, some one cried out: "Call it Ku Klux!"

The Klan at once suggested itself, and was added to complete the alliteration. So, instead of adopting a name, as was the first intention, which had a definite meaning, they chose one which was absolutely meaningless. This trivial and apparently accidental incident had a most important bearing on the future of the organization so singularly named. Looking back over the history of the Klan, and at the causes under which it developed, it is difficult to resist the conclusion that the order would never have grown to the proportions which it afterward assumed, or wielded the power it did, had it not borne this name, or some other equally as meaningless and mysterious. Had they caned themselves the "Jolly Jokers," or the "Adelphi," or by some similar appellation, the organization would doubtless have had no more than the mere local and ephemeral existence which those who organized it contemplated for it. Hundreds of societies have originated just as this one did, and, after a brief existence, have passed away. But in the case before us there was a weird potency in the very name Ku Klux Klan! Let the reader pronounce it aloud. The sound of it is suggestive of bones rattling together! The potency of the name was not wholly in the impression made by it on the general public. It is a singular fact that the members of the Klan were themselves the first to feel its weird influence. They had adopted a mysterious name. There upon the original plan was modified so as to make everything connected with the order harmonize with the name.

Amusement was still the end in view; but the methods by which they proposed to win it were now those of secrecy and mystery. So when the report of the committee on rules and ritual came up for consideration, the recommendations were modified to adapt them to the new idea. The report, as finally adopted, provided for the following officers:

> A Grand Cyclops, or presiding officer.
>
> A Grand Magi, or vice-president.
>
> A Grand Turk, or marshal.
>
> A Grand Exchequer, or treasurer.

Two Lictors, who were the outer and inner guards of the "den," as the place of meeting was designated.

The one obligation exacted from members was to maintain absolute and profound secrecy with reference to the order and everything pertaining to it. This obligation prohibited those who assumed it from disclosing the fact that they were Ku Klux, or the name of any other member, and from soliciting anyone to become a member. The last requirement was a singular one. It was exacted for two reasons. First, it was in keeping with their determination to appear as mysterious as possible, and thus play upon the curiosity of the public. Secondly, and mainly, it was designed to prevent unpleasantness following initiations. They wished to be able to say to novices: "You are here on your own solicitation, and not by invitation from us."

They desired accessions; to have them was indispensable; but they knew human nature well enough to know that if they made the impression that they wished to be exclusive and select, then applications for membership would be numerous. The result showed that they reasoned correctly. Each member was required to provide himself with the following outfit: A white mask for the face with orifices for the eyes and nose.

A tall, fantastic cardboard hat, so constructed as to increase the wearer's apparent height.

A gown or robe of sufficient length to cover the entire person. No particular color or material was prescribed. These were left to the individual's taste and fancy; and each selected what in his judgment would be the most hideous and fantastic, with the aim of inspiring the greatest amount of awe in the novice. These robes of different colors, often of the most flashy patterns of "Dolly Varden" calicoes, added vastly to the grotesque appearance of the assembled Klan.

Each member carried also a small whistle, with which, by means of a code of signals agreed upon, they held communications with one another. The only utility in this was to awaken inquiry.

And the object of all this was amusement. "Only this, and nothing more." A few young men, barred for the time by circumstances from entering any active business or professional pursuits, and deprived of the ordinary diversions of social life, were seeking in this way to amuse and employ themselves. The organization of this Klan was to them both diversion and occupation. But where did the fun come in? Partly in exciting the curiosity of the public and then in baffling it, but mainly in the initiation of new members.

The ritual used in the initiation was elaborate, but not worthy of reproduction. It is enough to say that it was modeled on and embraced the leading features of the ritual of an order which has long been popular in colleges and universities under various names. In one place it is the "Sons of Confucius"; in another, the "Guiasticutas"; but everywhere the "ancient and the honorable" and the mirth provoking.

The initiations were at first conducted in the law office where the suggestion for the formation of the Klan had been made; but it was not a suitable place. The room was small; it was near the business portion of the town, and while the members were in session there they never felt entirely free from apprehensions of interruption. On the brow of a ridge that runs along the western outskirts of the town there used to stand a handsome and commodious residence. The front or main building was of brick, the "L" of wood. In December, 1865, the brick portion of this house was demolished by a cyclone; the "L" remained standing. It consisted of three rooms. A stairway led from one of them to a large cellar beneath. No other houses stood near. Around these ruins were the storm-torn, limbless trunks of trees which had once formed a magnificent grove; now they stood up grim and gaunt like specter sentinels. A dreary, desolate, uncanny place it was; but in every way suitable for a "den", and the Klan appropriated it.

When a meeting was held, one Lictor was stationed at the house, the other fifty yards from it on the road leading into town. They were dressed in the fantastic regalia of the order and bore tremendous spears as the badge of their office.

As before stated, and for the reasons assigned, the K u Klux did not solicit anyone to join them; yet they had applications for membership. While members were not allowed to disclose the fact of their membership, they were allowed to talk with others in regard to anything that was a matter of common report in regard to the order. A member might express to an outsider his desire or intention to join. If the person addressed expressed a similar desire, the Ku Klux would then say to him, if he were a desirable person: "Well, I think I know how to get in. Meet me at such a place, on such a night, at such an hour, and we will join together." Usually, curiosity would predominate over every other consideration, and the candidate would be found waiting at the appointed place.

As the Ku Klux and the candidate approached the sentinel Lictor, they were hailed and halted, and questioned. Having received the assurance that they desired to become Ku Klux, the Lictor blew the signal for his companion to come and take charge of the novices. The candidate, under the impression that his companion was similarly treated, was blindfolded and led to the "den!" The preliminaries of the initiation consisted in leading the candidate around the rooms and down into the cellar, now and then placing before him obstructions, which added to his discomfort if not to his mystification. After some rough sport of this description he was led before the Grand Cyclops, who solemnly addressed to him numerous questions- some of them grave and serious, some of them absurd to the last degree. If the answers were satisfactory, the obligation to secrecy, which had already been administered in the beginning of the ceremony was exacted for a second time. Then the Grand Cyclops commanded: "Place him before the royal altar and adorn his head with the regal crown."

The "royal altar" was a large-looking glass. The "regal crown" was a huge hat bedecked with two enormous donkey ears. In this headgear the candidate was placed before a mirror and directed to repeat the couplet: "O wad some power the giftie gie us to see oursel's as ithers see us."

As the last words were falling from his lips the Grand Turk removed the bandage, and before the candidate was his own image in the mirror. To increase the discomfiture and chagrin which any man in such a situation would naturally feel, the removal of the bandage was the signal to the Klan for indulgence in the most uproarious and boisterous mirth. The Grand Cyclops relaxed the rigor of his rule, and the decorum hitherto maintained disappeared, while the "den" rang with shouts and peals of laughter. And worse than all, as he looked about him, he saw that he was surrounded by men dressed in hideous garbs and masked so that he could not recognize one of them. The character of these initiatory proceedings explains why, from the very first, secrecy was so much insisted on. A single "tale out of school" would have spoiled the fun. For the same reason the Klan was, at first, very careful in regard to the character of the men admitted. Rash and imprudent men, such as could not be fully relied upon to keep their obligation to profound secrecy were excluded. Nor were those received who were addicted to the use of intoxicants. Later on in the history they were not so careful; but in the earlier period of its existence the Klan was composed of men of good character and good habits. In some instances persons of objectionable character were persistent, even to annoyance, in their efforts to gain admission to the order. Occasionally this persistence was rebuked in a manner more emphatic than tender. For example, one young man, who was personally very unpopular, made repeated attempts to join the Ku Klux. They arranged to have an initiation not provided for in the ritual. A meeting was appointed to be held on the top of a hill that rises by a gentle slope to a considerable height, on the northern limits of the town. The candidate, in the usual way was led into the presence of the Grand Cyclops. This dignitary was standing on a stump. The tall hat, the flowing robe, and the elevated position made him appear at least ten feet tall. He addressed to the candidate a few unimportant and absurd questions, and then, turning to the Lictors, said: "Blindfold him and proceed." The procedure was to place the would-be Ku Klux in an empty barrel, provided for the purpose, and to send him whirling down the hill! To his credit be it said, he never revealed any of the secrets of the Ku Klux.

These details have an important bearing on the subsequent history of the Ku Klux. They show that the originators of the Klan were not meditating treason or lawlessness in any form. Yet the Klan's later history grew naturally out of the methods and measures which characterized this period of it. Its projectors did not expect it to spread; they thought it would "have its little day and die." It lived; more, it grew to vast proportions.

## II

## THE SPREAD OF THE KLAN

The devices for attracting attention were eminently successful. During the months of July and August, 1866, the Klan was much talked about by the citizens of Pulaski. Its mysteriousness was the sensation of the hour. Every issue of the local paper contained some notice of the strange order. These notices were copied into other papers, and in this manner the way was prepared for the rapid growth and spread of the Klan, which soon followed.

Six weeks or less from the date of the organization, the sensation in Pulaski was waning. Curiosity in regard to it had abated to such a degree that the Klan would have certainly fallen to pieces but for the following circumstances. By the time the eligible material in the town had been used up, young men from the country, whose curiosity had been inflamed by the notices in the papers, began to come in and apply for admission to the Klan. Some of these applications were accepted. In a little while the members so admitted asked permission to establish "dens" at various points in the county. No provision had been made for such a contingency, but the permission was granted; had it not been, the result would, in all probability, have been the same.

As the ritual followed by the Pulaski Klan could not be conveniently carried out in the country, various modifications and changes were permitted. But the strictest injunctions were laid on these new lodges, or "dens," in regard to secrecy, mystery, and the character of the men admitted. The growth in the rural districts was more rapid than it had been in the town. Applications for permission to establish "dens" multiplied rapidly.

The news that the Ku Klux was spreading to the country excited the attention of the country people as the existence of the Klan in town had not done. The same cause rekindled the waning interest of the town people. Every issue of the local papers in the "infected regions" bristled with highly mysterious and exciting accounts of the doings of the "fantastic gentry."

During the fall and winter of 1866 the growth of the Klan was rapid. It spread over a wide extent of territory. Sometimes, by a sudden leap, it appeared in localities far distant from any existing "dens." A stranger from West Tennessee, Mississippi, Alabama, or Texas, visiting in a neighborhood where the order prevailed, would be initiated, and on his departure carry with him permission to establish a "den" at home. In fact, it was done often without such permission. The connecting link between these "dens" was very fragile. By a sort of tacit agreement the Pulaski Klan was regarded as the source of power and authority. The Grand Cyclops of this "den" was virtually the ruler of the order; but as he had no method of communication with subjects or subordinates, and no way in which to enforce his mandates, his authority was more fancy than fact. But so far there had appeared no need for rigid rules and close supervision. The leading spirits of the Ku Klux were still contemplating nothing more serious than amusement. They enjoyed the baffled curiosity and wild speculations of a mystified public even more than the rude sport afforded by the ludicrous initiations. Such is the account of the Ku Klux Klan in the first period of its history, from June, 1866, to April, 1867. Yet all this time it was gradually and in a very natural way taking on new features not at first remotely contemplated by the originators of the order; features which finally transformed the Ku Klux Klan into a band of "Regulators."

The transformation was effected by the combined operation or three causes:

(1) The impression made by the order upon the minds of those who united with it;

(2) The impression produced upon the public by its weird and mysterious ways;

(3) The anomalous and peculiar condition of affairs in the South at this time.

The mystery and secrecy with which the Klan veiled itself made a singular impression on the minds of many who united with it. The most common conclusion reached by those whose attention was attracted to the Klan was that it contemplated some great and important mission; its rapid extension was regarded as confirmatory of this conclusion; and, when admitted to membership, this impression was deepened rather than dispelled by what they saw and heard. There was not a word in the ritual, or in the obligation, or in any part of the ceremony, to favor it; but the impression still remained that this mysteriousness and secrecy, the high-sounding tides of the officers, the grotesque dress of the members, and the formidable obligation to profound secrecy, all meant more than mere sport. This conviction was ineradicable, and the attitude of many of its members continued to be that of expecting great developments. Each had his own speculations as to what was to be the character of the serious work which the Klan was to do. It was an unhealthy and dangerous state of mind; bad results very naturally followed from it.

The impression made on the public was the second cause which contributed to the transformation of the Klan into regulators. When the Klan first began to hold its meetings in the dilapidated house on the hill, passers-by were frequent. Most of them passed the grim and ghostly sentinel on the roadside in silence, but always with a quickened step. Occasionally one would stop and ask: "Who are you?" In awfully sepulchral tones, the invariable answer was: "A spirit from the other world. I was killed at Chickamauga." Such an answer, especially when given to a superstitious negro, was extremely terrifying; and if, in addition, be heard the uproarious noises issuing from the "den" at the moment of a candidate's investiture with the "regal crown," he had the foundation for a most awe-inspiring story. There came from the country similar stories. The belated laborer, passing after nightfall some lonely and secluded spot, heard horrible noises and saw fearful sights.

These stories were repeated with such embellishments as the imagination of the narrator suggested, till the feeling of the negroes and of many white people at mention of the Ku Klux was one of awe and terror. In a short time the Lictor of the Pulaski "den" reported that travel along the road on which he had his post had almost entirely stopped. In the country it was noticed that the nocturnal perambulations of the colored population diminished or entirely ceased wherever the Ku Klux appeared. In this way the Klan gradually realized that the most powerful devices ever constructed for controlling the ignorant and superstitious were in their hands. Even the most highly cultured were not able wholly to resist the weird and peculiar feeling which pervaded the whole community. Each week some new incident occurred to illustrate the amazing power of the Unknown over the minds of men of all classes.

Circumstances made it evident that the measures and methods employed for sport might be effectually used to sub serve the public welfare - to suppress lawlessness and protect property. When propositions to this effect began to be urged, there were many who hesitated, fearing danger. The majority regarded such fears as groundless. They pointed to the good results which had already been produced and the question was decided without any formal action. The very force of circumstances had carried the Klan away from its original purpose; so that in the beginning of the year 1867 it was virtually, though not yet professedly, a band of regulators trying to protect property and preserve peace and order.

After all, the most powerful agency in effecting this transformation- the agency which supplied the conditions under which the two causes just mentioned became operative-was the peculiar state of affairs existing in the South at that time. As every one knows, the condition of things was wholly anomalous; but no one can fully appreciate the circumstances by which the people of the South were surrounded or pronounce a just judgment on their behavior, except from personal observations. On this account, not only the Ku Klux, but the mass of the Southern people, have been tried, convicted, and condemned at the bar of public opinion, and have been denied the privilege of having the sentence modified by mitigating circumstances, which in justice they have a right to plead.

At that time the throes of the great revolution were settling down to quiet. The almost universal disposition of the better class of the people was to accept the arbitrament which the sword had accorded them. On this point there was practical unanimity. Those who had opportunity to do so engaged at once in agricultural, professional, or business pursuits. But there were two causes of vexation and exasperation which the people were in no good mood to bear. One of these causes related to that class of men who, like scum, were thrown to the surface in the great upheaval. Most of them had played traitor to both sides; on that account they were despised. Had they been Union men from conviction that would have been forgiven them. But they were now engaged in keeping alive discord and strife between the sections, as the only means of preventing themselves from sinking back into the obscurity from which they had been up heaved. They were doing this in a way not only malicious, but exceedingly exasperating. The second disturbing element was the negroes. Their transition from slavery to citizenship was sudden. They were not only not fitted for the cares of self control and maintenance so suddenly thrust upon them, but they entered their new role in life under the delusion that freedom meant license. They regarded themselves as freed men, not only from bondage to former masters, but from the common and ordinary obligations of citizenship. Many of them looked upon obedience to the laws of the State - which had been framed by their former owners - as in some measure a compromise of the rights with which they had been invested.

The administration of civil law was only partly reestablished. On that account, and for other reasons mentioned, there was an amount of disorder and violence prevailing over the country which has never been equaled at any period of its history. The depredations on property by theft, and by wanton destruction for the gratification of petty revenge, were to the last degree annoying. A large part of these depredations was the work of bad white men, who expected that their lawless deeds would be credited to the negroes.

But perhaps the most potent of all causes in this transformation was the existence in the South of a spurious and perverted form of the "Union League." It would be as unfair to this organization, as it existed at the North, to charge it with responsibility for the outrages committed in its name, as it is to charge upon the Ku Klux Klan much of the lawlessness and violence with which it is credited. But it is a part of the history of these times that there was a widespread organization called the "Union League." It was composed of the disorderly elements of the negro population, and was led by white men of the basest and meanest type. They met frequently, went armed to the teeth, and literally "breathed out threatening and slaughter." They uttered the most violent threats against the persons, families, and property of men whose sole crime was that they had been in the Confederate army, and in not a few instances these threats were executed. It was partly to resist this organization that the Ku Klux were transformed into a protective organization. Whatever may be the judgment of history, those who were acquainted with the facts will ever remain firm in the conviction that the organization of the Ku Klux Klan was of immense service at this period. Without it, life for decent people would not have been tolerable. It served a good purpose, for wherever the Ku Klux appeared the effect was salutary.

It was a dangerous experiment, this transforming of the Klan into regulators; on the whole it was no more successful than other experiments of a similar character have been. Yet, as we have said, the immediate results were good, and, for that reason, in their final issue the more disastrous. Permanent good was also effected; but whether enough of it to counterbalance the attending evils, is doubtful.

For a while the robberies ceased. The lawless class assumed the habits of good behavior. Under their fear of the dreaded Ku Klux the negroes made more progress in a few months in the needed lessons of self control, industry, and respect for the rights of property and general good behavior, than they would have done in as many years but for this or some equally powerful impulse. The "Union League" relaxed its desperate severity and became more moderate. But events soon occurred which showed that the fears of those who apprehended danger were not wholly groundless, and it became evident that unless the Klan should be brought under better control than its leaders at this time exercised, it would cause greater evils than it suppressed.

## III

## THE TRANSFORMATION

Until the beginning of 1867 the movements of the Klan had been characterized in the main by prudence and discretion, but there were exceptions. In some cases there had been a liberal construction of orders. The limits which it had been agreed not to pass had been overstepped.

Attempts had been made to correct by positive means evils which menaces had not been sufficient to remove. Rash, imprudent, and bad men had gotten into the order. The danger which the more prudent and thoughtful had apprehended as possible was now a reality. Had it been possible to do so, the leaders would have been willing to disband the Klan. That could not be done. They had woken a spirit from the vast deep; it would not go down at their bidding. The only course which seemed to promise a satisfactory solution of the difficulty was this: to reorganize the Klan on a plan corresponding to its size and present purposes; to bind the isolated "dens" together; to secure unity of purpose and concert of action; to hedge the members up by such limitations and regulations as were best adapted to restrain them within proper limits; to distribute the authority among prudent men at local centers, and exact from them a close supervision of those under their charge. In this way it was hoped the impending dangers would be effectually guarded against.

With this object in view the Grand Cyclops of the Pulaski "den" sent out a request to all the "dens" of which he had knowledge to appoint delegates to meet in convention at Nashville, Tenn., in the spring of 1867 at the appointed time this convention was held. Delegates were present from Tennessee, Alabama, and a number of other States. A plan of reorganization previously prepared was submitted to this convention and adopted. After the transaction of some further business, the convention adjourned, and the delegates returned home without having attracted any attention.

At this convention the territory covered by the Klan was designated as "The Invisible Empire." This was subdivided into "realms," coterminous with the boundaries of States. The "realms" were divided into "dominions," corresponding to congressional districts; the "dominions" into "provinces," coterminous with counties; and the "provinces" into "dens."

To each of these departments officers were assigned. Except in the case of the supreme officer, the duties of each were minutely specified. These officers were:

The Grand Wizard of the Invisible Empire and his ten Genii. The powers of this officer were almost autocratic.

The Grand Dragon of the Realm and his eight Hydras.

The Grand Titan of the Dominion and his six Furies.

The Grand Giant of the Province and his four Goblins.

The Grand Cyclops of the Den and his two Night Hawks.

A Grand Monk.

A Grand Scribe.

A Grand Exchequer.

A Grand Turk.

A Grand Sentinel.

One of the most important things done by this Nashville convention was to make a positive and emphatic statement of the principles at the order. It was in the following terms:

"We recognize our relation to the United States Government; the supremacy of the Constitution; the constitutional laws thereof; and the union of States there under."

If these men were plotting treason, it puzzles one to know why they should make such a statement as that in setting forth the principles of the order. This statement was not intended for public circulation. It is now given to the public for the first time. Every man who was a Ku Klux really took an oath to support the Constitution of the United States.

This Nashville convention also set forth the peculiar objects of the order, as follows:

> (1) To protect the weak, the innocent and the defenseless from the indignities, wrongs, and out rages of the lawless, the violent and the brutal; to relieve the injured and the oppressed; to succor the suffering especially the widows and orphans of Confederate soldiers.
>
> (2) To protect and defend the Constitution of the United States and all laws passed in conformity there to, and to protect the States and people thereto from all invasion from any source whatever.
>
> (3) To aid and assist in the execution of all constitutional laws, and to protect the people from unlawful seizure, and from trial except by their peers in conformity to the laws or the land.

This outline of Klan legislation bears internal evidence of what we know from other sources to be the truth. Those who were attempting to direct the movements of the Klan were now principally concerned about devising such measures as would control the Klan itself and keep it within what they conceived to be safe limits. The majority had up to this time shown a fair appreciation of the responsibilities of their self-imposed task of preserving social order. But excesses had been committed, and it was foreseen and feared that, if such things continued or increased, the hostility of State and Federal governments would be kindled against the Klan, and active measures taken to suppress it. The hope was entertained that the legislation taken by the convention and the reorganization would not only enable the Klan to enact its role as regulators with greater success, but would keep its members within the prescribed limits and so guard against the contingencies referred to. They desired on the one hand to restrain and control their own members; on the other, to correct evils and promote order in society; and to do the latter solely by utilizing for this purpose the means and methods originally employed for amusement. They failed in both directions. How and by will be told presently.

By the reorganization no material change was made in the methods of the Klan's operations. Some of the old methods were modified, some new features were added. The essential features of mystery, secrecy, and grotesqueness were retained, and steps were taken with a view to deepening and intensifying the impressions already made upon the public mind. They attempted to push to the extreme limits of illustration the power of the mysterious over the minds of men. Henceforth they courted publicity as assiduously as they had formerly seemed to shun it. They appeared at different points at the same time, and always when and where they were the least expected. Devices were multiplied to deceive people in regard to their numbers and everything else, and to play upon the fears of the superstitious.

As it was now the policy of the Klan to appear in public, an order was issued by the Grand Dragon of the Realm of Tennessee to the Grand Giants of the Provinces for a general parade, in the capital town of each province, on the night of the 4th of July, 1867. It will be sufficient for this narrative to describe that parade as witnessed by the citizens of Pulaski. On the morning of that day the citizens found the sidewalks thickly strewn with slips of paper bearing the printed words: "The Ku Klux will parade the streets tonight." This announcement created great excitement. The people supposed that their curiosity, so long baffled, would now be gratified. They were confident that this parade would at least afford them the opportunity of learning who belonged to the Ku Klux Klan.

Soon after nightfall the streets were lined with an expectant and excited throng of people. Many came from the surrounding country. The members of the Klan in the county left their homes in the afternoon and traveled alone or in squads of two or three, with their paraphernalia carefully concealed. If questioned, they answered that they were going to Pulaski to see the Ku Klux parade. After nightfall they assembled at designated points near the four main roads leading into the town. Here they donned their robes and disguises, and put covers of gaudy materials on their horses. A skyrocket sent up from some point in the town was the signal to mount and move. The different companies met and joined each other on the public square in perfect silence; the discipline appeared to be admirable. Not a word was spoken. Necessary orders were given by means of the whistles. In single file, in deathlike stillness, with funeral slowness, they marched and countermarched throughout the town. While the column was headed north on one street it was going south on another. By crossing over in opposite directions the lines were kept up in almost unbroken continuity. The effect was to create the impression of vast numbers. This marching and countermarching was kept up for about two hours, and the Klan departed as noiselessly as they came. The public was more than ever mystified. The efforts of the most curious to find out who were Ku Klux failed. One gentleman from the country was confident that he could identify the riders by the horses. But, as we have said, the horses were disguised as well as the riders. Determined not to be baffled, during a halt of the column he lifted the cover of a horse that was near him, and recognized his own steed and saddle, on which he had ridden into town. The town people were on the alert to see who of the young men of the town would be with the Ku Klux, All of them, almost without exception, were marked mingling freely and conspicuously with the spectators.

Perhaps the greatest illusion produced was in regard to the numbers taking part in the parade. Reputable citizens were confident that the number was not less than three thousand. Others, whose imaginations were more easily wrought upon, were quite certain there were ten thousand. The truth is that the number of Ku Klux in the parade did not exceed four hundred. This delusion in regard to numbers prevailed wherever the Ku Klux appeared. It illustrates how little the testimony of even an eyewitness is worth in regard to anything which makes a deep impression on him by reason of its mysteriousness.

The Klan had a large membership; it exerted a vast and terrifying power; but its influence was never at any time dependent on, or proportioned to, its membership. It was in the mystery in which the comparatively few enshrouded themselves. It is an error to suppose that the entire male population of the South were Ku Klux, or even a majority of the people were privy to its secrets and in sympathy with its extremist measures. To many of them, perhaps to a majority, the Ku Klux Klan was as vague, impersonal, and mysterious as to the people of the North or of England; they did, to this day, attribute to it great good.

One or two incidents will illustrate the methods resorted to play upon the superstitious fears of the negroes and others. At the parade in Pulaski, while the procession was passing a corner on which a negro man was standing, a tall horseman in hideous garb turned aside from the line, dismounted, and stretched out his bridle-rein toward the negro, as if he desired him to hold his horse. Not daring to refuse, the frightened African extended his hand to grasp the rein. As be did so, the Ku Klux took his own head from his shoulders and offered to place that also in the outstretched hand. The negro stood not upon the order of his going, but departed with a yell of terror. To this day he will tell you: "He done it, suah, boss. Seen him do it."

The gown was fastened by a drawstring, over the top of the wearer's head. Over this was worn an artificial skull made of a large gourd or of pasteboard. This, with the hat, could be readily removed, and the man would then appear to be headless. Such tricks gave rise to the belief - still prevalent among the negroes - that the Ku Klux could take themselves all to pieces whenever they wanted to. Some of the Ku Klux carried skeleton hands. These were made of bone or wood, with a wrist or handle long enough to be held in the hand, which was concealed by the sleeve of the gown. The possessor of one of these was invariably of a friendly turn, and offered to shake hands with all he met, with what effect may be readily imagined. A trick of frequent perpetration in the country was for a horseman, spectral and ghostly-looking, to stop before the cabin of some negro needing a wholesome impression and call for a bucket of water. If a dipper or gourd was brought it was declined, and the bucketful of water demanded. As if consumed by raging thirst, the horseman gasped it and pressed it to his lips.

He held it there till every drop of the water was poured into a gum or oiled sack concealed beneath the Ku Klux robe. Then the empty bucket was returned to the amazed negro with the remark: "That's good. It is the first drink of water I have had since I was killed at Shiloh." Then a few words of counsel as to future behavior made an impression not easily forgotten or likely to be disregarded.

## IV

## THE DECLINE

For a while after the reorganization of the Klan, those concerned for its welfare and right conduct congratulated themselves that all was now well. Closer organization and stricter official supervision had a restraining influence upon the members. Many things seemed to indicate that the future work of the Klan would be wholly good. These hopes were rudely shattered. Before long official supervision grew less rigid, or was less regarded. The membership was steadily increasing. Among those who were added were bad men who could not be - at least, were not - controlled. In the winter and spring of 1867 and 1868 many things were done by members or professed members of the Klan which were the subject of universal regret and condemnation. In many ways the grave censure of those who had hitherto been its friends was evoked against the Klan, and occasion was given its enemies to petition for the intervention of the Government to suppress it. This was done. The end came rapidly. We must now trace the causes which wrought the decay and downfall of the "Invisible Empire."

Men of the character of the majority of those who composed this Klan do not disregard their own professed principles and violate self-assumed obligations carelessly. To see men who were just now the advocates of law and order defying the one and destroying the other, is a sight singular enough to elicit inquiry as to the causes that wrought the change. The transformation of the Ku Klux Klan from a band of regulators, honestly, but in a mistaken way, trying to preserve peace and order, into the body of desperate men who in 1869 convulsed the country by deeds of violence, and set at defiance the mandates of both State and Federal governments, is greater than the transformation which we have already traced. In both cases there were causes adequate to the results produced; causes from which these results followed naturally and almost necessarily, and which have never been fully and fairly followed out. They may be classed under three heads:

> (1) unjust charges; (2) misapprehension of the nature and objects of the order by those not members of it; (3) unwise and over-severe legislation.

As has already been pointed out, the order contained within itself, by reason of its purpose and methods, sources of weakness. The devices by which the Klan deceived outsiders enabled all who were so disposed, even its own member's, to practice deception upon the Klan itself. It placed in the hands of its members facilities for doing deeds of violence for the gratification of innate deviltry or personal enmity, and having them credited to the Klan. To evilly disposed men membership in the Klan was an inducement to wrong-doing; in fact, it presented to all men a dangerous temptation. In certain contingencies, at any time likely to arise, it required a considerable amount of moral robustness to withstand this temptation. Many did not withstand it, and deeds of violence were done by men who were Ku Klux, but who at the time were acting under cover of their connection with the Klan, but not under its orders; and because these men were Ku Klux, the Klan had to bear the odium of their misdeeds.

In addition to this, the very class which the Klan proposed to hold in check and awe into good behavior, after a while became wholly unmanageable. Those who had formerly committed depredations to be laid to the charge of the poor negroes now assumed the guise of Ku Klux, and returned to their old ways with renewed ardor. In some cases even the negroes played Ku Klux. Outrages were committed by masked men in regions far remote from any Ku Klux organization. The fact that these persons took pains to declare that they were Ku Klux was evidence that they were not. In this way it came about that all the disorder prevailing in the country was charged upon the Ku Klux. The Klan had no way in which to refute or disprove the charge. They felt that it was hard to be charged with violence of which they were innocent. At the same time they felt that it was natural and not wholly unjust that this should be the case. They had assumed the office of regulators. It was therefore due society, due the Government, which so far had not molested them, that they should at least not afford the lawless class facilities for the commission of excesses greater than any they had hitherto indulged in; and, above all, that they should restrain their own members from lawlessness. The Klan felt all this; and in its efforts to relieve itself of the stigma thus incurred, it acted in some cases against the offending parties with a severity well merited no doubt, but unjustifiable. As is frequently the case, they were carried beyond the limits of prudence and right by a hot zeal for self-vindication against unjust aspersions. They thought the charge of wrong was unfairly brought against them. They did worse wrong than that charged to clear themselves of the charge.

The Klan, from the first, shrouded itself in deepest mystery, and out of this grew trouble not at first apprehended. They wished people not to understand; they tried to keep them profoundly ignorant. The result was that the Klan and its objects were wholly misunderstood and misinterpreted. Many who joined the Klan, and many who did not, were certain that it contemplated some mission; far more important than its overt acts gave evidence of. Some were sure it meant treason and revolution. The negroes, and the whites whose consciences made them the subjects of guilty fears, were sure it boded no good to them. When the first impressions of the awe and terror to some extent wore off, a feeling of intense hostility toward the Ku Klux followed. This feeling was all the more bitter because founded, not on overt acts which the Ku Klux had done, but on vague fears and surmises as to what they intended to do. Those who entertained such fears were in some cases impelled by them to become the aggressors. They attacked the Ku Klux before receiving from them any provocation. The negroes formed organizations of a military character, and drilled by night. These organizations had for their avowed purpose "to make war upon and exterminate the Ku Klux." On several occasions the Klan was fired on. The effect of such attacks was to provoke counter hostility from the Klan; and so there was irritation and counter-irritation, till the state of things became little short of open warfare. In some respects it was worse; the parties wholly misunderstood each other. Each party felt that its cause was the just one; each justified the deed by the provocation.

The Ku Klux, intending wrong, as they believed, to no one, were aggrieved that acts which they had not done should be charged to them; and they felt outraged that they should be molested and assaulted. The other party, satisfied that they were acting in self defense, felt fully justified in assaulting them. And so each party goaded the other from one degree of lawlessness to another.

The following extracts from a General Order of the Grand Dragon of the Realm of Tennessee will illustrate the operation of both these causes. It was issued in the fall of the year 1868. It shows what were the principles and objects which the Klan still professed, and it also shows how it was being forced away from them:

"HEADQUARTERS REALM NO. 1."

"DREADFUL ERA, BLACK EPOCH, DREADFUL HOUR."

"General Order No. 1."

"Whereas, information of an authentic character has reached these headquarters that the blacks in the counties of Marshall, Maury, Giles and Lawrence are organized into military companies, with the avowed determination to make war upon and exterminate the Ku Klux Klan, said blacks are hereby solemnly warned and ordered to desist from further action in such organizations, if they exist.

"The G. D. (Grand Dragon) regrets the necessity of such an order. But this Klan shall not be outraged and interfered with by lawless negroes and meaner white men, who do not and never have understood our purposes.

"In the first place this Klan is not an institution of violence, lawlessness and cruelty; it is not lawless; it is not aggressive; it is not military; it is not revolutionary.

"It is essentially, originally and inherently a protective organization; it proposes to execute law instead of resisting it and to protect all good men, whether white or black, from the outrages and atrocities of bad men of both colors, who have been for the past three years a terror to society and an injury to us all.

"The blacks seem to be impressed with the belief that this Klan is especially their enemy. We are not the enemy of the blacks, as long as they behave themselves, make no threats upon us and do not attack or interfere with us.

"But if they make war upon us, they must abide the awful retribution that will follow.

"This Klan, while in its peaceful movements and disturbing no one, has been fired into three times. This will not be endured any longer; and if it occurs again and the parties be discovered, a remorseless vengeance will be wreaked upon them.

"We reiterate that we are for peace and law and order. No man, white or black, shall be molested for his political sentiments. This Klan is not a political party; it is not a military party; it is a protective organization and will never use violence except in resisting violence.

"Outrages have been perpetrated by irresponsible parties in the name of this Klan. Should such parties be apprehended, they will be dealt with in a manner to ensure us future exemption from such imposition. These impostors have, in some instances, whipped negroes. This is wrong! Wrong! It is denounced by this Klan as it must be by all good and humane men.

"The Klan now, as in the past, is prohibited from doing such things. We are striving to protect all good, peaceful, well-disposed, and law-abiding men, whether white or black.

"The G. D. deems this order due to the public, due to the Klan, and due to those who are misguided and misinformed.

"We therefore request that all newspapers who are friendly to law, and peace and the public welfare, will publish the same.

"By order of the G. D., Realm No. 1.

"By the Grand Scribe."

Granting that this order expressed the principles which the Klan was honestly trying to maintain, it also illustrates how it was driven to violate them by the very earnestness and vehemence with which they attempted to maintain them. If it is asked why, under these embarrassing circumstances, the Klan did not disband and close its operations, the answer is plain. The members persuaded themselves that there was now more reason than ever for the Klan's existence. They felt that they ought not to abandon their important and needful work because they encountered unforeseen difficulties in accomplishing it. It is an illustration of the fatuity which sometimes marks the lives of men, that they did not perceive that these evils grew out of their own methods, and must continue and increase while the Klan existed. Men are not always wise. They frequently persist in a course which, to others differently situated, appears not less absurd than wicked. We cannot apologize for their course. We cannot excuse it. But justice requires that a fair and truthful statement be made of the embarrassments and temptations which surrounded them.

Matters grew worse and worse, till it was imperatively necessary for the State authorities to interfere. There was a general feeling that legislation on the subject was necessary. But few were prepared to expect such legislation as that enacted by the famous - or infamous, as the reader chooses - Legislature called together by Governor Brownlow in September, 1868.

Tennessee was the first State to pass an anti Ku Klux statute. In September, 1868, Governor Brownlow called the Legislature together in extra session to devise measures for the suppression of the order. A relentless and bloody statute was passed; and to enforce it the Governor was authorized, if be deemed it necessary, to declare martial law on the infected counties and to call out troops. The law passed, and the method of enforcing it increased rather than quieted disorder. The statute is long, and, as a whole, not worth quoting. Its leading provisions were the following:

> (1) For association or connection with the Ku Klux a fine of five hundred dollars and imprisonment in the penitentiary not less than five years; and "shall be rendered infamous."
>
> (2) Persons impaneled for jury service were required to answer under oath whether they were obnoxious to the first section of the act.

(3) Prosecuting attorneys and grand jurors were directed to summon persons whom they suspected "or had cause to suspect" and to force them to testify what they knew the Ku Klux. If those so summoned failed to appear or refused to testify, the penalty was a fine of five hundred dollars.

(4) Every "inhabitant" of the Slate was constituted an officer extraordinary with power "to arrest without process" any one known or expected to be a Ku Klux.

(5) To feed, lodge, entertain or conceal a Ku Klux exposed the offender to a fine of five hundred dollars, and imprisonment for five years.

(6) It was made unlawful to publish any order emanating from the Klan.

(7) There was but one clause in the law which bears the semblance of mercy. Its provisions are so odious as to be shocking. The one way by which a man could relieve himself of liability to this law was by turning informer. As additional inducement to do this, a reward of half the fine was offered.

(8) But, most remarkable of all, the statute was made penal against offenses committed previous to its passage. The last section of it reads: "Nothing herein contained shall be so construed at to prevent or exempt any person heretofore guilty of any of the offenses herein contained from prosecutions under the law at it now stands."

There were hundreds of men in the Klan who were not law-breakers. There had been no law against association with the Ku Klux. They had no personal participation in the excesses in which some of the Klan had indulged. They were ready to admit that the movement bad proven to be injudicious. Good had been done, but harm bad followed. They would cheerfully have obeyed a legal command to sever their connection with the Ku Klux and desist from further operations. But when these men were declared infamous, made liable to fine and imprisonment, and exposed to arrest "without process" by any one who chose to inform against them, the effect was to drive them to absolute desperation.

In some sections of the State a reign of terror followed the passage of this act. The Ku Klux were now almost in the attitude of men fighting for life and liberty. There was no hope in submission except on terms which to men of honor were more hateful than death.

## V

## DISBANDMENT

On the 20th of February, 1869, Governor Brownlow resigned his position as Governor to take the seat in the United States Senate to which he had been elected. The last paper to which he affixed his signature as Governor of Tennessee proclaimed martial law in certain counties, and ordered troops to be sent thither. This proclamation was dated February 20, 1869. In a few days it was followed by a proclamation from the "Grand Wizard of the Invisible Empire" to his subjects. It recited the legislation directed against the Klan, and stated that the order had now in large measure accomplished the objects of its existence. At a time when the civil law afforded inadequate protection to life and property, when robbery and lawlessness of every description were un-rebuked, when all the better elements or society were in constant dread for the safety of their property, persons, and families, the Klan had afforded protection and security to many firesides, and in many ways contributed to the public welfare.

But, greatly to the regret of all good citizens, he further said, some members of the Klan had violated positive orders; others, under the name and disguises of the organization, had assumed to do acts of violence, for which the Klan was held responsible. The Grand Wizard had been invested with the power to determine questions of paramount importance to the interests of the order. Therefore, in the exercise of that power, the Grand Wizard declared that the organization heretofore known as the Ku Klux Klan was dissolved and disbanded.

Members were directed to burn or destroy all regalia and paraphernalia of every description, and to desist from any further assemblies or acts as Ku Klux. They were told further, that they would continue in the future, as heretofore, to assist all good people of the land in maintaining and upholding the civil laws, and in putting down lawlessness.

This proclamation was directed to all Realms, Dominions, Provinces, and Dens in "the Empire." It may be that there were portions of the Empire never reached by it. The Grand Wizard was a citizen of Tennessee; and as no paper in that State could publish the order, because of the stringent law against such publication, there was no way in which the proclamation could be fully distributed. Where it was promulgated, obedience to it was prompt and implicit.

But whether obeyed or not, this proclamation terminated the Klan's organized existence as decisively as General Lee's last general order, on the morning of the 10th of April, 1865, disbanded the army of Northern Virginia. When the office of Grand Wizard was created and its duties defined, it was explicitly provided that he should have "the power to determine questions of paramount importance, and his decision shall be final." To continue the organization or to disband it was such a question. He decided in favor of disbanding. Therefore, the Ku Klux Klan had no organized existence after March, 1869.

The report of the Congressional Investigating Committee contains a mass of very disreputable history, which belongs to a later date, and is attributed to the Klan, but not justly so. These persons were acting, in the name of the Klan and under its disguises, but not by its authority. They were acting on their own responsibility.

Thus lived, so died, this strange order. Its birth was an accident; its growth was a comedy, its death a tragedy. It owed its existence wholly to the anomalous condition or social and civil affairs in the South during the years immediately succeeding the unfortunate contest in which so many brave men in blue and gray fell, martyrs to their convictions. There never was, before or since, a period of our history when such an order could have lived. May there never be again!

[Captain John C. Lester was one of the Klan's founding members, as well as, a member of the Tennessee State House. In 1884, he and the Reverend David L. Wilson (also a Klansman and a fervent supporter of the 1920s Klan revival) co-authored a book about his experiences in the Klan, THE KU KLUX KLAN, ITS ORIGIN, GROWTH, AND DISBANDMENT, which was the first published work to cite General Nathan Bedford Forrest as the Klan's first leader. Interestingly enough, Bedford himself claimed in 1868 that he was not a member of the Ku Klux Klan, but did hold sympathy for their cause. Forrest also contended that he saw "carpetbaggers" and Southern whites who were members of the Republican party as greater threats to the fabric of America. It should be noted, however, that Forrest did order the Klan to disband in 1869 due to the steady increase in violence being enacted in its name (this order was ignored by many members of the Klan throughout the country).]

# NEW LIGHT ON THE KU KLUX KLAN OF 1866

An Editorial Response to the Previous Article

In the present number of THE CENTURY may be found a chapter of the inside history of the Ku Klux Klan, which is, in many respects, remarkable. It describes the somewhat trivial origin of the Klan out of circumstances which account for the mystery attending its rise and growth; it traces the causes which changed the Klan into a powerful organization called the Invisible Empire; and it leaves the history at the point where, in 1869, the "Grand Wizard" disbanded the Empire, though, for a long time after, bands of men calling themselves Ku Klux continued to "regulate" affairs in the South, on secret mob principles.

In its specific statements of fact, the narrative, we think, bears inherent marks of authenticity. It is proper to say that the writer of the paper is an active minister in the Southern Presbyterian Church. We may state also that he has no personal knowledge of the Ku Klux, although he has had abundant opportunity to know as much of the inside history of the Klan as if he had been a leading member; he has had access, besides, to authentic private documents.

Many of the facts related by him will be as new, probably, to most readers at the South, who were personally acquainted with the "mission" and deeds of the "Invisible Empire," but not with its origin, as to those readers at the North who remember the name Ku Klux only as the synonym for midnight murder and political infamy. These are harsh terms, but they are none too harsh if one is to characterize frankly that unfortunate period in our history, which has come to be regarded at the South with solid, though softening, satisfaction, and at the North with lessening disapproval of the results, though with lasting abhorrence of the methods.

In its drift, the paper may be regarded as a moderate apology for the Ku Klux, on the score of unpremeditated mission and extenuating provocation. Its conclusions in this regard are partly unsound, because the writer does not properly bring into the premises the real impelling idea of the Invisible Empire. Its members were a people who had sought by revolution to insure the perpetuity of a slave system, which was the corner-stone of their social and industrial life. The penalty of defeat required that they should be governed in large part by the politically unskilled and mentally ignorant race which had been in servitude to them, and which was being organized and led by a few whites, who were even more odious to them. Here was a state of affairs, it is now plain to see, as perfectly arranged to breed trouble as the juxtaposition of fire and powder. No race on the face of the earth would have accepted such moral and political subjugation to another race regarded as of a lower type, and which had just been transported from barbarism, or recently reared out of it. Probably the nearest approach to such moral and political servitude observable today, is the ease with which the native intelligence of some of our Northern cities is ruled by a horde of ignorant foreign-born liquor-dealers, and their more ignorant foreign-born clients. We certainly favor a reform of this anomaly, but not by bloodshed. There are stronger agencies for social and political regeneration than mob violence; and a mob of the higher elements of society is worse than a mob of the ignorant and of the dregs, because its example is more pernicious and lasting.

So, when we are told that many members of the Ku Klux were originally in search of amusement, and did not premeditate outrage, terrorism, and murder in giving wide-spread organization to the Klan, we cannot help thinking that they might have stilled the evil power they had raised if their hearts had not been fired by a general purpose to subjugate the blacks, who, by the operation of the law of the land, had become their political masters. What was an overmastering wish with some was a lawless determination with others, and with all it meant revolution at any cost. The ordinarily peaceable men in the Klan had helped to fashion it into an effective instrument, and the rebellious spirits of that unsettled time seized the weapon, some to wage private warfare, and all to vent their hatred of the political situation. It was the worst kind of mob violence; and, as in every deviation from legal methods, the worst elements came to the top.

In estimating the minor provocations which, it is claimed, led the Ku Klux into the role of regulators, and in weighing the tone of injury and innocence which pervades the manifestoes of the Klan, we must not forget who, in the eyes of the law, were the aggressors. It is not uncommon for an aggressor, of whatever kind, to view with alarm and abhorrence a natural act of self-defense or retaliation. The Government, which placed the blacks in their strange position, in the end left them to defend themselves. Naturally, they were made to yield to the whites the power they had not the physical courage and the mental ability to hold. They are entitled to the fullest sympathy, for they were politically without blame and were grievously sinned against. And perhaps we should also regard their trials and the place they have accepted as necessary features of the discipline which is to make intelligent freemen of a once barbarous and ignorant race of bondmen.

On the other hand, there is a growing sympathy with the whites of the South, and a willingness to admit that on the ground of human sentiment that great changeable force which now seems to differentiate human law and the law of heaven, and again seems to override both the whites had great provocation. In the same spirit men are beginning to accept the success of the Ku Klux revolution as being in the result the inevitable solution of an anomalous political situation. Peace and happiness never could come to the South so long as the political lines were co-existent with the color lines, with the blacks in the ascendancy. Every well-wisher of the blacks will counsel them to accept the foot of the political ladder, and it is not without fitness that they should begin at the bottom rung and work up, because they were the last to be apprenticed to citizenship. Already the whites, as in Charleston, are giving them a share of the public employment, by making them street-cleaners, firemen, and policemen. This is not sharing according to numerical importance, but it is a beginning, and the education which is being placed within their reach will fit them for better things to come.

But let us not be misunderstood. If it was a questionable device to place the power of the ballot, suddenly and without limitations, in the hands of an emancipated and uneducated race, none the less immoral, unjustifiable, and brutalizing were the means adopted by the whites to rid themselves of an intolerable rule. And because the blacks are still restrained from the free exercise of their legal rights, the situation at the South is to-day morally unsound. For it is for ever true, as a Southern orator has said, that "the political devil is no more to be fought with fire, without terrible consequences to the best interest of the community, than is the devil of avarice, or of envy, or of ambition, or any other of the numerous devils which infest society."

The lessons to be drawn from the Ku Klux period are mainly for statesmen, but they also teach the individual citizen, in a new way, that mob force is a barbarous and dangerous remedy for real or fancied wrongs.

Originally published as FACTS, HARPER'S WEEKLY, January 30, 1915

# FACTS ABOUT THE LYNCHINGS OF 1914

Booker Washington's report on lynching for 1914 has the merit of stating facts and making no argument whatever. Often that is the most effective way to carry conviction. Of the 52 persons lynched last year, only seven were charged with rape and two of those were white. Three of the persons lynched were women, and one of the women was seventeen years of age. She was charged with killing a man who was reported to have raped her. One woman, charged with burning a barn, was killed in the presence of her four-year-old child. One man was lynched for biting another; one for stealing mules; one for being under a house.

The lynchings were distributed as follows: Alabama, 2; Arkansas, 1; Florida, 4; Georgia, 2; Louisiana, 12; Mississippi, 12; Missouri, 1; New Mexico, 1; North Dakota, 1; North Carolina, 1; Oklahoma, 3; Oregon, 1; South Carolina, 4; Tennessee, 1; Texas, 6.

[FACTS was generously provided by Matt Jacobsen from OLDMAGAZINEARTICLES.com.]

ONLY AMERICANS MAY PASS  photograph by J. A. Murdoch, Atlanta, Ga.

Reprinted from, THE LITERARY DIGEST, January 27, 1917

# LAST YEAR'S LYNCHING

Last year's lynching figures suggests Principal Robert R. Moton, of Tuskegee Institute, may well be kept in mind when we consider the northward migration of the negroes. The latter movement, says the New York Age, a negro paper, "is following a natural economic pull, but back behind it, increasing and hastening it, are lynching and all the other forms of oppression and injustice practiced against the race." This is not believed due to the number of lynchings, for there were only fifty-four last year, as compared with sixty-seven in 1915, but, so the negro editor thinks, to "the horrible atrocity of several cases: the burning alive of the victim at Waco, the lynching of two women in Florida, and the lynching of a respectable and well-to-do colored man at Abbeyville." All but four of the victims, it might be added, were negroes, and all but one of the lynchings took place in Southern States, according to the figures sent out from Tuskegee.

The geographical distribution of these occurrences interests the anti-prohibition National Herald (Philadelphia), which notes "that forty-four of them were in prohibition States, or prohibition territory of 'wet' States," and that the only Northern lynching occurred in prohibition Kansas. So, it observes, "prohibition at least, does not prevent mob murder any more than it prevents mob confiscation of property by ballot."

Georgia keeps the lynching record, which she held in 1915, a fact that leads the Montgomery Advertiser in the neighboring State of Alabama to remark that there are people "who meekly hold that it might be good for this whole section of the nation if Georgia would kindly mend its ways and quit spilling human blood on the picturesque theory that 'it's no harm to kill a nigger.'" We come to the end of 1916, admits the Atlanta, Constitution, speaking for Georgia, "with fourteen out of a total of fifty-four to our credit, or more than 25 per cent. Of the whole." And it adds:

"The seriousness of it all is stressed the fact that in only three of the fifty-four cases was the victim lynched for the particular crime which many have held to justify mob action, and which first gave rise to it. In nine cases there was attempted assault, while in forty-two, or 77 per cent of the whole number, the crime varied from murder down to slapping the face of a boy. Men were lynched for aiding suspected prisoners to escape, and there is one recorded instance where a man was killed because he protested with a mob about to put another to death."

In face of the scorn and criticism which have been directed at Georgia, says The Constitution regretfully, "we have done nothing." Another Georgia daily, the Savannah Press believes "the lynchings in this State can be traced almost wholly to the fact that none is punished for complicity in such unlawful and dastardly acts. Indeed, more energy is expended probably in getting evidence against a man accused of violating the prohibition law in the average Georgia community than there is in getting the data together upon which to convict a man of the crime of murder for lynching is only murder by the many instead of by the individual."

[LAST YEAR'S LYNCHING was generously provided by Matt Jacobsen from OLDMAGAZINEARTICLES. com.]

# K.K.K.

## The Strangest Secret Society on Earth

### by Shaw Desmond

*From time immemorial secret societies have had a fascination all their own. Here is an authoritative account of one of the most remarkable underground organizations in the world. Suppressed by law after the American Civil War, the "Ku-Klux-Klan" has been resuscitated during recent years, and has now spread far and wide throughout the United States. The name of only one member is known - the supreme head - but the society has representatives in every walk of life and metes out justice in its own extraordinary fashion. Mr. Desmond tells some remarkable stories concerning the "K.K.K." and its masked, white-robed night-riders.*

An "invisible empire," an "Imperial Wizard," "Ku-Klux-Klan." In this matter-of-fact twentieth century of ours, these three things sound like the worst kind of jiggery-pokery. There seems to be something about the very name "Ku-Klux-Klan" that suggests the "abracadabra" of ancient incantations.

Yet behind these seemingly ridiculous things stands one of the most remarkable movements in the word.

The Ku-Klux-Klan is a secret society with ramifications throughout the whole of the North American Continent.

Originally formed in the strenuous days of reconstruction following the American Civil War for the purpose of holding the negro in subjection, and sternly suppressed by the Federal Government in the year 1870, it has now been revived, but with a program far transcending the original.

The objects of this formidable organization are as clear-cut as a diamond. They are stated with a directness that is almost brutal, and backed by a force that is ruthless. Here they are :

To maintain white supremacy everlastingly over all other races, whether black, or brown, or yellow. The Klan stands for the permanent and perpetual predominance and rule of the white race in America.

Other principles follow, such as:

"The organization stands for the protection of woman's honour and the sanctity of the home." The Klansmen in their work on this side of the society's activities are amazingly quick and, apparently, all-knowing. Only a few months ago the negro boot-boy in an Atlanta hotel insulted a white woman believing that his conduct would never come to light. But the "Klan Eagles" as they are called, see everywhere.

He was dragged from his bed at dead of night by masked men and taken to the slopes of Stone Mountain, where he given five minutes in which to forswear forever any further communication with white women or else be burnt alive! The wretched man fell on his knees, terror-stricken, and swore. His captors then vanished into the night. From that moment however, that negro knows that his every movement and every word will be watched wherever he may try to hide himself in the United States.

There is not a city where such black undesirables do not receive their mysterious warnings. If they ignore them, vengeance follows, swift and sure.

The K.K.K. occupies a unique position amongst the secret societies of the world. Formed originally in 1866, and apparently blotted out but actually only driven underground, its official titles, paraphernalia, regalia, emblems, symbols, secret signs, and intricate regulations were nursed carefully in Southern hearts, waiting for "The Day." It is, moreover, the only secret society on earth of its type duly and officially recognized by the Government of the country in which it exists. In the words of a New York journalist, its members believe they have an idea that it is as great as the Government of the United States, which admitted the incorporation of the Klan under the laws of the State of Georgia in the years 1915 and 1916.

When one realizes that in this amazing organization every member has to be "one hundred per cent American" - that is, born in America of

American parents - and that it has in its ranks some of the highest judges on the American bench; members of Congress; ministers of the gospel; lawyers and bankers; city officials of every rank; doctors; skilled and unskilled working men and, finally, some of the chiefs of the police and police officers of all ranks from captains to ordinary policemen, one begins to understand the significance of the machine which is now once more being called into and its to shake the country.

## ONLY ONE MEMBER

Yet of all the tens of thousands in its ranks and no man can say what its actual membership only one solitary member is known to the world. That man is Colonel William Simmons, formerly a Methodist preacher of blood and fire, now the fiery protagonist of the Klan and preaching another sort of blood and fire. Of all its countless adherents, the name of this man, whose headquarters in Atlanta are known as the Aulic of the Imperial Wizard, is the only one published, and only he, with perhaps three others, is in possession of the roll-call of the Klan, so that he holds in his hands the lives and reputations of hundreds of thousands of human beings.

Colonel Simmons, who is Professor of Southern History at Lanier University, Atlanta, has a piercing eye, a firm-set mouth and wears an expression of invincible will and determination. He is a clean-shaven man, with smoothly-parted hair and tortoise shell-rimmed glasses, and he frankly conveys a sensation of fear to the average man - especially after his visitor has seen the staring pictorial representation of a human eye painted upon the outer door of the temple of the Wizard. Of his absolute sincerity there can be no doubt. Of his capacity to write his name in American history there is also no doubt.

It was this man who, nearly twenty years ago, believed that the time had come to revive the Ku-Klux-Klan. For fourteen years he spent all his tremendous energies to his task, studying, working, organizing.

In October, 1915, he disclosed his ambition to friends, among whom were three members of the original Klan, and from that nucle1us has sprung the modern Klan, which in its sweep from the South, sending out its thousands of "Klan Eagles," as they are called or "gospel spreaders," is gradually dragging within its vortex the youth of the North and the great Middle West, the hub of America. Its symbol is the Fiery Cross, which it carries aloft through the dark night to strike terror and win adherents. He believes frankly in the right of might or as a member of the Klan would put it "the right of the white-born free-born American to make his country the first in the world."

One of the favorite methods of the K.K.K. is to strike terror into evildoers and opponents without resorting to violence if it can be avoided.

Quite recently in a little Southern town a single horsemen appeared, apparently from nowhere, in the awe-inspiring dress of the Klan and stated in a sepulchral voice from behind his mask that within a few minutes a band of solemn, determined men would pass and that nobody should follow them. In the distance could be heard the thunder of hoofs coming out of the shadows. Then, headed by a herald bearing a flaming cross, two hundred night-riders each man clad in the robes of the masked and armed to the teeth. As they passed under the arc lamps, the lights were switched off, coming on again only when the uncanny riders had vanished. This was a silent recognition of their power and authority.

One result of this melodramatic appearance was that not a single negro of ill-repute could be found in the precincts of the city the next morning. It was not even necessary for the riders to state the object of their demonstration. Every colored man knew it.

The K.K.K. has been thought out with meticulous care. Its plans are claimed to be laid for twenty-five years ahead, and the whole organization is on the strictest military lines. Eight States are already completely mapped out and enrolled - Florida, Georgia, Tennessee, Alabama, Texas, Kentucky, Virginia, and South Carolina. Twenty-one others, at the moment of writing, are coming into line with startling rapidity. In New York City itself there are already many thousands of members, and the immediate objective of the society is a roll-call there of a quarter of a million. The Klan has representatives in every State in the Union. A score of members of the House of Representatives at Washington have enrolled and also many United States Senators from the Upper House. All these people, inside the society, are under strict military discipline. In the words of an American sympathizer "They can't quit! They won't quit!"

"No man is wanted in the Klan," said Colonel Simmons on one occasion, "who hasn't manhood enough to assume a real oath with serious purpose to keep the same inviolate." Behind those words stands a purpose and a threat.

One of the most terrifying things about the Klan is its method of "weeding out," a process which is always going on.

When a member of the society is deemed "undesirable" he finds one day upon his dressing-table, perhaps, a slip of paper which tells him to clear out. Or it may be that a voice comes to him in the crowded street, giving him the same warning. In either case he obtains unmistakable evidence of the genuineness of the communication by certain symbols.

If he is a wise man, he goes, and at once. If he is not a fool he respects rigidly any secrets of the Klan which he may have learned. If he does not, there is no power in the North American Continent to protect him. The Klan never forgets.

One of the rules of the order is that any member who violates the law of the land in any way can be at once expelled from the Klan. This, apparently, is done without trial, on the order of Colonel Simmons, acting upon information presented to him and after independent investigation. It is by the rigid backing of the law of the United States that the organization has gathered into its ranks in all States the local law officers, including mayors, sheriffs, and captains of police, as well as soldiers and sailors.

That is why in Birmingham, Alabama, and other cities it has been impressed upon the people that all the operations of the Klan - some of them, as will be seen, of an extraordinary nature - have had the full sanction of the legal authorities of the community.

## STAMPING OUT A CRIMEWAVE

Recently, in Birmingham, where a wave of crime had been troubling the community, a mysterious message was conveyed to the local police by the K. K. K. offering to stamp out crime inside a few days. Within a short time after the acceptance of the offer, some seven hundred the finest riders, and shots in Alabama were turned loose upon the crime-wave, with the result that, in the words of a resident, "the fear of God was put into the hearts of evildoers and crime practically disappeared." In this case the Klansmen tracked the "wanted" men remorselessly, risking their lives with the utmost coolness. In the duels to the death which ensued they almost invariably came out on top owing to their quickness with the rifle and magazine-pistol.

The first reappearance of the Klan in recent times was in Houston, Texas. Like all the appearances of "the Knights of the Invisible Empire," as they call themselves, the Houston materialization was accompanied by the triple combination which has always struck terror into the spectator-secrecy, ruthlessness, and the suggestion of hidden force.

It was at the Confederate Veterans' reunion parade. As the long lines of men who fought in the Civil War of 1861 passed down the streets, rank on rank, there suddenly appeared pouring out of alleyways, from back streets, and from all sorts of hiding places a body of horsemen who might have stepped out of Dante's Inferno.

They were clad in high white conical-shaped head-dresses and robes of flowing white, the headgear having eye-slits like those of the old Inquisition of Spain. These men wheeled silently into line behind the veterans, the muffled hoofs of their horses making practically no noise. Every man carried his loaded rifle at the ready across his breast, whilst under the white robes could be seen the outlines of magazine pistols.

For a moment the great crowds were dumb. The negroes, knowing full well what that body of men portended, trembled and turned away. And then, full-throated, there burst from the crowd a great roar of welcome. In a moment the years had spun backward to the days of the Civil War, when the grandfathers of these very men had lined up in the same guise to destroy the

Republican administration of that day. The ghosts of the night were riding once again. The Fiery Cross was aflame! Only, this time, it was not a Southern movement only, but one destined to embrace the whole country.

Think for a moment what this thing means. It means that half-a-dozen members of a family might be seated around a table. Perhaps two of the sons are members of the Klan, but the father will not know it. Or it may be that it is the father who is a member yet his nearest and dearest will have no more knowledge of it than if he did not exist. It might well happen that a man who has offended the Klan will receive his punishment at the hands of his own brother.

Already through the Southern night is heard the pad-pad of the hoofs of the night-riders, galloping to some unknown destination on some unknown purpose. The belated negro, hearing that muffled thunder, drags himself into the nearest ditch, his face twitching, his frame trembling, for he remembers the stories of his grandfathers and of what the Klan did in the old days.

It is only fair to the Ku-Klux-Klan to say, in the words of Colonel Simmons, that it repudiates some of the terrible accusations which have been brought against it, not only in its old but in its modern form. What he calls "foes of the South" and "enemies of the Southern people" viciously assailed it as a band of murderers who stopped at nothing and whipped, murdered, and terrorized not only blacks but whites when they incurred its displeasure, and who used its machinery to avenge personal spite and wrongs. "No fouler slander was ever perpetrated," he said. "Instead of being murderers and cut-throats, the members were men of the highest type and were working to safeguard life and property."

However that may be, such authorities as Henry William Elson, in his "History of the United States," assert that the Klan after the Civil War carried out operations "marked by violence and disorder in the extreme" to prevent the newly enfranchised negro using his vote, leading to Ku-Klux Act of 1871.

Goldwin Smith, D.C.L., in his "Outline of Political History," asserts that the Klan "did horrible atrocities upon the negroes" in their night-rides.

So far as lynching is concerned, the force behind these outrages is often ascribed to the Klan, although the society formally repudiates anything that is against law and order. However, where the law is slow or inefficient, there is little doubt that the Klan would not fear to step in.

The other day, for instance, a negro who, with others, killed a policeman in a police raid on a gambling saloon in Arkansas was taken to the local jail. The curious thing about this case was that several other negroes had also fired at the policeman who was hit by a single bullet and these negroes were also lodged in the jail. All at once three hundred men appeared and asked the jailer quite politely for his keys. The jailer equally polite and possibly a member of the Klan himself, first requested the very determined gentlemen who faced him "to allow the law to take its course," and then handed over the keys! The men sent in a posse who went unfalteringly to the cell where the negro was confined, deliberately ignoring the other negroes, took him out and hanged him to a telegraph pole near the scene of his crime.

Here as in all similar cases, the Klan, or the men who do these things in its name, was absolutely sure of its ground. Doubtless the bullet in the policeman's body had been fitted to the negro's pistol and the real murderer found.

It is this deadly certainty that so terrifies evildoers in the South, and it is often most uncanny. Thus, at a place called Bristol, in the South, an aged merchant was recently killed by some unknown person, who robbed him and then vanished. It looked "all Lombard Street to a China orange" against the murderer being found, as be had apparently left no traces. Yet, within a few hours, the offender, a negro, had been caught and dealt with.

It would be wrong to imagine, however, that the Klan only directs its efforts against black men. Quite recently, in Santa Rosa, California, there was a desperate pistol battle between four white men, who had kidnaped some twenty girls whom they had locked up in a shack, and the police. After three officers had been killed, help suddenly appeared and the men were overpowered. Infuriated citizens, seemingly under organized direction, insisted upon justice being meted out on the spot, producing a telegraph pole for the purpose and even attacking the jail after the men were lodged in it. Finally, after they had been assured that justice should be done, somebody gave the order to disperse and they silently melted away.

If the Klan directed this affair, as is believed, it gives full proof of the perfection of its discipline.

The present revival of the K.K.K. is nominally due to the recent enfranchisement of the millions of black women, and the danger of black supremacy in the South, but its scope is likely to be much wider and more epoch-making.

Already the negroes are stirring uneasily under the new materialization. In Virginia in particular, one negro publisher has suggested that a burying-ground be at once selected for the Klan; and there is this to be said about his threat. Many thousands of young negroes, trained in arms during the Great War, are not likely to sit down quietly under what they regard as a new menace. It is at any rate a fact that in the Gulf States many negroes have gone over the border to obtain arms and ammunition, which they have been smuggling into the South. Any man who has been in America will see the ugly significance of this in its potentialities for the future.

What is more, the leaders of the negroes state point-blank that if the Klan seeks once more to prevent the use by the negroes of the ballot, the negroes will resist to the utmost of their power. If the Klan persists in its determination to secure white supremacy at all costs and anybody who knows the type of men from whom its strength is drawn, and its history, will know that nothing has ever been able to turn it from its purpose then the first clash between white and black will take place down in these Southern States, whence, nerve-racking tales are coming.

The trouble is that, whether members of the Klan have or have not taken part in lawless scenes, the tendency is to give the Ku-Klux full credit for their inception. And this is one of the chief dangers with which the Klan is faced, and one about which it sometimes bitterly complains

What is actually happening is that the bands of desperados are breaking loose in certain States. Calling themselves the Ku-Klux-Klan, wearing the spectral white helmets and robes of the order and even murdering under the guise of "Klanishness" as it is called.

It is this sort of thing which has led to the recent solemn pronouncement issued by the Imperial Wizard, couched in the usual crude but earnest language of the proclamations of the Klan.

"Beware! Beware! All ye people of the earth. There is one and only one Ku-Klux-Klan; therefore shun as a poisonous serpent and other organization of a similar name. We warn you. Beware!"

## THE NIGHTRIDERS

At the moment of writing some very ugly things are being done in the name of the Klan, although, possibly, without its sanction. The Southern roads are covered with the riders of the night, whose white-robed forms, on horses with muffled hoofs, are to be seen galloping along under light of the moon, the fiery cross at their head. These night-riders, appearing from nowhere. have been destroying cotton burning crops and barns, and generally carrying dismay and consternation amongst the farmers of the South, white or black.

So secret are the methods the night-riders and so perfect their intelligence department that they are able to do their will with apparent impunity. Barns containing tobacco worth thousands of have been burnt almost under the noses of their owners and even whilst close watch was being kept about them, some of the guards themselves, perhaps, being night-riders. This work is often done in the name of the Klan, although the Ku-Klux-Klan repudiates it.

A little while ago, a farmer named Joseph Arrington, living near Ohio, had in one of his tobacco barns some ten thousand pounds of the finest Burley leaf tobacco, which he purposed on selling at the prevailing low prices. To protect such a store was to him a matter of life or death, yet, despite his efforts, he woke one night to find the sky lit up by flames spouting from his barn which had been so thoroughly impregnated with combustible stuff that it was burned to the ground and all the tobacco destroyed. This is an example of what has been done by the night-riders throughout Robertson Mason counties.

At Louisville in western Kentucky, there is a place called Owensboro where seven "loose leaf" houses had been buying tobacco from the farmers at very low prices. In a flash some two thousand "day-riders," as they are called to distinguish them from the men who work at night materialized, rode up to the seven business houses, and quietly gave the managers the alternative of shutting their houses and refusing to receive any more tobacco at the low prices prevailing or "taking the consequences."

Faced by two thousand desperate and angry men it is not difficult to understand what the decision of the managers finally was.

In certain districts men go to sleep with their hearts in their throats, fearing to hear that muffled thunder which heralds a visit from the dreaded night-riders. Perhaps it is some lonely farmhouse miles from anywhere, which is the object of a visit. There is the padding of hoofs, and a banging on the door, which the scared proprietor, in his night attire, will open. If he does not open the door is smashed and he is lucky if no worse befall.

He is then taken outside by the masked riders, whilst his wife and children look on terrified from the house, and sometimes placed under a tree with a noose about his neck. He is told the most minute things about his cotton and his crops. Every single plan which he thinks he has made in secret is disclosed to him, the most minute acts of his life are mentioned. All this is done to show him that the Klan has an eye that sees everything and a hand that reaches everywhere.

It may be that this man has been negotiating the sale of his cotton at a price below that of wartime - the unforgivable sin in the South - or it may be that he has threatened the Klan or the night-riders who pretend to be members of the Ku-Klux. In either case, unless he professes humility and promises amendment, Heaven help him! He generally promises.

This burning of cotton gins and the threatening of cotton growers and dealers is sternly disavowed by the staff officers of the Ku-Klux-Klan, so

It would seem that the Klan must be more or less exculpated from blame in this connection. But, however this be, it shows the menace let loose upon South by the newly-revived organization. For it is now open to evilly-disposed persons to form bands, call themselves the Ku-Klux-Klan, and rob and murder with impunity under the of "One hundred per cent Americanism."

Perhaps in nothing is the religious nature of the organization shown more than in its fanaticism and its ceremonies. There is scarcely a member of the Klan who is not as assuredly convinced of the righteousness of his cause and its objective as was ever any follower of Mohammed. Its strength, in fact, lies in its terrible earnestness and sincerity.

How seriously the Ku-Klux takes its ceremonies and mysteries will be seen from that paragraph in its constitution which declares that all these things "are held sacred by us as a precious heritage; this precious heritage we shall jealously keep, and valiantly protect from profanation."

Not only must the members of the K.K.K be native-born white American citizens, but it is specifically laid down, following that "religious" note which runs through everything "Klannish," that such citizens "must believe in the tenets of the Christian religion and owe no allegiance of any degree or nature to any foreign Government, political institution, sect, people, or persons." This is part of the solemn oath which is sworn at midnight in the forests and on the lonely mountain sides. Heaven help the man who breaks it!

This at once rules out all Irish-Americans; it rules out too, Roman Catholics, because they owe allegiance to His Holiness the Pope; it automatically excludes all German-Americans; and, as the Klan states, "it rules out Bolshevists and foreigners who would bring foreign political nostrums into this country." The Ku-Klux-Klan shares its "invisible empire" with nobody.

One of the rarely humorous sides of the Klan's activities is shown in its decision to fight all those Protestant bodies which have been uniting in certain American communities for a "Blue Law" propaganda - that is, for the purpose of following up the recent prohibition legislation against alcohol by laws prohibiting dancing, theatres, smoking, and so on. The Klan declares that it has no sympathy whatever with the communities which have been formed to further these "Blue Laws." It claims that such laws "destroy the sanctity of the home by permitting law officers to enter it and to pry into the most private affairs of the citizen." The "Blue Law" officer, when he seeks such entry, will now have to reckon with the secret powers of the Klan. Which is all keeping the American statesman awake at night and giving him furiously to think.

The latest move of the K.K.K. is the branding of offenders against public morals. Only a few weeks ago a body of a masked men suddenly appeared in the home of Alex Johnson, a negro bell-boy at a hotel in Dallas, Texas, and, without speaking a single word, took him into a fast automobile without head-lights. Driving at a furious pace, the boy the whole time screaming in terror and pleading incoherently for his life, they drove to a lonely place.

Here, Johnson, despite his frantic appeals, was tied to a fence-post and, having been stripped to the waist, was given twenty-five heavy lashes by a powerful man.

As he sagged unconscious from the whipping, a bottle of acid was produced and the letters, K.K.K. were indelibly marked on his forehead. He was taken back in the car and flung into the road outside the hotel where he was employed.

During the whole of these proceedings not a word was spoken by any of the masked men. Such branded men, of course, will carry the mystic K.K.K. symbol to their graves for all to see.

Now, as these lines are being written, Colonel Simmons, the "Imperial Wizard," is preparing for a great tour of the cities of the North in order to extend the active operations of the K.K.K. He is to address secret conclaves in these cities and hold giant public demonstrations, and each of States like those in the South, is to have a sort of sub-Wizard, whose name is to be made public. One of the chief divisions of the Klan is to be in New York City itself, where a public headquarters is to be opened with a full staff of officials, the names of none of whom will appear, with the exception of that of the sub-Wizard. There is no doubt at all that the K.K.K. is a force to reckoned with in modern American life.

### MASKED MORALISTS.

#### KU KLUX KLAN REVIVAL.

**FROM OUR OWN CORRESPONDENT.**

NEW YORK, Sunday.

Gangs of masked and hooded raiders sweeping the country after the manner of the famous Ku Klux Klan bands are spreading terror in the State of Texas

They proclaim as their object the "upholding or the supremacy of the white race" and the enforcing of a code of morals laid down by themselves Their victims include both Whites and Negroes, who are subjected to tarring and feathering, branding with acid, surgical operations, flogging, and banishment.

Facsimile of a paragraph from the London "Daily Mail" Referring to the activities of the "K.K.K."

[Shaw Desmond is an accomplished author who, in later years turned his attention to the field of psychic research. He founded the INTERNATIONAL INSTITUTE FOR PSYCHICAL RESEARCH as well as authoring many books including REINCARNATION FOR EVERYMAN, THE POWER OF FAITH HEALING,: PSYCHIC AND DIVINE, and YOU CAN SPEAK WITH YOUR DEAD.]

Reprinted from THE LITERARY DIGEST for December 2, 1922

## THE KLAN AS A NATIONAL PROBLEM

Half the State in the Union are now the scenes of Ku Klux activities, according to a study of the news dispatches made by a Massachusetts paper, the Worcester Gazette. The Klan carried the State elections in Texas and Oregon on November 7th. In Louisiana the situation is such that Governor John M. Parker makes a special trip to Washington for help to handle "horrifying crimes" in his State attributed to clansmen there and to others coming over the borders from other States. The announced readiness of the Federal Government to cooperate with Louisiana or any other State, "whenever Federal interests are involved," seems to the New York Tribune "a definite warning to the Ku Klux Klan that its leaders will do well to heed." While at present there is apparently to be no actual aid given by Federal agencies, The Tribune notes that several States are now ready to cooperate with Louisiana against the "Invisible Empire." The Governor of Georgia, where the present Ku Klux Klan started, says he will cooperate. Governor Olcott of Oregon says the Klan has been an "active menace" in his State, that "no greater menace confronts the United States today" and that "the time has come for Americans to assert themselves in a nation-wide battle against this political iniquity." The Governor of Connecticut says the State police have been watching the Klan there. Governor Allen of Kansas recently announced that the Klan officials would be expelled from his State and the Supreme Court of that State has been asked to halt all Klan activities in Kansas.

While Governor Parker denounces as "extravagantly inaccurate" the Washington Post's recent assertions that the Ku Klux Klan "has virtually reduced the sovereign State of Louisiana" to vassalage, and that "the machinery of State Government has almost ceased to function," the press are convinced by his request for assistance that the problem has outgrown State boundaries and must now be dealt with by the nation as a whole. The organization, as the Washington Star notes, is found now North, South, East and West. It is only right, declares the New York World, "that the Federal authority should take cognizance of a subversive movement that is far wider than any State."

The Klan in its new form and spirit is not confined to the South. It raises its ugly head even in New York pulpits. It is an issue in Oregon. No State between is free from it. Nor is it confined to the old purpose of terrifying ignorant Negroes in the black belt into what the local white minority considers good conduct. It has taken on sinister attribute from the old Know-Nothing movement. Its aim in the negation of constitutional government in order that it may set up a super-government of its own for the tyranny of an arrogant and narrow intolerance.

It may not be true, as the Ku Klux have claimed, that there are more than seventy members of the organization in Congress. The fact that such a claim can be made plausible shows that the movement has invaded the Capital in such strength that it can not be ignored. President Harding and the Department of Justice have a plain duty to perform in using all the resources of the Government for the repression of a cabal that aims to make of free government a mockery.

Although New Orleans correspondent of the Philadelphia Public Ledger says the Ku Klux Klan boasts 145,000 members in Louisiana - more than two-thirds of the vote cast in the last State election-representatives of Louisiana in Congress deny that there is any absence of normal order, or anything like a Ku Klux "menace" in their State. The New Orleans Item wires us that "no grave nor unhappy situation exists as yet, and wise action and considerate action may avert it." From the Louisiana capital the Baton Rouge Slate Times telegraphs that the Ku Klux Klan has not at any point "usurped the functions of the State Government" although there may be instances where a few weak-kneed parochial and district officials have joined the Klan where it is politically powerful." This paper offers a very simple explanation of the Governor's trip to Washington:

"The Governor in his investigations in Morehouse Parish, of the murder of two citizens-Richards and Daniels -who are supposed to have been done away with by the Ku Klux Klan, found some leads the State could not follow out. They led into other states. It was to seek the cooperation of the Federal Government in this particular, that Governor Parker went to Washington."

The Ku Klux "Bureau of Information," according to the <u>Albany Journal</u>, claims that "the Klan is growing at the rate of about 10,000 new members every week." What, asks the <u>Washington Star</u>, "explains the growth of this organization?" We might let the Klan's spokesmen help furnish an answer. For instance, in an issue of <u>Colonel Mayfield's Weekly</u> (Houston, Tex.), appearing after the Ku Klux candidates won the Texas "run-off" primary last summer, the editor, who must not be confused with Senator-elect Mayfield, sets this down as the Ku Klux Klan's mission in Texas Hind the rest of the world:

"It is going to drive the bootleggers forever out of this land and place whisky-making on a parity with counterfeiting."

"It is going to bring clean moving pictures to this country; it is going to bring clean literature to this country. It is going to drive the Catholics back into their church and keep them there. It is going to protect and preserve our public schools at all hazards. It is going to break up roadside parking, and see that the young man who induces a young girl to get drunk is held accountable. It is going to enforce the laws of this land; it is going to protect homes; its conduct is going to be such that to be a Klansman will be greater than a king. The Klan means a new era in the life of America. It means the return of old time Southern chivalry and deference to womanhood; it means that the married man with an affinity has no place in our midst."

In paid newspaper advertisements and in letters to editors, defenders of the Klan say it is anti-Catholic because the Catholic Church is "un-American" and controlled outside of America. Its secret methods are said to be necessary to fight the "Jesuits" and to "slip up on crooked public officials." The Klan is said to be wrongfully blamed for acts of violence because "the daily press is almost wholly owned or controlled by the Romanists and Jews." Nevertheless, if officers of the law will not enforce the law, the Klansmen must "ride forth" and do it. So, it is argued, officials can easily keep the Klan from activity by performing their own duties effectively. It is interesting to note that a reader of <u>The Literary Digest</u> writes from a Pennsylvania town to say: "If the Ku Klux can assist our courts to secure justice and throw fear into the hearts of men that make mockery of our laws, then I am ready to be a, Klansman."

In his recent book, The Modern Ku Klux Klan, Mr. H. P. Fry, once a "Kleagle," or organizer, tries to explain the success of Ku Klux propaganda by the growth of discordant groups among the American people. He thinks that favors shown to Negroes by northern politicians and the activities of the National Association for the Advancement of Colored People have been powerful recruiting forces for Ku Kluxism. The Ku Klux organizer constantly uses the cry that "social equality is to be forced on the South." On the Pacific coast the Klan "is attempting to win the people by putting forth the doctrine of 'white supremacy' in relation to the Japanese question." The writer believes that of late there has been a great increase of antagonism between the Christian and the Jew, between the Protestant and the Catholic. Klan organizers work largely upon "a feeling of jealousy" of the Jews' great advance in America along all lines of commercial and professional activity. Mr. Fry says that there is more anti-Catholicism in this country than the average person realizes, and in his study of the Ku Klux movement he has found that "one of its greatest bids for popular favor was in its attitude to the rise of Catholicism in America." He explains:

"Basic causes of group antagonism between Protestant and Catholic lie partly in the fact that the government of the Catholic Church is outside of the United States, and partly on account of the attitude of the Church itself toward certain American institutions, notably the public-school system and the laws in this country governing marriages."

To rid the United States of the "Invisible Empire," Mr. Fry suggests first, publicity, and then Congressional legislation against organizations with secret membership lists or engaged in promoting racial or religious discord. The States, he says, can help stamp out Ku Kluxism through laws directed against organizations "stirring up religious and racial prejudice against unwarranted interference with the law enforcing branches of the Government and against going about the community in disguise."

[THE KLAN AS A NATIONAL PROBLEM was generously provided by Matt Jacobsen from OLDMAGAZINEARTICLES.com.]

Reprinted from THE LITERARY DIGEST for December 23, 1922

# NEW YORK'S ANTI-KLAN OUTBURST

Leave the Ku Klux Klan "to us Protestants," said James W. Gerard, former Ambassador to Germany, recently in an address before a New York Jewish congregation; "no Jewish organization need take any action. We Americans," he went on, "should not suffer any such organization as the Ku Klux Klan to exist." Meanwhile the Klan has set New York by the ears; Mayor Hylan has ordered the police to investigate the activities of an accredited representative of the Invisible Empire, and, save in one instance reported in the press, the order has been denounced in Protestant, Catholics and Jewish circles alike. Judge Francis X. Mancuso has gone a step further by instructing a Grand Jury to scrutinize the activities of the secret organization as a potential breeder of racial hatred and religious strife, and Ferdinand Pecora. Acting District Attorney of New York County, is said to have come into possession of about eight hundred names of reputed members of the Klan and to have secured other information, which may result in legal proceedings being brought against the hooded hosts. Among the interesting pamphlets which came into the possession of the District Attorney were announcements of ambitious phrasing. The Klan is described in these documents as "the most dauntless organization known to man," and as having "the most sublime lineage in history." Mr. Pecora is reported to have remarked that "compared with these fellows, the Crusaders were a bunch of pikers."

Exciting much comment was the accusation that Calvary Baptist Church, the largest of its denomination in New York, was a hotbed of Klan propaganda; but the charge was vigorously denied in a statement signed by leading members and by Dr. John Roach Straton, pastor, who, before a congregation that is said to have overflowed into the streets, virtually read Dr. Oscar D. Haywood, self-announced apostle of the Klan, out of office as evangelist of Calvary Church, and denounced the Klan's methods, though admitting that its motives might be sincere and good. Other developments in Klan activities near New York to inspire comment include a new secret society, "The Royal Riders of the Red Robe," seemingly affiliated with the larger organization, which is reported to have backed the demand of the Leif Ericson Klan of Paterson, New Jersey, that German should not be taught in the high schools of that city, and the permitted address of a hooded evangelist in a Reformed Church in West Sayville, Long Island. While the Klan is thus reported to be busying itself in and about New York, its strategy is to be seriously challenged. The American Unity League of Chicago, an anti-Klan organization which has been making public the names of Klansmen in Chicago, is reported to be preparing to launch a similar campaign in New York. The hoods and sheets, it is said, are to be lifted. Another rebuke comes from Arthur S. Tompkins, of Nyack, New York, Grand Master of the Grand Lodge of Masons of the State of New York, who denies an allegation that 75 per cent of the Klan members throughout the country are Masons. As quoted in press reports, his statement runs:

"The Masons are utterly opposed to the Ku Klux Klan as un-American and un-Masonic. We know of only a few Masons who are members of the Klan, and we don't consider them good Masons. The Grand Lodge of the State of New York, its officers and the great body of Masons throughout New York State are absolutely opposed to the Klan and its activities."

Objecting strongly to the "color scheme of today," Dr. Straton said in his sermon against secret societies:

"White Ku Klux Klanism, green sectarianism (a reference to Irish Catholic societies), yellow journalism and general blackguardism are equally distasteful to my eye and heart." Grasping the fringe or a flag draped near the pulpit; he called all Catholics, Protestants and Jews to rally around its red, white and blue as being a good enough color scheme for all Americans, and the congregation, according to reports, arose, applauding and joining in singing "America." As for his opinion on the Klan itself, Dr. Straton is quoted in press reports as declaring:

"The ideals of the Ku Klux Klan, as stated in their literature and by their lecturers, beyond any question are fair and good enough, but they fail to see that their ways are necessarily contrary to our American principles. I believe, therefore, to put it concisely, that their motives are good and their methods are bad their principle's are virtuous, but, their practices are vicious. I think recent history in this country will support me in this contention."

"Here we have already not only a 'labor group' and a 'capitalistic group,' but also the Catholic group, with its secret societies, and the Jewish group, with its secret societies, and the negro group, with its secret societies, and now comes the Ku Klux Klan, with many imitators and auxiliaries springing up around it. We have recently been treated to an account of the startling doings of the 'Royal Riders of the Red Robe,' and even the women, we are told, are organizing, tho they seem to be troubled somewhat for an appropriate name, since the men have already usurped all the robes, both red and white, and for both day and night."

Catholic comment hails the Klan as another organized breeder of bigotry. The "organized fanaticism, bigoted nationalism, subsidized prejudice, and hate-dispensing propaganda as represented by the Ku Klux Klan in America has gone just far enough without drawing the attention of the officials of the country," declares The Tablet, official organ of the Catholic diocese of Brooklyn, in a bitterly resentful denunciation. Instead of a Government by the people in Lincoln's happy phrase, the Klan, we are told, seeks to "subvert the Government of Lincoln and Washington and to give us a Government 'of the Klan, by the Klan, and for the Klan.' And it has the blasphemous gall to assert that such a Government would be Christian and American. A more dastardly plot, a more repulsive conspiracy, has not been born this side of hell in our day." The Tablet further relieves its pent-up feelings against the Klan and "constant misrepresentation and calumniation indulged in by anti-Catholic papers, tracts, lecturers and organizations" by exclaiming:

"We are sick and disgusted of being charged that we are 'in politics' when there are less than six Senators are Catholics out of nearly a hundred, and less than forty out of over four hundred Congressmen, and not one in the President's Cabinet; no denomination has less men in national politics than we, and those who manufacture this calumny are guilty of drawing a red herring across their own trail. We are sick and disgusted of hearing the Knights of Columbus lied about and slandered, by a motley crew who know their charges are false. We are sick and disgusted of hearing that we are plotting to destroy the public schools, or opposed to public education, a charge concocted by knaves and meant to he swallowed by ignoramuses. We are sick and disgusted of all of this, and similar charges, made either through hatred or ignorance, and frequently for personal profit."

Opposition to the Ku Klux Klan, on the ground that it, is un-American as well as anti-Semitic, is also expressed in a resolution adopted by 700 representatives of 250 organizations at a conference in New York of the American Jewish Congress. The resolution expresses the delegates' "abhorrence" of the policies and acts of the secret order, and says:

"The conference believes the Ku Klux Klan to be a menace to the unity and integrity of American life, and declares its purpose to cooperate with all groups prepared to oppose the Ku Klux Klan as hostile to American ideals and subversive of the spirit of American and democracy."

But this is the very reverse or the true spirit of the Klan, declares Dr. Haywood, who, as he is quoted in press interviews, recalls that the Congressional investigation of the Klan "failed to find anything to condemn it as opposed to the Constitution of the United States or the Federal statutes." He goes on to assert that the organization is a "secret, fraternal order devoted to the cultivation of race pride, racial purity, religious liberty, patriotism and social ideals of Protestant Christianity, its ultimate objective being to establish and maintain the solidarity and supremacy, of the Gentile white Protestant American in America." Those who do not come under this classification are not excluded because of hatred of them, Dr. Haywood asserts, but "because of the desire to bring together those elements that will be congenial respecting the development of American ideals. "The Klan is, therefore, not anti-Catholic; it is not anti-Jewish; it is not anti-negro;, it is not anti-alien."

Defense of the Klan comes also from a pulpit. Canon William Sheafe Chase, rector of Christ, Protestant Episcopal Church, Brooklyn, says that while he may not approve of all of the methods of the Klan, he is "glad to find a strong band of men who are organized to resist the corruption of politics and the lawlessness of our times." As press reports quote him further, he avers:

"A society, like a man, may be loved for the enemies it has. The bootleggers, the professional gamblers, the producers of vile songs and plays, the Sabbath breakers and corrupt leaders are attacking it and using every effort to destroy it. Personally, I think that the violent enemies of the Klan are more of a menace to the public welfare than the Klan itself."

[NEW YORK'S ANTI-KLAN OUTBURST was generously provided by Matt Jacobsen from OLDMAGAZINEARTICLES. com.]

THE EMPEROR ADDRESSING THE FIRST IMPERIAL KLONVOKATION
photograph by J. A. Murdoch, Atlanta, Ga.

## PROTESTANTS DISOWNING THE KU KLUX

The Ku Klux Klan has not infrequently marked its approval of certain Protestant pastor's by contributing small sums of money to their churches, but it is a mistake, we are told, to think that the Klan deserves and is receiving the support of the Protestant Church at large. Much more frequently the Klan and all its works have been denounced from the Protestant pulpit. To make this all the more clear, though the Klan is not mentioned by name, the Administrative Committee of the Federal Council of Churches of Christ in America recently issued a statement declaring that any organization whose membership is secret, oath-bound, and disguised, and which tends to foster racial or class prejudice, has no real right to speak in the name of the Protestant Church. As it is quoted in The Herald of Gospel Liberty (Christian), the statement is as follows:

"The Administrative Committee of the Federal Council of the Churches of Christ in America records its strong conviction that the recent rise of organizations whose members are masked; oath-bound, and unknown, and whose activities have the effect of arousing religious prejudice and racial antipathies is fraught with grave consequences to the Church and to society, at large. Any organization whose activities tend to set class against class or race against race is consistent neither with the ideals of the churches nor with true patriotism, however vigorous or sincere may be its professions of religion and Americanism.

"Evils of lawlessness and immorality, however serious can never be remedied by secret, private, and unauthorized, action. They must be handled by the State and by the recognized forces of education. For groups of individuals wearing masks and concealing their identity to pass judgment on men and women and to carry out humiliating measures of their own devising is subversive of every principle of civilized government, and undermines respect for the established agencies of law and order.

"Any body of men, unidentified and banded together to achieve in a partisan spirit the purposes of a sectional, political, racial, or sectarian group, is almost certain to fall into the very evils of mob rule against which the spirit of Christian democracy, and Americanism makes vigorous and constant protest. Even If they resort to no unworthy deeds themselves, their practice of carrying on their plans in disguise or under cover of darkness, encourages others to do likewise, and so affords the opportunity for all manner of lawlessness to be carried on with immunity from arrest or punishment. However true it is that in some communities religious organizations seek a control over municipal administration which is undemocratic and highly undesirable, yet for another body of men, secret and oath-bound, to undertake to get control is equally intolerable, even if they seek with all sincerity to wrest it from the control of other groups.

"The Administrative Committee of the Federal Council of the Churches is opposed to any movement which overrides the processes of law and order, and which tends to complicate and make more difficult the work of cooperation between the various political, racial and religious groups in the Republic. No such movements have the right to speak in the name of Protestantism, and the churches are urged to exert every influence to check their spread."

[ PROTESTANTS DISOWNING THE KU KLUX was generously provided by Matt Jacobsen from OLDMAGAZINEARTICLES.com.]

# WHEN THE KLAN RULES

## The Giant in the White Hood

### by Stanley Frost

*In this, the first of a succession of independent but related articles, Stanley Frost gives reasons for considering the Ku Klux Klan very seriously. He shows that it is very much alive, and that, whether the desire be to change, use, fight, or destroy it, nothing but facts will serve as ammunition.*

The Ku Klux Klan has become the most vigorous, active, and effective organization in American life outside business. Its influence, though intangible and often secret, affects every public question and every activity which depends in any degree on public opinion; its power is incalculable, since it is different from that of any other known force. It controls, in a way in which no political party has ever controlled, hundreds of cities, towns, and counties, a few States; it has elected its picked men mayors, sheriffs, and judges, legislators and Governors, Representatives and Senators in Congress. It is reaching for the Presidency.

Moreover, it is growing with tremendous speed. Its members are already beyond two millions, and may be near four; certainly they will increase by hundreds of thousands in the next few weeks. All efforts which have been made to check or destroy it have failed; indeed, they seem only to have speeded its growth. It is not yet able to impose its will on the Nation, but it is surely on the road towards supreme power. The cloud which two years ago was no bigger than a man's hand has covered a great part of the heavens and is still spreading.

This is the first of the reasons why there should be a new and careful consideration of the Klan. It is a reason which appeals to every man or woman to whom it makes a cent's worth of difference whether or not their opinions and judgments on public affairs are accurate and well founded. All such people must from now on know the real facts as to the strength, the methods, the habits, and the intentions of this white-hooded giant, as well as the dangers his existence creates. All thought regarding the body politic is subject to discount in exact proportion to the lacks and inaccuracies of this information.

But there are other reasons for a reappraisal of the Klan which will appeal equally to all fair-minded men and women; reasons which seem to indicate that earlier judgments found against it were at least partly wrong, or have become wrong.

One is the quality of the people who are in the Klan or are joining it. They are not always, though sometimes, the best in the community, but they are usually the good, solid, middle-class citizens, the "backbone of the Nation." It is absurd to continue to believe that these people, so many and of such standing, are all criminally minded; that they are any more likely to commit outrages than any other equal-sized body, such as the Presbyterian Church, or that they can or will become a menace to the country through any other cause than ignorance.

It is clear that the opinion most of us formed two years ago, that the Klan was an attempt to gather the wild and lawless elements into a power, that it was composed of gangs of night-riding hoodlums, probably criminal and certainly crazy, along with a scattering of feebleminded people whom they had hoodwinked-it is clear that this judgment is no longer correct, no matter how well founded it seemed.

It is clear too that the Klan can no longer be dismissed as an unimportant though distressing outbreak of a few morons. Instead it has become a great National movement, with all the power and entitled to all the dignity and respect-yes, "respect" even if joined with fear and nervous ridicule--which belong to such movements.  Whether for good or bad, whether insane or inspired, it must be studied, judged, and dealt with on that basis.

It is clear, finally, that since it has become such a movement quick action must be taken if it is to be stopped, diverted, or controlled. Its power is very real; already there are strong influences getting into motion to use that power. If its leadership or program is wrong, the time when either can be changed will soon pass. When it has added the momentum of another million members or so, it will be as hard to divert from its course as a comet.

It is, for example, pure folly any longer to attack it as "lawless." It is true that lawlessness may be argued from its methods; true, too, that lawless acts have been committed under cover of its hoods; true, finally, that a trusted official recently killed a man in Atlanta. But when the great number of Klansmen is considered, with the fact that in many States there has never been an outrage that could even remotely be charged to them-and this in States where their strength is undoubted-and when it is further considered that of all the outrages charged against the Klan not a dozen have been proved, fairness must admit that the charge falls as to actual conduct.

Since that is true, the charge of lawless intent gets nowhere. In almost all communities the Klan now has members who are known; they are not lawless either actually or in intention, and such charges therefore seem absurd equally to them and to their non-Klan neighbors. They simply are not believed, and he who spreads them discredits himself.

The shoe, in fact, is now on the other foot. It is the legal officials who have become lawless and the Klan which is suffering illegal persecution. The case of Oklahoma is the worst, but hundreds of minor officials all over the country are stretching their powers, as Governor Walton did his, in their efforts to suppress the Klan.

To give a single instance: A certain county judge ordered the arrest on sight of any Klan organizer who appeared, and when he caught one shipped him out of the county. There was no trial, no charge could be proved against him, and the punishment is not one provided by any law.

Perhaps that county will do as well as any other to illustrate the kind of people who are now joining the Klan. In that county it today includes, if not the "best people," at least the next best. There are bankers, lawyers, doctors, probably a majority of the preachers, a handful of teachers, scores of small business men, and hundreds upon hundreds of farmers.

But the Klan also reaches into higher places. In New York City three men may be mentioned as typical of its upper layer: a man very near the top of one of America's biggest manufacturing corporations, a doctor who is recognized as close to the head of his profession, and the owner of a powerful magazine. All, by the way, are active churchmen.

I learned of one problem of Klan membership which has its elements of humor. The conscientious president of a large and highly respected fresh-water college is greatly disturbed in his mind as to whether or not he shall discharge the dozen or score members of his faculty who have joined. The Klan is watching him, rather hopefully, since such a raid would be splendid advertising and would also provide some very able "martyrs" for its propaganda bureau!

The total membership in the Klan today is of course a secret of the order. Klan officials refuse to give any figures. Others, whose information mayor may not be good, say the total, including both men and women, is now near 4,000,000. Detailed estimates, not by Klansmen, are that there are 500,000 in Indiana and 415,000 in Texas, 450,000 in Ohio; more than 200,000 each in Oklahoma, Oregon, California and New York State; and from 50,000 to 100,000 each in Arkansas, Washington, Kansas, Missouri, Michigan, Illinois, Kentucky, West Virginia, Maryland, New Jersey, Louisiana, Mississippi, Alabama, Georgia, Florida, and Tennessee. This would give a total of 3,850,000, which is not far from the Klan guess when allowance is made for scattered membership.

These figures, however, are undoubtedly extravagant, for Klansmen are inclined to boast, and politicians are scared and very liable to the complaint of "seeing things at night." But they will not be at all extravagant if the increase in Klan membership goes on long at the present pace.

It is fairly amazing. I have spoken of the county where the judge helped the Klan get 2,000 members. It took five men four weeks to do it, an average of 100 a week each. This is probably a conservative average, for at one single meeting of which a report reached me-not from a Klansman-an organizer got above 5,000 recruits. That man held five meetings that week. And there are -again the figures are approximate- some 800 Klan organizers at work. That would give a total "naturalization" of 80,000 a week! Even if both figures be discounted pretty heavily, it leaves a weekly increase of around 50,000, and this agrees with an estimate I received from one of the leading Klan opponents. I believe it is approximately correct, but on the side of conservatism.

These people are all joining with a definite idea, for a definite purpose, and willing to work under strict discipline to achieve that purpose. The result is a tremendously effective force. It is also tremendously active. Recent elections showed that the Klan is politically entrenched in seven States: Oregon, Texas, Oklahoma, Arkansas, Indiana, Ohio, and California. It is so powerful in a dozen others that no politician can by any possibility be driven into any remark (for publication) hostile to it. It is to be noted that even in States which have passed anti-Klan laws they are not being enforced, as with the celebrated Miller Law in New York. Moreover, with few exceptions, the daily press has stopped making gratuitous attacks. Everywhere there is the shadow of a power that those who depend on public goodwill do not offend without compelling reasons.

Entrenched in seven States, great in power in others, the Klan figures that before the next election it can carry on intensive membership campaigns in at least twenty-one more States! The possibilities from these campaigns may be guessed from the fact that similar ones gave it Ohio and Indiana in a few months.

So much for the power and importance of the Klan in our National life of today and tomorrow. It can hardly be exaggerated, but to be estimated correctly it must be taken in connection with the fact that the history of the country has been filled with movements which were, in a general way, very similar. Time after time there has broken out organized effort to restrict the power of alien-born and, particularly, of Roman Catholic citizens. Each has raged with bitterness, each has gained some headway, and each has vanished suddenly.

These movements have been dubbed "nativistic" by certain historians and political writers. The word has rather a horrendous sound and is undoubtedly intended to express contempt. Yet the fundamental idea in which they all agree is at least debatable. It is merely this: That native-born citizens, trained in the National schools, sons and heirs of the men who built up the Nation, are on the whole better interpreters of National thought and purposes, and hence more fitted to rule the country, than are people of alien blood, tradition, and training, whom those natives have admitted to a share in their advantages.

This idea hardly seems criminal. It may fairly be called illiberal, with whatever stigma that adjective implies in view of the recent demonstration that liberalism may wander far from common-sense patriotism.

The first, then, of the "nativistic" movements came in the very first years of the Republic. The Federalists wished a firm Central Government; the newly arrived preferred a weak one. So the Federalists made the alien vote an issue, and in 1795 raised the term of naturalization to fourteen years. The Republicans, under Jefferson, restored the term to five years in 1802, and grew powerful on the alien vote-as other political parties have done many times since. The issue was kept alive till it vanished in the War of 1812.

It revived in New York City in 1835, when the alien voters definitely banded together to control the city, parading with banners which read, "Americans must not rule us!" The response of the Americans was instant. They rallied under the leadership of men of whom Samuel F. B. Morse, inventor of the telegraph, was one of the best known. He wrote the famous "Brutus" letters, charging that there was an alien, Catholic conspiracy to seize control of America. He attacked the "compact and clannish body of immigrants, avid of office and openly allying themselves as foreigners against the Nation." The movement resulted in practically driving foreigners from office in the city, spread to Boston and Philadelphia, where there were riots, and then slumbered.

The next outbreak was in 1843, when the Democrats again carried New York City and gave the majority of offices to foreigners. Again it won control, and again there were riots and bloodshed and much bitterness. One notable outrage was the looting and burning of a nunnery. Having accomplished its immediate purposes, it again died.

But the alien issue became a tremendous one in 1853. The big immigration from Ireland following the famine of 1847 and from the Continent as a result of the abortive revolutionary movements in 1848-50 swamped the American voters. This resulted in the formation of "The Sons of 1776, or the Order of the Star-Spangled Banner," the lower lodges of which were pledged to vote for none but native Protestants-there was no Negro question then-and the higher orders to force foreigners and Catholics out of all public service. The members were instructed to answer "I don't know to all questions, and so got the name of "Know-Nothings."

My own boyhood study of history left me with the impression that the Know Nothings were a queer, obscure and rather disreputable lot, without any particular influence. Nothing could be further than the facts. They nearly got control of the country. Operating at first by endorsing local candidates  as the Anti-Saloon League has done and the Ku Klux Klan is doing now  they upset all political calculations in 1853 and 1854. In 1855 their success went to their heads and they came into the open as the American Party.  This, as events proved, was a fatal mistake, but it won great immediate success.  In that year they carried nine States and narrowly missed six more; the next year they had eight Governors and fourteen legislatures. A sidelight on their standing and membership is the fact that they elected twenty-four ministers to the Massachusetts Legislature. Their strength was chiefly in New England and the South, though they showed sporadic power in all parts of the country.

But the movement died fast. Being a political party, it was forced to take a stand on the burning slavery question, tried to straddle, lost everything but the boarder States in 1858, and by 1860, after a vain effort to avert the war, had almost vanished. Professor George M. Stephentheson, the historian, says that "about the only definite thing it accomplished was the binding together of the different racial stocks," but its temporary achievement was much greater. It did, for the time, clean up much local political corruption and drive from office many foreigners and Catholics.

They remembered it after its power was gone, and their efforts, combined with its pusillanimous record on slavery, covered it with obloquy. Its members hunted cover, and it has never had a friendly historian. Perhaps it did not deserve one, for its propaganda was based on the most lurid stories about the Catholic Church and was from first to last little but an appeal to prejudice, lacking the dignity of the Morse movement, but it very nearly won complete success.

Following the Civil War there was one other outbreak, the American Protective Association, but it fell under the disrepute left over from the Know-Nothings, and, though it once claimed two million members, never achieved any power. The last flicker from it was the famous "Rum, Romanism, and Rebellion" of the Rev. Dr. Burchard, which defeated Blaine for the Presidency. That debacle convinced politicians once for all that the anti-alien, anti-Catholic agitation was too dangerous to monkey with.

So, in spite of all the talk of unfit immigration un-assimilated aliens, hyphenism, and perversion of Americanism which has been heard in the last few years, the Ku Klux Klan is the first to "dare raise the fundamental issue openly once more. History, as well as the Klan's own success, shows how powerful an appeal that issue may have. And the Klan has not yet made, and its leaders declare that it will not make, the mistakes which wrecked the Know-Nothings. It is evident that the possibilities in such a situation confuse the imagination.

It is evident, too, that an organization which has grown so fast and won such support from so solid a class of citizens and all in the face of such bitter opposition, possesses enormous vitality. There is some deeper reason for its existence than a desire to masquerade in white hoods, or even to go night-riding and reform the neighbors with a blacksnake whip. Such a growth in itself proves that the movement has an appeal to some deep-seated sentiment, instinct, prejudice, condition, or whatever you care to call it, but something widespread, fundamental, and very much alive.

*In the article which follow this, Mr. Frost will undertake to explain with as little prejudice as possible the facts about the Ku Klux Klan, its purposes, its methods, and the extent of its success, the sort of people who endorse it and who join it, its possible results, and its undoubted dangers. In those articles it is assumed that for anew judgment on the Klan neither mere denunciation nor vague indignation will serve, but only a careful estimate of the value or danger of the purposes and ideals professed, a determination whether the Klan furthers those purposes and ideals or not, and a decision whether its methods and propaganda are a greater menace than the evils it assumes to cure. The Klan cannot be dealt with or resisted effectively unless it is measured by this sort of enlightened judgment based on facts. Stanley Frost's next article in his series on the Klan will tell of the great change that has taken place in the Klan in the last two years, how its methods have been reformed in an effort to avoid criticism, and how it is now prepared for defense.*

WILLIAM JOSEPH SIMMONS
Founder of the Knights of the Ku Klux Klan and Emperor
photograph by J. A. Murdoch, Atlanta, Ga.

Reprinted from THE OUTLOOK magazine, December 26, 1923

# THE GIANT CLEARS FOR ACTION

## by Stanley Frost

The Ku Klux Klan today is a very different organization from that of two years ago, which was investigated by Congress and found guilty by public opinion of serious crimes. This is the first fact about it which strikes an inquirer. It is different in leadership, in personnel, in purposes, and in methods. Its leaders, to be sure, declare that the difference is merely a change of emphasis, but this seems to be nothing more than an attempt on their part to hold traditional strength. In fact, there has been a deliberate overhauling. In it whatever of the old Klan seemed useful has been kept, but there have been important rejections and much that is new has been added.

These changes are carefully calculated by a shrewd and understanding mind. The new leaders recognized that the position of the Klan and its reputation were fatally weak for any great success. They had large ambitions, and set about to make the Klan at once less easy to attack and far more effective in its appeal to the average decent citizen. They developed new strategy and tactics. In short, the Giant in the White Hood attempted to "clear the decks" for action. How well it succeeded is partly proved by the growth that followed.

The first result is that the Klan today does stand far less subject to the kind of criticism which has a direct, simple, emotional appeal than it did two years ago. The Giant is wearing better armor. The old indictments for violence and graft have less and less truth; also they are less and less effective with those who know the new Klan-and it is taking pains to be known by those whom it wishes to enlist. It is putting out a strong propaganda, and with much success, to show that it is not in any way a champion or defender of lawlessness. Behind the propaganda is an effort to make sure that no such showing can ever again be made against it as was made before the Congressional investigating committee.

Moreover, it has adopted a rather different objective; at least a very different definition of its old objective. Though it has kept the fundamental idea unchanged-"America for Americans"-it has attempted to formulate a propaganda which does not appeal to hate nor stimulate violent prejudice except as the idea itself does so, and a program which is broader, more definite, and offers opportunity for lawful and satisfying action. It has tried to hold the most effective of its appeals, to make them proof against attack, and to widen their scope.

Finally, it is using very different methods. In place of the blacksnake whip and physical terrorism it has adopted new weapons far more subtle and mote dangerous and far less open to simple and obvious criticisms. It has not abandoned terrorism, but refined it. It has added the most effective methods of a political minority and other methods, even more deadly and effective, which are not exactly new to American politics, but have never been employed by so tremendous an organization.

The first step in the reform was the simple and obvious one of removing the cause for attacks based on its reputation for graft, for fomenting disorder and violence, for being a menace to law and order, and for attempting to substitute itself for the government. It considers that this has been done.

When I asked H. W. Evans, the Imperial Wizard, how much success his reform campaign had achieved, he said: "As much progress has been made as it seems to me could have been expected in the short time since the change in control of the Klan took place. The Klan is now on the whole as nearly free from those evils in personnel as can be expected, so far as we have definitely ascertained. Naturally failures on the part of members are continually occurring-a situation which is perfectly sound may become unsound within a few weeks or a month-but whenever such a situation arises it is corrected as soon as the facts are learned."

"Failures on the part of men to live up to their teachings and convictions are always betrayals of trust. Klansmen are not free from them.

But we have arrived at the point where the Klan recognizes all such actions as in direct conflict with its teachings and oath."

This statement, which admits the previous charges against the Klan and the fact of the house cleaning, and which admits also that the organization is not yet perfect, is quite typical of Dr. Evans. Before taking up the story of what he has done to the Klan let us stop for a moment to look at the man himself. His position as Wizard makes him one of the most influential men in America today. On him depends largely whether the achievements of the Klan be good or bad.

Hiram Wesley Evans, then, is in the middle forties; of middle height, too, and tending to put on flesh. He is smooth shaven, round-headed, and rather round-faced, with the slightly prominent eyes so commonly found in politicians.

He is a Texan born, a dentist by profession, an active member of the Christian or Disciples Church, a thirty-second degree Mason, as are many of the Klan leaders. He is a natural orator and speaks with the softness and peculiarities of the South and with something of the tang and rotundity of the old-fashioned political oratory. He gives the impression of tremendous activity, backed by great force. His address would lack appeal to an "intellectual" audience; it is extremely effective with "common people."

I was told before I saw him, by one of his intimates, that he was not a great man; that the strength of the Klan was in its ideas rather than in its leaders; but that he was decidedly efficient. My contacts with him confirmed this estimate. He described himself to me as "the most average man in America," and that cannot be improved as a thumbnail sketch.

The story of what Dr. Evans has done to the Klan and for it came mostly from other people. He said little about it, except as to results; and he was always careful to identify himself with the mass, to appear no more than their leader and spokesman. Yet the evidence is that he has almost single-handed taken control of the organization and changed it to his purposes. There seems no doubt that these purposes include personal ambitions for power, probably for position and possibly for wealth, but there seems also no doubt that he expects to achieve these through carrying the Klan to power and success, and that he is too canny to risk the great triumph for any minor gratification.

There is no need to devote much space to the early history of the Klan. It was founded in 1915 in Atlanta by Colonel W. J. Simmons, a preacher, dreamer, and -even according to his enemies- something of an idealist, however warped. His imagination had been stirred by outbreaks of race and religious prejudice in Georgia and by the hyphenism which was already appearing; he felt that the law was failing to protect the rights either of America or Americans against organized conspiracies, and he set out to correct this. He founded his order along the lines of the Ku Klux Klan of reconstruction days, which many believe saved the South from Negroes and carpetbaggers. He won some immediate success in enlisting members through the appeal of the honor in which the South still holds the Klan of the sixties.

Whether he intended it or not, the tradition of the lawless methods of the sixties was also carried over, with far less justification. Many parts of the South and West take easily to nightriding, and a good many men took the cover of the Klan to indulge this. The result was to bring the Klan into immediate disrepute throughout the country. The story of these outrages is too well known to need repeating here.

Colonel Simmons, as has been said, is a dreamer; he is nothing of an organizer. The Klan grew very slowly. So, presently, he made a contract with E. Y. Clark, who had been highly successful as an organizer of drives, by which Clark was to get eighty per cent of the initiation fees of $10 each. Clark had considerable success, though his organizers are accused of appealing to the worst motives and prejudices and did the Klan great harm. After paying them, Clark's profits were considerable; he is said to have made as high as $40,000 a month. Charges of graft and corruption naturally followed.

## THE GIANT CLEARS FOR ACTION

The Congressional inquiry, the exposures in newspapers and magazines, and the storm of condemnation which followed nearly broke Simmons's heart. He understood it very little. Although the Klan was so organized that he could never have been ousted, he resigned, undoubtedly under pressure from the Evans crowd.

"Texas was the star Klan State, and we came to the meeting all ready to go ahead and do something," one man said. "But when we got here we found the Klan was not going anywhere or aiming to do anything. So we got busy, and Simmons saw the need of a change."

About the first thing Evans did was to cancel Clark's contract. This precipitated a fight, which is still going on. Simmons stood by his friend and they were backed by the Atlanta Klan. The Evans group revoked its charter. Although the fight is hot in Atlanta, I have found little evidence of it elsewhere, and none at all in the North. It is certainly having little effect on the power or growth of the Klan under Evans, and does not seem to threaten his control. Its chief importance has been to bring out some facts about the Klan and to show how complete is the divergence between the old Klansmen and the new. Colonel Simmons declares that Evans has utterly betrayed and perverted the Klan and its ideals.

One result of the Evans regime was apparent at once: big personal profits were stopped; Clark had built a splendid home in Atlanta; Evans lived for a while in a $65-a-month flat, and his present home is a modest one. When Evans took charge, the Klan treasury held only about $100,000. The finances, by the way, are under complete control of the Wizard. By July 31, 1923, the treasury held assets of $1,087,273 and liabilities of $1,705 (balance, $1,085,568), as against assets of $403,173 and liabilities of $247,227 (balance, $155,946) a year before. Dr. Evans and his friends feel that they are pretty well clear of the charge of graft.

This matter being attended to, Dr. Evans took up the question of lawlessness. His practical mind saw clearly that it not only accomplished nothing, but that it aroused opposition, gave enemies of the Klan their best ground for attack, and emphatically blocked all possibility of carrying the Klan into the Northern States or among the better classes anywhere, and so making its real power. This is apart from his personal views on the morals of violence. On those he spoke to me as strongly as any enemy of the Klan could speak.

At first he gave his attention to specific instances of violence, often going to places where trouble was brewing. One story is told of a town in which the anti-Klan forces had organized to break up a Klavern (Klan assembly). Evans managed to get to the meeting after it had assembled, and found some 140 men, all armed to the teeth, ready to go forth to battle. Around the house was a mob, not well organized but dangerous. Evans took his stand before the door and for four hours argued with his followers. In the end he induced them to leave their arms in the building and go out defenseless. Some were wounded, many were mauled, but not one struck a blow. By this and similar means he tried to establish the idea that a Klansman must not use violence.

But he soon found that this was not enough, and made an open and direct fight inside the order. This culminated in an Imperial Klonvocation (a meeting) of the Grand Dragons (State heads) with minor officials, at Asheville, North Carolina, last July. At this meeting he not only defined the new purposes and methods he had been perfecting, as will be told in a later article, but laid down the law on the subject of violence. In closing his address he said: "We have not been appointed by Almighty God or any Imperial Wizard to go out meddling in other people's business. Our duty is to get behind the constituted officers of the law, as everyone of you have sworn to do. Let's get a National law enforcement program - let's fix it so people will have to go to the penitentiary for violating law. You cannot enforce laws in the form of a super-government trying to force your will or your government on the law of the land. The first time one of your Klansmen violates the law, thus breaking his obligation, thus doing a thing in direct conflict with that for which we stand, let us administer on him as Klansmen for breaking his obligation. Let us then get them outside the Klan and let the judge and jury and the penitentiary take care of them. When we do this, the thing will fade like the morning dew.

"The Wizard is not responsible for any violation. I am going to tell you now, you go home and do your duty and the first time you have a bunch of Klansmen that break a law do not get behind them. Put your influence with the constituted officers of the law, and go with the law and act through the law, and thus once and for all and eternally end this accusation."

This, mind you, was to Klansmen alone, and not a public statement. Dr. Evans may have intended to make it public later, but the Klansmen gathered could not know that.

Dr. Evans soon succeeded in getting to the head of the Klan in various States men who supported this campaign. One such is General Nathan Bedford Forrest, Grand Dragon of Georgia, and son of the famous Confederate general, who was head of the Klan of 1866. General Forrest is an unusually high type of man, strong and clean, and he has made an open fight. His "realm" was one of the worst, since it was the first organized under the old methods. His record, however, is typical of several other Southern Grand Dragons.

General Forrest told me, with some bitterness, how people were continually calling on the Klan to redress grievances by beating up some neighbor. He denied vigorously that the Klan touched any such affairs, except to send all complaints to the regular law officers. "If they fail in their duty, then we tell the local Klan and let it bring pressure to bear in the next election," he added.

He admitted that there were cases in which people had used the Klan regalia to cover crime, and fewer cases in which Klansmen themselves had broken the law, always without sanction of the Klan. Wherever this is suspected to have occurred the local Klan is under orders to help bring the offenders to justice. General Forrest as Grand Dragon has offered a reward of $1,500 for the conviction of any offending Klansman, and in Macon, where some nightriders were on trial and Klansmen were suspected, he sent detectives to work under the sheriff. Men were finally brought to trial on their evidence, and he had a statement made in court that the Klan did not endorse, support, or protect the men. In at least four cases where local Klans have misbehaved he has revoked their charters and given his evidence against them to the courts.

He has got results. "The Klan used to be made up of riffraff-not criminals, but rowdies and low class folks," one of the best-known men in Georgia told me, and others agreed. "Now it is getting the reputation of being a decent organization and a lot of much better men are joining it. This is mostly since violence has been stopped. There has been very little for quite a while."

The final measure taken to stop violence is perhaps a good test of the sincerity of the reform. In many States no member is now permitted to take his regalia from the Klavern without permission. All hoods and robes are checked with a doorkeeper, and are never in possession of a Klansman except for official business. This measure destroys the chief excuse of the Klan in case of outrages -the plea that the regalia was used without permission.

In every place where I investigated or from which I have reports this reform of the Klan has been made clear to every member and is insisted upon in all propaganda. Thus, officially at least, the Klan has cleared its skirts. The extent to which the change has been accepted by the members is another matter, which will be taken up later. But, since there are now so few reports of Klan violence, it seems clear that until new evidence appears the new orders must be accepted as a real position, fairly well maintained. So far as the leaders are concerned or can make their orders effective, the Klan does not take the law into its own hands nor permit its members to do so.

Opponents of the Klan naturally deny this reform. They charge that it was forced by the exposures and the prospect of internal disruption, that it is purely hypocritical, a matter of tactics adopted for the expediency of the moment, which will be abandoned whenever some new expediency dictates.

There is, of course, no means at the disposal of a reporter to determine men's motives. I put the question to a leading Klansman.

"I can't prove to you that it isn't so," he smiled. "But I will point out two things. First, the Klan is absolutely committed, inside and out. If it fails to live up to the reform, it will be damned much more completely than before. Second, the great influx of members has come since the law-and-order program was made clear. They prove that this program is good policy. The Klan will not be foolish enough to change. Moreover, the new members agree with this principle; they now constitute a majority, and they will see that it is lived up to."

Whatever the motive, it is certain that the Klan must be handled on the basis of the reality of this reform, so far as any efforts go either to detach present members or to prevent its spread. Its propaganda is so unequivocal and its record so greatly improved that with these men the argument of lawlessness carries no weight.

This reform, then, is the first and most important step of the Klan in preparing for its great campaign. So far as it is successful and gains credence it will protect the movement from the charges which have been the only basis for most of the attacks on it. Dr. Evans calculates, with some reason, that the whole attack will fall if those charges become untenable. Certainly enemies of the Klan would be forced to a change of base - not a great hardship in view of the poor success of their efforts to prevent the growth of the Klan so far. Certainly also new attacks would have to be based on the new ideals, program, and methods of the Klan, even though such attacks would be more difficult than the old, calling for argument and education rather than simple condemnation.

Violence and graft, however, are not the only things that have been charged against the Klan. There are certain features of the Order which are a part of its very growth and structure which are obviously dangerous, and which are far more difficult to reform.

IMPERIAL SYMBOL OF THE KLAN
designed by William Joseph Simmons

Reprinted from The Literary Digest for June 10, 1922

# THE KU KLUX IN POLITICS

The closeness of the Oregon vote in the Republican primary contest for the governorship, in which Governor Olcott narrowly, won over State Senator Hall, focuses attention for the first time in months on the Ku Klux Klan and its entry into politics. For Senator Hall was openly backed by the hooded organization and a "Federation of Patriotic Societies," we are told by Oregon dispatches. In Texas, too, the Klan is reported to be active in politics. Senator Culberson, one of the veterans of the Senate, who has declared against the "K.K.K." as a menace to civil law and organized society, is opposed by Congressman Henry, who indorses and praises the secret body, while Judge Napier, of Wichita Falls, who promises to drive the Ku Klux Klan from Texas, is out after the governorship.

While no active political campaigns are reported from other States, we learn that a recent search of the office of the Grand Goblin of California, at Los Angeles, after one man had been killed and two shot in frustrating a Ku Klux raid, brought to light two automobile loads of documentary evidence of the Klan's connection with the raid; the home of the Mayor of Columbus, Ga.,was ransacked and the City Manager was assaulted; although the Klan declares that it is innocent in this instance. Among picturesque bits in the dispatches, we read that in Tulsa, Okla., a band of seven men, who said they were members of the Klan, forced a young man to marry a widow; near Hartford, Conn., there was held a ceremony in which some 1,500 white-robed members are said to have participated, and in New Albany, Ind., masked Klansmen donated $25 toward a new church. Other recent and diversified activities in different sections of the country are reported from Kansas, where Governor Allen is investigating the charge that members of the National Guard are also members of the Klan; in Kansas City, Kans., where the Klan visited a hospital and left $402 with the superintendent; in Sacramento, where a secret ceremony was reported in full by the Sacramento Bee; and in a New Jersey village, where forty members of the Klan conducted their own services, much to the surprise of the widow, over the grave of a member.

It is only in Texas and Oregon, however, writes Mark Sullivan, political correspondent of the New York Evening Post, that the Ku Klux Klan will be "a major political issue" in the State elections. The recent Oregon primary campaign was" the bitterest and closest political campaign in Oregon's history," according to a Portland dispatch to the New York World, yet, this paper points out editorially, "Oregon has no negro problem." The anti-alien and religious questions," however, served the Klan's purposes, observes the Buffalo Express. In fact, the Portland (Ore.) Telegram charges that "a religious dust-storm obscured the real issues." As the Baltimore American tells us:

"On the one side was the 'Federation of Patriotic Societies,' under the acknowledged leadership of the Ku Klux Klan, and on the other side were arrayed the alien-born citizens and the negroes. The chief contest was on the gubernatorial nomination. In Multnomah County, which includes the city of Portland, the Federation of Patriotic Societies made a clean sweep in the local offices, including judicial nominations, and gave a plurality of 1,059 for the candidate for Governor. Hall was not nominated, but his vote is large enough to show the Ku Klux strength."

"The closeness of the vote ought to be a warning," agrees the New York Evening World. "If the Ku Klux Klan insists on entering politics, good citizens must show it the way out," declares the Detroit Free Press, for, as the Brooklyn Eagle views it, "if the movement were to become permanent, it would be the greatest sort of peril to the nation." "There is no excuse for the Klan," asserts the Fresno Republican, "for our Governmental structure places the responsibility for enforcement of law and the maintenance of order on certain authorized persons." "Good government can not be achieved by privately organized force," agrees the Milwaukee Journal, and the Los Angeles Times reminds us that "a mob is a mob; it doesn't matter what secret pins or regalia it wears."

## THE KU KLUX IN POLITICS

In fact, this is the tenor of all editorials which we have seen regarding the Ku Klux Klan, which the *Sacramento Bee* calls "infamous" and "un-American." "In a vicious and degrading campaign, Oregon has made a lamentable exhibition of itself," thinks the New York World. But hope for the future is held out by the Buffalo Commercial, which says:

"These so-called patriotic societies arouse public sentiment and at times appear to sweep all before them. But there is nothing in the movement that is based upon right principles, hence it cannot permanently enter the political field."

[ THE KU KLUX IN POLITICS was generously provided by Matt Jacobsen from OLDMAGAZINEARTICLES. com.]

THE KLANSMEN  photograph by J. A. Murdoch, Atlanta, Ga.

Reprinted from The Literary Digest for November 25, 1922

# KLAN VICTORIES IN OREGON AND TEXAS

The Ku Klux Klan victories in Texas and Oregon, where the influence of the hooded organization is said to have elected a United States Senator in one instance and a Governor in the other, indicates to The Nation (New York) that "the Ku Klux Klan has now passed out of the amusing stage and has entered the domain of practical politics to challenge our existing parties." The Senator-elect from Texas; a former member of the Klan, and State Commissioner of Railroads when he announced his candidacy, "has never denied that he was the Ku Klux candidate, " we are reminded by the New York Times, which sees a possibility, if his election is challenged, of a "fight in the Senate that will parallel in national interest the battle to unseat Senator Newberry." "Never was there a worse tangle," admits the San Antonio Light (Ind.), which brings this report from Texas:

"There were injunctions for this and against that, injunctions against injunctions, counter decrees of courts, rehearings, reversals, citations for contempt, orders for one thing and then an other, until the average voter was ashamed of his State and exasperated with the whole thing. Many men absolutely refused to go to the polls because of their disgust over the matter."

Senator-elect Mayfield, who is a Democrat, favors the repeal of the Esch-Cummins Transportation Act, is "dry," is for the soldiers bonus, and will be one of the "farm bloc," we are told. In the opinion of the Dallas Journal (Ind. Dem.), "the factors that made for Mr. Mayfield's success were his personal following; the support of the Ku Klux Klan; the fact that his name was printed on the ballot in a considerable number of counties, whereas his opponent's name was not printed on the ballot in any county; and the pull of the primary election pledge." But the Houston Post, which is of the same political complexion, says in a column editorial in which the words Ku Klux Klan are not to be found, that the election of Mayfield is "a triumph for Democracy and Decency." Continues this Texas paper:

"His election comes as a tribute not only to the candidate, but as an evidence of the splendid solidarity" of the Democratic party of Texas, and its power to resist the mightiest attacks both from within and without the party."

"In view of the character of the combined attack upon the Democratic nominee for the Senate, Senator Mayfield's victory stands out as tremendously significant. It stands as a fitting rebuke to the discordant elements in the Democratic party in Texas for their effort to dismember and destroy the party. It serves notice to all outside interests, political, ecclesiastical, and otherwise, that Texas is capable of running her own affairs, and intends to do so. It presents evidence that the people of Texas stand unreservedly for the great moral and social reforms wrought under the administration of the Democratic party. Particularly, does it mean that Texas is stronger than ever for Prohibition, and that it will not tolerate any movement designed to revive the legalized liquor traffic, either openly or by subterfuge. The election of Mayfield is among other things a tremendous triumph for Prohibition. It insures not only another dry Senator from Texas, but it spells the doom of the pro-liquor movement in this State."

When we move beyond the Rockies, down the valleys of the Snake and Columbia, we find an entirely different situation in Oregon. There the Compulsory School Bill, which requires parents to send children between the ages of eight and sixteen years to a public school during the entire school year, unless the child is taught by parent or private teacher, "was the most upsetting factor in the history of Oregon since the agitation over slavery," notes the <u>Portland Oregonian</u> (Ind. Rep). Only two Oregon newspapers declares the <u>Fort Wayne News-Sentinel</u>, opposed this measure, and none supported it.

Oregon has no "negro problem," but "a religious dust-storm" is said to have obscured the issues in the recent campaign, and to have made possible the election of the Klan candidate for Governor, former State Senator Walter M. Pierce, Democrat. The issue, as the political editor of the <u>Portland Telegram</u> (Ind. Rep.) saw it, was "whether the religious liberty guaranteed in the State Constitution" should be preserved, This issue was a vital one; he declared the day before election, because "it strikes at the very foundation of the Government itself." Nevertheless, we learn from Portland dispatches to New York papers that the Compulsory School Bill, sponsored originally by the Scottish Rite Masons and later taken up by the Ku Klux Klan, was approved by the voters.

When we look for an explanation of the Oregon victory, in which the reduction of taxes also was a prime issue, we learn from the Portland Oregonian that "Mr. Pierce bargained for the vote of the patriotic societies and the Ku Klux and he got it. It helped greatly. He is an adroit campaigner and that helped. The Republican party was more or less divided, and the position of Mr. Olcott within the party was not so strong as to bring about a union of factions or to inspire great enthusiasm for him among men to whom party has a genuine appeal. Doubtless there are other contributing reasons for the Democratic sweep; but these are enough, and more. The public was determined on a change."

"The whole campaign was carried on without speakers and without press support or opposition. It was really all done by secret propaganda. Thus Governor Olcott goes down to defeat for supporting the principles on which the Government of the United States was founded. He was defeated for protesting against intolerance and bigotry," asserts this paper. "The State Of Oregon seems to be suffering from an acute attack of Ku Kluxism, which has taken the form of a violent anti-Catholicism" observes the Baltimore Evening Sun. As for Governor Olcott, "it is better to have character than to win any election," maintains the Portland Oregonian.

"Until now parents have had the alternative of sending their children to private or parochial schools," notes the New York Times, "but the new bill takes from the parent all discretion, and makes the child a compulsory ward of the State. "It will fan the flames or religious hatred," predicts the Portland Telegram, editorially.

"Since full religious freedom is guaranteed by the Constitution, and since no attempt has ever been made by any State to impair that sacred constitutional right, the country will wonder what sinister influences had been at work in Oregon to impair the reason of a majority of her citizens."

"The school law just ratified by the voters of Oregon is a virtual attempt to Ku Klux education in that State," avers the Baltimore Sun; "it applies the Ku Klux principle, of force to educational training." In the Sun's opinion:

"The motive is, of course, to force Catholic children to attend the public schools. But it strikes not only at Catholics but at Episcopalians, Presbyterians, Lutherans, and other Protestant denominations who prefer parochial or private educational institutions for their children."

"This Oregon law is a challenge to a religious civil war. It undertakes to deprive parents of the liberty of educating their children in schools of their own selection, against which nothing can be said except that they generally combine certain features of religious with mental training. It is an approach to this country that a single State in the American Union should have yielded to this degrading and shameful spirit of bigotry."

[KLAN VICTORIES IN OREGON AND TEXAS was generously provided by Matt Jacobsen from OLDMAGAZINEARTICLES. com.]

Reprinted from THE OUTLOOK magazine, September 6, 1922

# THE KU KLUX AND POLITICS

There has been much discussion as to the influence of the Ku Klux Klan in the political situation. Sensationalists have been inclined to exaggerate it. In National matters it is practically nil; in the East and the Southeast it is negligible; in the West and Southwest it has had local effects in different ways, but has not acted consistently or for definite issues.

An example of this was seen the other day in the announcement that in Texas Earle Mayfield, "Ku Klux candidate" as the newspaper called him, had won in the "run off" primary for the United States Senatorship which followed the first primary, in which six candidates engaged. An examination of the facts shows that his Ku Klux support was only a minor matter. The Ku Klux candidates for State offices made a poor showing and were defeated by large majorities. The prohibition issue was prominent in the State campaign. Mayfield was "dry." His opponent, Ferguson, was moderately wet; and the fact that when Governor he was impeached and removed from office told heavily against him. If the Texas primary showed anything, it was that Mayfield was the stronger man personally, and that the prohibition sentiment is still strong in Texas. It is even intimated that the Democratic situation is so un-satisfactory in Texas that a good liberal Republican might have a chance.

There have been some queer developments in the Ku Klux Klan. Thus in Georgia, it has been alleged that Negroes were being asked to join, and in New York it has been charged that the Negro "'Moses," Marcus Garvey, had been approached by the Klan. There are many indications that the Ku Klux is soon to pass away as a disturbing element. Yet not many weeks ago newspaper accounts stated that a crowd totaling nearly 30,000 from Chicago and northern Illinois gathered to witness the initiation of nearly 3,000 new members into the secret council of the Ku Klux Klan. The ceremonies were performed in an immense, field three miles northwest of

Springfield. Similar ceremonials celebrating the initiation of tens of thousands of new members, have taken place in other parts of the country.

Officially the Ku Klux Klan has promised not to wear its regalia in night raids and disclaims any intention of regulating supposed evil-doers by violence. As a terrorizing agency it is practically dead. But its attractiveness to the great class of "joiners" is strong, for it combines mystery and publicity uniquely; it is a "secret society" which as the Chicago incident above quoted shows, thrives on flashlight photographs and press notices.

[THE KU KLUX AND POLITICS was generously provided by Matt Jacobsen from OLDMAGAZINEARTICLES.com.]

## GOVERNOR ALLEN ON THE KU KLUX KLAN

Kansas is engaged is engaged in trying out the Ku Klux Klan through an action brought in the State Supreme Court to restrain its secret activities. Naturally, Governor Henry J. Allen is much interested in the question. In an interview in New York recently Governor Allen gave such a vivid description of the Klan as he sees it that we quote at some length from it in the New York Herald:

"In my State the thing has gone beyond a laughing matter. Every day my mail is choked with letters from people who have received threats-pitiful letters from poor people so frightened they know not what to do. Every one who has a private grudge is using Klan to scare his enemy. Bigotry and religious intolerance are rife. Pulpits where once was preached the brotherhood of man now thunder denunciations against each other, and neighbors who in years gone by lived in peace and harmony now hate each other with a hatred which passes understanding. And they say that all this is the aftermath of a feeling engendered by the war. There is no doubt that many excellent men have joined the Klan from misdirected zeal. In New Orleans its activity is directed against the Jewish element. In other parts of the South the object is the Negro. In Kansas it is the Catholic. I myself have been branded by the Klan as a Catholic and all of my family, Catholic. They must have been somewhat surprised when they discovered that I am a Methodist, a thirty-second degree Mason and a lot of other things which a Catholic cannot be."

What is proposed in Kansas is to have the Supreme Court uphold the State Charter Board in denying the Klan a charter, and thereby make it illegal for the Klan to carry on its organization work. Other States take notice!

[GOVERNOR ALLEN ON THE KU KLUX KLAN was generously provided by Matt Jacobsen from OLDMAGAZINEARTICLES. com.]

THE OATH  photograph by J. A. Murdoch, Atlanta, Ga.

Reprinted from THE OUTLOOK magazine, December 27, 1922

## INVISIBLE GOVERNMENT

If there is one thing more than another that Americans require of their political affairs, it is that they should be open, aboveboard, and discussable by all. Invisible government and secret influences form the antithesis to democracy. We have and will maintain freedom of speech and of the press, subject only to the apothegm stated the other day in these columns. Personnel liberty ends where public injury begins.

The most moderate program put forth by defenders of the revived Ku Klux Klan shows its purpose to influence legislation, public opinion, and political elections. It has a right to do all this if it acts openly and fairly. It has no right to work secretly by underground methods to inflame racial and religious prejudice in order to bring about political or legislative action. If one says this to a defender of the Klan, he replies "Well, the Knights of Columbus do the same thing." We have seen no evidence of this; but if it so, then that or any other organization so acting is subject to precisely the same criticism. Meanwhile it is notorious and self-evident that the Klan cunningly tries to twist into one chord the three hateful strands of anti-Jewish, anti-Catholic, and anti-Negro prejudice. Help yourself in effect the Klan says, to your own special hatred! All distinctly un-American.

There is no objection to secret societies in themselves. Anyone can name offhand several that are admirable as sources of social enjoyment, of mutual benefit, of fraternal benevolence. Ceremony and ritual are attractive to many people, and it is true that many secret societies are merely harmless, but beneficial. Yet in order that the worthy associations should not be confounded with the objectionable, it is at least desirable that all should be registered with the State authorities and the names of their responsible officers be available for purposes of inquiry. Emphatically this is the desire in the case of an organization like the Ku Klux Klan, founded originally as an instrument of terrorism, and lately revived in an effort to foster race and religious animosity and to throw the influence of its secretly banded members on this or that side of a political issue. We are not permitted to know when and why the Klan's influence is thus exerted, and in such a situation fair discussion is impossible. Just lately, for instance, one newspaper correspondent remarked:

"One of the surprises of the year's election was the success of a candidate for Governor of Oregon, with Ku Klux support, and the adoption by the voters of that State of a law designed to do away with all parochial schools at which a feature of teaching is instruction in religious matters."

It may be that the Ku Klux Klan was influential in the election of a Governor in Oregon and in the adoption of the school law and it may not; how can we tell what oath bound society has done? The same thing applies to the election of Senator Mayfield in Texas, "said to be" due to Klan efforts. We don't want "said to be" in American political life, we want open politics as well as diplomacy.

When the present Klan revival was new, there were several acts of violence charged against local Klans. The National officers of the Klan in one or two instances expelled the local chapter; in other cases the Klan was declared to be wrongly accused. Thus was exposed instantly one danger attached to those who ride by night "to do justice to wrong-doers;" others may imitate them from evil and personal motives. The Klan saw the light; and it is fair to say that this sort of lynching a la masquerade seems to have ceased. Their remains to the mystery of the oddly mingled delight of mask, gown and torch, with joy of alliteration, and inconsistent pleasure of seeing in newspaper flashlight photographs of their midnight ceremonies.

[INVISIBLE GOVERNMENT was generously provided by Matt Jacobsen from OLDMAGAZINEARTICLES. com.]

Reprinted from THE OUTLOOK magazine, November 14, 1923

# NIGHT-RIDING REFORMERS

The Regeneration of Oklahoma

Special Correspondence from Stanley Frost

*The Outlook sent Stanley Frost to Oklahoma to study the amazing political conflict which has taken place in that State. The forces at odds in this State may have a far-reaching influence upon National politics.*

The first stage in the regeneration of Oklahoma is over. The revolt against visible corruption and official despotism has won. J.C. Walton has been impeached on charges which, in addition to telling of the pitiful, picayune graft so common in American politics, remind one of the ancient struggles of the British Parliament against the Stuart kings. Walton seems sure to go, but whether he is convicted or not all that remains of this phase of the fight is merely to mop up the political trenches.

This is no small job, to be sure. It has been years since American politics have revealed such a mess. Even while the Walton affair held public attention, the papers of Oklahoma were full of stories of other official misdeeds. A penitentiary warden was under indictment; legislators were accused of graft; bribery was hinted at; judges were attacked; literally hundreds were charged with minor peculations; the very air whispered reports of connivance with bootleggers, dope-peddlers, and more violent criminals; the Walton expose itself has ramifications involving scores in varied crime. Probably most of these will escape, but the dirt will at least be swept behind the door.

As the dust settles it becomes easier to see into the causes and motives behind the recent struggle, and to the student of modern politics these are even more important than the immediate issues. There are involved many of those factors which are problems in other States, the farmer-labor movement, the trades union in politics, the enforcement of prohibition, even the Fundamentalist movement in religion. But above and beyond all is the Ku Klux Klan, with its appeal to the narrowest instincts of a reawakening Americanism along the lines of racial and Protestant supremacy. Without an understanding of these motives and causes the Oklahoma crisis must seem meaningless factional disturbance.

The situation is particularly important because of the intention of Klan leaders to use the record here as the basis for an intense campaign to recruit members of the better sort, particularly in the North. That campaign is only awaiting the final disgrace of Walton to be set in motion, and may have been begun before this is printed. And it is no longer possible to think the fact that the Klan is already an immense power and that it may easily become the dominant force in politics.

The Klan issue has not been settled in Oklahoma. It existed before Walton seized upon it, and it will survive his fall. It is quite possible that if he had been a different man, had kept his own record clean and had been able to hold the issue to moral grounds instead of playing cheap politics with it, he might have become a National figure, with a Senatorship - even the Presidency - in reach, as he had hoped. But that egg is broken and the anti-Klan movement in the State is for the present leaderless, its members having been forced by Walton to join the Klan in fighting for fundamental liberty.

It may as well be admitted that, on the surface at least, the Klan record can be made to appeal to many good, sincere, and patriotic men who are now seeking leadership toward the recovery of the Anglo-Saxon ideal of socially responsible individualism. In Oklahoma the Klan can prove by its enemies themselves that it has been on the side of public safety, of enforcement of law (at least of most laws), of the suppression of graft and connivance with crime. It has opposed from the beginning the Governor whom the whole State now sees as a dangerous public enemy. Although it had the power to meet his illegal attacks with force of arms and was goaded by him in. every possible way toward violence, it held its members under strict control and averted what might have been a serious civil war. Finally, it has been the center and the backbone of the fight to restore constitutional government and has carried that fight to a triumphant and legal conclusion.

This is a compelling record. But it is not all the record, and it must not be forgotten for a moment that the secrecy which is one of the Klan's chief weapons puts it in a position to escape or confuse judgment on its sins and failures, while claiming more than its share of credit. Nor does this record touch, except at a few points, the fundamental purposes and methods of the Klan. Later I hope to be able to report adequately on these, for there have been important changes in the organization since the exposures of two years ago. The present articles, however, can deal only with Oklahoma.

Lawlessness is nothing new there. It was about the last Territory to be opened to settlement, and the traditional lawlessness and easy tolerance of lawbreaking which mark frontier life have only partly died out. In addition, the population is mixed and much of it vicious. A large part of the State was taken from the old Indian Reservation, and such whites as had lived there had been renegades, many of them criminals, whose very presence in the Territory was in violation of law and often an attempt to escape it. This degenerate breed hampers and often defeats every effort of the State toward progress.

As a State, Oklahoma is only sixteen years old. The conflicting elements in her population caused serious trouble and lacks in her Constitution which have not yet been entirely cleared up. There has not been time for the growth of civic solidarity or much State pride. Her schools are within six of the bottom of the list and her general literacy and consequently the possibility of education through the press in political morality is low. Add great discrepancies between the poverty of the farmers and the wealth of the oil boomers, a mixture of Indians with moral standards quite different from those of white men dissatisfaction as a result of recent hard times, the rough element drawn to the oil fields, and a great preoccupation with material development, and you have the rough outline of conditions with which decency and progress must contend.

Thus political morals are necessarily low. In the southeast corner of the State they are about as bad as may be. In the north they rise greatly and there has grown up among the better classes a sort of civic idealism. This, however, has been confused by self-interests and prejudices and has been expressed largely in material things: new hotels, better pavements and roads, better water works, and, with some, better schools. Ordinary law enforcement has come behind these; there has been almost no thought even, for good government in the larger sense.

Moreover, there is no leisure class which might take leadership in civic affairs, and the better people generally consider political activity rather disgraceful. It has been perfectly hopeless for them as well, since no man of even moderately decent standards could compete with the professional liars and spoilsmen.

With few exceptions, the latter had control of the governments-State, county, and local. Politics was almost entirely a matter of spoliation enriched by corrupt catering to financial interests. A political campaign was most likely to succeed if based on impossible promises to class or special interests; combined with a play upon prejudices and a discreet connivance with the criminal elements.

The simpler kinds of reform had been making progress, however, steadily if not rapidly. Corruption was less and less open, crime more and more furtive. W.E. Disney, who leads the fight against Walton in the Legislature, tells of his own experiences as a prosecuting attorney in Muskogee. He, by the way, is a descendant of the Kansas fighters of the fifties.

Ten years ago he told me, bootlegging in particular was so open that even to talk of prosecution was a joke. When finally some thirty members of the gang were jailed, they made huge mirth. They organized a "jail-birds union" and issued membership cards certifying that the "bearer

## NIGHT-RIDING REFORMERS

is a jail-bird in good and regular standing and as such is entitled to free board and keep in any jail in Oklahoma." One member recently held a State office, but on the whole the campaign succeeded, and Muskogee is now a clean county.

Other counties and towns did as well, but some did not. Tulsa was one of the latter, and her story may be taken as typical of conditions in many parts of the State. Two years ago Tulsa was under almost absolute control of the criminals. Bootlegging and dope-peddling flourished unabashed. Highway robbery -called "hijacking"- was a common means of livelihood. Hardly a night passed without it, and on one celebrated evening a gang took possession of one of the main roads and for hours systematically winnowed the traffic. Murder was common. No decent woman and few men left shelter at night. Officers seldom attempted to interfere; those who did were shot down with impunity, and in the few cases where the criminals were caught and convicted they were usually promptly pardoned.

As has been the case so often in this country, where legal means failed to curb crime, illegal means were taken up. The reformers became night-riders. Vigilante law had been sporadic in the State, now it became organized. There is no question that the Klan played a large part in this- how large a part will be discussed later; but there is also no doubt from the stories of a dozen of the best-informed men in Tulsa that night-riding had been going on before the Klan appeared, that it was not wholly chargeable to the Klan at any time, and that many reputable and solid citizens took part in it. From other parts of the State come stories that peace officers themselves finding their legal efforts nullified by the pardon mill the Capitol, were among the vigilantes.

The methods used were direct, brutal, and effective. Around Tulsa men armed themselves, went out in autos in a deliberate attempt to lure the "hijackers," and then shot to kill. They suffered some casualties, but within a few months "hijacking" became so highly hazardous an occupation that it ceased. With bootleggers, dope-peddlers, and caterers to sexual vice the method was less defensible. Men suspected of these things were caught abroad or taken from their homes, sometimes, though not always, given rump trials, and soundly whipped-the kind of raw-hiding from which it takes the strongest man weeks to recover. The traffics were not entirely stamped out, but they were reduced to more or less normal dimensions, and the worst gangsters were driven away.

"In actual results," one judge commented, "the thing worked pretty well. I don't defend it, of course, but from what I've seen I should say that the night-riders averaged nearer justice than the courts do."

The most important result of the night-riding, however, at least in Tulsa, was the destruction of the political power of the gangs. There has been a reform movement in Tulsa for years, but it was not until the night-riders subdued the criminals that it carried any office. In the spring of 1922, however, the city government was at last cleaned up, and last January a sound county government was put in. Both are also solidly "Klux."

From that time on night-riding practically ceased. It had been dwindling for months. Recent investigations have shown that in the later stages it had degenerated into private vengeance and punishment for very minor offenses, but these outrages were seldom known; the burden of proof in the then state of public opinion was upon the victim, and they had almost no effect on either public sentiment or the political situation at that time. So far as known, there were only two cases after January $1^{st}$ - a very minor affair in a distant corner of the county and a severe whipping in Tulsa itself, which was the immediate cause of the imposition of martial law.

Because of its results this case deserves a little mention. The victim, Nate Hantaman, was accused of peddling dope. He was stripped and beaten, and it was charged that he was mutilated. On the testimony of the doctor who attended him this is not true and he was able to walk home two hours after the whipping. The case was much like scores of others, but it was skillfully press-agented and aroused a very considerable indignation. Incidentally, Hantaman has since been arrested on a charge of bank robbery, and his wife, whose tears to the Governor brought the soldiers to Tulsa, is under Federal indictment for selling opiates.

This, then, was the situation at Tulsa early last August: night-riding had almost stopped, reform administrations were in power, and the citizens had once more turned the enforcement of the law over to them. An isolated outrage brought the most drastic action possible under American laws from Governor Walton. Let us return for a moment to look at his record.

He is one of the "mixer" type of politicians, and a good one. He is of medium size, round-faced, with a weak mouth and in personality which he makes engaging by a chameleon-like adaptability. If he has character of his own, it has not been made manifest. He is a good speaker, too ignorant to be far-sighted, too adaptable to be trustworthy. I found no one who would now accept his most solemn promises. He is vain; he is also of a temperament which finds comfort in being surrounded constantly by gunfighters, and his most frequent companions are policemen.

Walton was for one term Mayor of Oklahoma City, and he is the kind of man who, given a little success, would surely run for Governor, though his election in the beginning seemed hopeless. His only support at first was from labor, no great power in the State. Presently two alliances were made; the first birth of the Socialists, a body of some 60,000, of whom perhaps 5,000 or 6,000 are convinced Socialists and the rest "protest voters." The other was with the Farmer-Labor workers, who had recently come into the State and were organizing the discontent among the farmers with the poverty-stricken and unblessed element in the southeastern corner -the old Indian reservation- as a nucleus. These combined and held a convention, which nominated him to run in the Democratic primaries, and all these elements went into those primaries in a deliberate attempt to force him on the party.

Opposed to him were Bob Wilson, for many years State School Superintendent, and Judge Owen, a lawyer with a fine record. Wilson was the avowed candidate of the Klan; Owen had the Catholic support. Walton in his campaign made the usual reckless promises; on the same day in the same town, he promised farmers that he would get them $3 wheat and labor that he would reduce the loaf to five cents! But with all this, and in spite of the division of the opposition, Walton could not have won, local politicians agree, but for one complication.

This was that there had been initiated and was to come up at the same election a bill to forbid the Catholic pariah schools. Wilson, the Klan man, was making a strong run and the Catholics were badly scared.

"If that bill and Wilson had both won," I was told by one of the men who took part in the maneuvering for the Catholic vote, "the Catholics would just naturally have had to leave the State. It was a matter of life and death with them. We tried to make them see that Owen could win if they'd stand by him, but the Klan was circulating nasty stories about him and they didn't dare. So on the last day. They swung to Walton-about 60,000 votes. That gave him the nomination, and the worst thing that can be charged against the Klan in this State is that they brought about conditions which made Walton possible."

In the actual election some 75,000 decent Democrats bolted Walton-partly under Klan influence - according to the same authority. But his campaign of promises and the farmers' hardships were enough to make up the deficit and, besides, to give him the biggest majority in the States history.

"It took three years drought to give us a man like that," is the way another politician analyzed the action of the farmer vote.

Walton's record as Governor need not be repeated - it has been told in the story of his impeachment.

A movement for his impeachment had already started when, in August, he launched his attack on the Klan by declaring martial law in Tulsa. His avowed object was to use military courts to stop the whippings and ferret out the night-riders. He very justly charged that these were not likely to be prosecuted by the local authorities.

Apart from the fact, already told, that the whippings had almost stopped, so that there was no immediate need of drastic action, he had found an excellent issue. There was already much public indignation against the Klan, and more was speedily aroused as the result of the investigations he ordered. The issue was a moral one, but if there is a man in the State who believes that Walton was actuated by any other motive than political expediency -or worse- I failed to find him. "If you ever on the assumption that the man could have a conscientious motive for anything, you'll get off the track," a dozen men said.

Various reasons for his action were given. Some people offered wild rumors, the fact that Walton had been refused membership by the Klan; the fact that Tulsa had voted against him; the suspicion of a desire to "shake down" the rich oil men there; even a story of a secret agreement during the campaign with the classes proscribed by the Klan -all these were alleged. Klan members point out as significant the fact that Hantaman, over whose whipping the fight started, is a Jew.

All these explanations seem to me needlessly involved. Walton is a politician, he hoped to become Senator, possibly President; but he was losing ground, and naturally reached out for the most popular issue he could find. That happened to be the Klan.

[Journalist Stanley Frost dedicated his literary talents by accurately surveying the Klan at the height of its power with a series of articles for THE OUTLOOK magazine, as well as an authorized interview with The Imperial Wizard of the Ku Klux Klan for THE FORUM, Vol. LCCIV, No. 6 (December, 1925). His book, THE CHALLENGE OF THE KLAN (Indianapolis, Bobbs-Merrill Co., 1924) is considered a vital source for researchers of the Klan's involvement in the twenties.]

GOD IS OUR REFUGE AND STRENGTH   photograph by J. A. Murdoch, Atlanta, Ga.

Reprinted from THE OUTLOOK magazine, June 4, 1924

# THE KLAN SHOWS ITS HAND IN INDIANA

### Special Correspondence from Indianapolis

### By STANLEY FROST

"The Ku Klux Klan has destroyed party lines in Indiana so far as the voters are concerned. Reports from all over the State show that the old parties are forgotten and only the shells of the machines remain. The Klan is the issue, the one thing that will have any important effect in deciding votes."

This was the estimate given me by one of the most honored and experienced of Indiana politicians as to the effect of the Klan's sweeping victory in the recent Republican primaries. Since we have been watching so long to see the old parties break up, this is likely to seem the most important result of that victory, though it is by no means completely accomplished. The old shells are still valuable political assets and already show signs of returning life. And a great effort is being made to suppress the Klan issue. Nevertheless Indiana is today nearer political realignment than any State has been since 1858.

There are, however, other results almost as important. The Klan for the first time has emerged as an open political power in a Northern State. The Klan issue has been forced to the front, in spite of great efforts to keep it quiet, and the Indiana situation may give it a first place in the National campaign. The power and possible menace of the Klan in politics were both demonstrated. Finally, the difficulties and dangers which face the Klan itself in the very moment of its victory were made so clear that, since the primaries, Klan leaders in Indiana have spent fully as much time and effort in trying to forestall those dangers as in gathering the fruits of success or preparing for the future.

In short, the Indiana campaign has definitely brought the Klan into Northern and National politics, and has given a demonstration of its methods, its power, and its dangers both to others and to itself. Indiana has been a laboratory. "It is the best State in the Union for trying out a new political idea," one of the Klan leaders told me. "If we can get away with it here, we're all set to go."

## Flabbergasted Politicians

The Klan victory was as unexpected as it was complete. Six months ago every sane politician avoided Klan support as being deadly and damning. Before he had the Klan endorsement Edward Jackson, for whom it won the nomination for Governor, was not believed to have a chance. The Klan campaign was waged with very small funds. The success, in view of all these adverse influences, is little less than a political miracle.

It has had about the same effect on the politicians that armed rebellion by the Friends would produce. They have lost touch, are in a panic, flabbergasted. They have not yet found out exactly what happened to them, or how, or why, or what it all means. "The situation is the most vague, elusive, and puzzling that I have ever seen or heard of," one man of nearly thirty years of political experience told me. The only people who are at all happy or sure of themselves are the Klan leaders. They know what they want and how they expect to get it, but they do not advertise either thing. It is significant that not one of the scores of men in both parties and the Klan with whom I talked was willing to be quoted by name on anything at all. To any except those who know the secrets of the Klan the situation is even yet far from clear, though it is clearing. The possibilities it contains are quite impossible to estimate. But the broader outlines of the campaign that is closed and the main factors in the campaign to come can be seen. Before taking them up, however, a brief outline is necessary of the situation in which the recent drama was enacted.

# THE KLAN SHOWS ITS HAND IN INDIANA

## The Stage Setting for the Klan Drama

The Indiana Klan is one of the most powerful in the country; it ranks behind only Texas and Ohio, and has an advertised membership of half a million and an active membership of perhaps half that. It is made up largely of people of substantial and decent standing, most of them active members of Protestant churches, fairly well educated with definite if somewhat narrow ideals. It inclines to youth, it is aflame with enthusiasm. It has never been accused of violence, and in a recent riot which I happened to see at South Bend the aggression was entirely from the other side. That bloodshed was prevented was due to the strenuous efforts of Klan leaders.

Quite naturally, both because of these facts and because in Indiana politics is played more persistently and intensely than anywhere else, the Klan sought an outlet for its energies in that field. Its membership is divided, but with the majority Republican. A large proportion had been Bull Moosers, some have leanings toward La Folletteism. Besides this, its natural field is in the Republican Party, since almost ninety percent of the Catholics are Democrats, making control of that party much more difficult.

The political situation was favorable to the entry of a new power. The Democratic machine is in the hands of Taggart, growing old and perhaps a trifle unsteady. The Republican machine was led by Senator Watson, but he is hardly friendly with ex-Governor James Goodrich, a leader of great skill, who is rather more feared than trusted, but is likely to control the sources of financial supply, no matter who controls the machine. Neither is Watson on good terms with ex-Senator Beveridge, to whose defeat two years ago Watson contributed more or less, and who is always powerful in spite of the fact that he has withdrawn from politics and devoted himself to authorship. In this confused situation any solid and cohesive body had great opportunities.

The Republican organization had been further weakened by the conviction of crime and removal from office of Governor McCray. The effect of this was less than might have been expected, however, as there was a general tendency to regard his case as personal rather than political, and there was little mention of it. It was nevertheless a weakness, and will have an effect this fall.

### Enter the Klan, Right Center

In this situation the Klan very naturally elected to make its main drive for power through the Republican Party. It gave its support to Jackson, now Secretary of State. It is denied that he was a Klansman. But it did not neglect the Democratic Party, and had its candidates in those primaries also. This is in line with the usual policy of the Klan, which aims so far as possible to remain invisible, working inside both parties, but concentrating in each race on the party or candidates which seem to be most able and willing to give it what it wants. Thus in general it follows the tactics of the Anti-Saloon League, with the difference that, while the League operates openly, the Klan prefers to keep its hand covered, and to veil both its actions and its power with as much secrecy as possible. This policy was followed in the early stages of the Indiana campaign, but was presently upset by D. C. Stephenson, then Klan leader of the State. He is a man of powerful personality and great magnetism, very energetic, and had been largely responsible for the Klan's rapid growth there. A large part of the Klan looked up to him with an almost fanatical devotion, and his influence in other States and in the Imperial Klan was great. In fact, it led him into delusions of grandeur, and he began an attempt to undermine Dr. H.C. Evans, the Imperial Wizard.

It was partly in pursuit of this ambition and partly because of his naturally flamboyant disposition that he sent out letters calling on the Klan to support Jackson. Of course some of these letters became public.

Jackson's opponents instantly fastened the Klan label on him, and the Klan was forced to accept an open issue or suffer a serious loss of prestige with its own followers. Lew Shank, the spectacular Mayor of Indianapolis, who was also candidate for Governor, made his run on an anti-Klan platform, and this helped to draw the lines tighter. The leaders of the Republican organization, afraid either to support or to offend the Klan, maintained a careful neutrality in public, but secretly worked against Jackson.

As has been said, few people at that time -last October- believed there was any chance for the Klan to win. Jackson was not an overly strong man; the enemies of the Klan were many and active, the Klan itself was torn by the struggle between Stephenson and the Imperial Palace, there was grave doubt whether it could deliver its strength, and there was little money. Yet the Klan dared not lose. To handle this very difficult task Dr. Evans put in charge Walter Bossert, then head of the Propagation Department, who is generally conceded to be the most skillful politician in the Klan. Stephenson was reduced to the ranks, where he devoted himself to his fight against Evans and Bossert. It is to Bossert that almost the entire credit for the Klan victory is given, both by his friends and enemies, and, since a good deal is likely to be heard of him in the future, he is worth a brief sketch.

## The Leading Actor

Bossert is now about forty, tall and heavy without being fat, showing almost unimpaired the physique which twenty years ago made him fullback and pitcher for the University of Indiana. He has a calm, clean-cut face, a shock of black hair touched with gray, piercing black eyes, and a manner that, while slow to kindle, strikes fire often and has a remarkable charm when once aroused. He is somewhat after the pattern of Boise Penrose, but distinctly finer and with the marks of both culture and idealism. He is a graduate of the Law Department of the University of Indiana and has practiced, though not much. He spends his time by preference on his farm near Liberty, Indiana, where he raises police dogs and Belgian chickens.

He is a seasoned political strategist, trained by "Slick Jim" Goodrich and Will Hays, and has been a trusted organizer for the Republican National Committee. He has no delusions about politics, and plays the game skillfully, on a hard-pan basis, and according to the accepted standards. Yet he is an idealist, a reformer, in politics for an idea, and now in the Klan for the same idea. From his boyhood up he had been controlled by the desire to make the public schools give to all children real training for liberty and democracy; this includes an attack on parochial schools. It is typical of the rather inconsistent combination of idealism and adaptation of means to end which characterizes him and to a large extent the whole Klan leadership- that he deliberately went into training as a practical politician as the best way to achieve his reform.

When he took over the Indiana campaign, Bossert staked his success almost entirely on intensive organization. Though he was cramped for funds, he did have the Klan to work through, and in this one thing Stephenson was not opposing him. His method was education through organization, by an endless chain system. He called together small groups of men, filled them with the issue he had picked, and sent them out to evangelize other men. His issue was the Klan -the need of it, what it could accomplish, its ideals, its opportunities, and, above all, the fact that it is simply must win that campaign. Jackson in his own campaign took care of the other issues. He did not mention the Klan, but talked about good government and the need of new blood in the party. Bossert himself says that the only thing that made success possible was that he began work months before the primaries, instead of waiting till the last few weeks, as is customary.

## The Spotlight on the Klan

At any rate, on the eve of the primaries, politicians estimated that Jackson would be the leading candidate, but that he would not have a majority. This meant that the actual nomination would be made in the State Convention -where the machine would control and Jackson would be beaten. It became Bossert's job to make sure that Jackson had a majority over all other Republican candidates. No one thought he could.

It was the fact that he did that stunned the politicians. When the count was made, it was found that Jackson had 227,785 of the 413,333 Republican votes, a clear majority of 42,348 and a plurality over Lew Shank, anti-Klan and his nearest opponent, of 132,291. Bossert had beaten the organization, the anti-Klan sentiment, and the other candidates. He seemed in a position to become boss of the Republican Party in the name of the Klan. He was generally expected to do so.

But the victory had been dearly bought. The Klan was out in the open, a fair target for all its enemies, who are legion. Stephenson again added to the difficulties by a public statement that the Klan was out to elect Jackson by 300,000, although the Democrats had not yet made their nomination. This was followed by an anti-Klan statement from Dr. C.B. McCulloch, the leading Democratic candidate, which was indorsed by Taggart, the Democratic organization leader. Finally, it was found that in nearly half the counties the anti-Klan forces had controlled the Democratic primaries, nominating Catholics for local offices. The issue had been sharply drawn.

The Klan could not afford to have it so drawn. There was grave doubt whether Jackson could win, even in Indiana and in spite of his big primary vote, on a straight Klan issue, or even with an obvious Klan label. There are 15,000 Negro votes which politicians figured would probably be lost to the party, the 15,000 or 20,000 Catholics who are normally Republican, and a considerable anti-Klan vote which is also usually

Republican but might easily desert if the issue was forced. Finally, the machine was lukewarm, if not hostile, and Stephenson's attacks on Bossert and Goodrich had closed the sources from which Republican campaign funds usually come. The normal cost of an Indiana State campaign is around $300,000 and the chances of raising that inside the Klan were small.

Worst of all, the Democratic Klansmen could not be depended upon. Thousands of them had voted in the Republican primaries to put Jackson over, but might desert him in November. Thousands of Catholics and other anti-Klan Democrats, also, had voted for Shank, and their return to their own party would be a further deduction from the apparent Republican strength. Finally, Stephenson's blunder had given the Democrats a weapon which might draw off every Democratic Klansman.

### The Clash in the Klan

"You'll notice that the Klan came out for Jackson even before we had nominated our man," a Democratic politician told me. "That proves that it was not waiting to decide between candidates and that it is simply a Republican outfit, first, last, and all the time. It claims to be non-partisan, but has really merely betrayed its followers into the Republican ranks. When the Democratic Klansmen find that out -as they will- how many of them will stand for it?"

So Bossert's problem, if he was to win with Jackson in the fall, was worse than before. He had, in the first place, to escape the straight Klan issue; if he could remove the Klan label from the Republican Party, all the normal Republican strength would be held and the added weight of secret Klan support would insure victory. He had, too, to win the help of the regular organization and to open the sources of revenue. And, since Stephenson was responsible for the blunders and was upsetting the whole Klan by his rebellion, he had to make the Indiana Klansmen repudiate their idol.

The latter problem was left to Dr. Evans himself. The Wizard came to Indianapolis with a strong staff, fought the Stephenson forces on the floor of a State Klerero and routed him utterly. Stephenson, who a few weeks ago was boasting that he would take the whole State with him away from Evans and divide other States, was thrown out of the Klan. He is now threatening to organize a rival order, but previous attempts along that line have been dismal failures.

## Close Harmony Behind the Scenes

Bossert handled the politics, with some aid from the Wizard. He began making bargains. One was with Goodrich, but nothing has yet happened to show how successful that was, nor what its terms are. He went to Washington and saw Watson, and some of the results of that arrangement are already visible. He saw many State leaders. Finally, he was made Grand Dragon by the Klerero and confirmed by the Imperial Wizard, thus getting full authority over the Indiana Klan forces. The result of all this was that Watson came out strongly for Jackson. When the county and district committees met, the old officers were re-elected-the Watson men. Watson was boomed for Vice-President. The State Convention nominated a list of officers who are not known to be either Klansmen or under Klan control -one may suspect that they have been OK'd by Bossert, but cannot prove it.

So in two weeks Bossert has won harmony with the State machine, the beginnings of harmony inside the Klan, with the probability that before the real campaign begins the internal troubles will have been entirely ironed out. Far more important, he has taken the Klan label off the Republican party; no one can prove that it is in any respect under Klan control; no one can make it accept the Klan as an issue. The Klan -whatever its power- has once more become invisible in Indiana politics. This is an even greater triumph than was Jackson's majority.

It also is deep political wisdom, for there is no question that his failure to take over the Republican machine was a voluntary renunciation, that he could have done it with the utmost ease. There are many now who boast that the Klan has been beaten -it is noteworthy that the Klan is quite willing to admit it -but no one thought it could be beaten till the committees voted. There would be no mystery about what happened if people could realize, as no machine politician can, how an organization like the Klan may not wish to show how much power it really has.

I cannot prove it, but I believe it will be found in time that Bossert, as head of the Indiana Klan, is also actually Republican boss, with almost absolute power. An invisible boss.

How far his maneuver will be successful in the fall campaign it is impossible to say. The Democrats make no secret of their intention to make Jackson, at least, wear a Klan label. They are counting heavily on the Stephenson statement, already mentioned, and hope to split the Klan with it. If they can do this, they ought to win in November; it seems at this distant date about their only hope.

### Ralston's Role

The one other chance is that Ralston, an Indiana man, may get the Democratic nomination for President and that State pride would give him the State and carry the State ticket along with him. But the Klan victory in the primaries here makes it even less likely than before that he will be nominated. Although Indiana is a State that knows how to split its tickets, many Democrats doubt that he could carry it in the face of local complications, and the Democratic National Convention certainly will not nominate a man from a State which it believes is already lost beyond hope.

Moreover, and this is even more serious, with the Klan irrevocably committed to a Republican State victory in Indiana, it can hardly afford to risk losing through having Ralston nominated. The National Klan will have to support the State Klan in this, and so will probably fight Ralston. Since much of his support has been from the Klan, he will thus lose a large part of the strength he might have had. So the Ralston boom was badly deflated at those same primaries, and only some unusual combination of political expediencies can revive it.

### The Moral of the Play

There are two important lessons that can be drawn from the Indiana demonstration; lessons that are doubly important since the Klan will bid for control in at least twenty-one States this fall, will have a powerful influence in the Democratic National Convention (the Republican Convention offers fewer opportunities for activity), may be itself an issue in the campaign, and will certainly take an important and probably a dominant part in that campaign.

The first lesson is the immense power of the Klan when it goes into politics. In Indiana it has shown better leadership, greater stability, more power to take care of internal quarrels, and a stronger unity than had been expected by any but its own leaders-far above the average of political organizations. It plays politics with a crusading spirit which is willing to make greater sacrifices and work harder than any organization has done in recent times. Its evangelistic enthusiasm wins many converts who are not members, so that it casts considerably more than its own vote. It also makes its members desert their usual party affiliations, split tickets, and put the Klan ahead of any other consideration to an extent never before known in American politics. Its organization is not only permanent but self-sustaining, so that it has no need of spoils and the quarrels they bring. I am convinced that it is-while it lasts-the most effective political organization the country has ever seen, not excepting Tammany.

The second lesson is that the Klan is in danger of defeat whenever it comes into the open, and of disruption whenever it becomes tied to any party. Its power lies in invisibility and impartiality. It may secretly endorse issues or men, but never parties and seldom openly. When it becomes identified with any party, it will surely lose much of its membership, it will lose the power of controlling either party through balance of power and implied threats, it will become merely an adjunct, like Tammany, of the party which it has captured. It will have to take what it can get. Moreover, it will be divided Nationally, since in some States it must work through one party, and in some through the other. And when it comes into the open it gives its enemies a chance to unite against it, and there are few States where it can win.

## The Final Act to Come

All this means that in the coming campaign the Klan has staked its life, not merely on victory, but on skillful manipulation and on its ability to hold the confidence of its members through thick and thin. If it is to win what it hopes this fall, it must give National support to one of the big parties, and must give local support here to one, there to the other. It must often switch back and forth half a dozen times between candidates for the Presidency, the Senate, the House, Governor, legislators, county officers, and city or town officials. It must induce its members to forget their old party loyalties utterly and to split their tickets in a way that no politician has ever thought even remotely possible. And it must do all this in secret, and without weakening the faith of its members.

There are troubled days and nights ahead for the Klan leaders. Also for the regular politicians. But it will give us an interesting campaign.

Reprinted from THE KLAN UNMASKED by William Simmons, Wm. E. Thompson Publishing Co. 1924

# SYMBOLISM OF THE KLAN

By William Joseph Simmons

The Emperor of the Invisible Empire

Much ado has been made about the strange symbolism of the Klan. I stated at the beginning that the regalia now in use by the organization, like the terminology, was selected as a memorial to the original Ku Klux Klan. It has been generally regarded as grotesque and ghostly, designed to intimidate and terrify persons against whom the displeasure of the Klan might be directed. But the only purpose in adopting the white robes and incidental trimmings was to keep in grateful remembrance the intrepid men who preserved Anglo-Saxon supremacy in the South during the perilous period of Reconstruction.

The regalia of the Klan, however, expresses something more in the present organization than a mere memorial. Its symbols convey to the initiated the highest sense of patriotism, chivalry and fraternalism. These symbols were designed by myself during the years that pondered a revival of the old order, and contemplated the endangered position of the native-born American throughout our commonwealth. Every line, every angle, every emblem spells out to a Klansman his duty, honor, responsibility and obligation to his fellow men and to civilization. None of it was wrought for mere ornamentation, and none of it designed as mere mysticism. All of it was woven into the white robes of the Ku Klux Klan for the purpose of teaching by symbolism the very best things in our national life.

Emblematic robes are not uncommon to organizations of men banded together for either religious or fraternal purposes. My affiliations with the church and my connection with a number of fraternal orders have convinced me that the impelling truths which grapple and hold the loyalties and convictions of men are taught better by symbolism than ritualism. The

Roman Catholic church proclaims the authority of its mission to the world through the insignia of its clergy and its rulers; while its service of sacrifice and sanctity, of separation and consecration, is expressed in the robes of its nuns and its celebrants. In that colossal pile, St. Peter's at Rome, the most splendid edifice of Christianity in all the world, is to be found a vast collection of stones and gold, an array of art so magnificent that it dazzles even the imagination, an amazing accumulation of trophies torn by conquest from pagan temples-all symbolizing the universal dominion of the church not only over all things material but also over all things religious. The robes of the cathedral are elaborate and impressive throughout all the grades and ranks of service, from the drab garb of the keeper of the portals to the flashing colored uniforms of the Swiss guard, and on through the white, red, and black trappings of the attendants in the inner courts to the vivid scarlet of the cardinals and the gorgeous purple of the pope. All are designed to express some function, or mission, or doctrine of the church in its vast system of evangelism.

The Anglican church of Great Britain and the Protestant Episcopal church of America, as well as various other Protestant organizations have found it to be impressive and inspiring for the clergy and the sisterhood to wear robes designed to mark them as men and women set apart for service to humanity. Perhaps the Greek Catholic Church has the most elaborate system of teaching great religious truths by symbolism of any other religious organization. It undertakes to convey to the world the idea of its virility as a Christian organization by an extensive and artistically wrought out symbolism in its robes and insignia.

It goes without saying that nearly all, or perhaps all, of the great fraternal organizations of the world are characterized by the robes they wear. There are different robes of different orders and various robes for the same order in different degrees. These carry the message of fraternalism in the garments that are worn. Why should we, Knights of the Ku Klux Klan, be singled out and condemned for adopting a symbolism altogether unique, to represent our particular service to the age in which we live?

Some objections, probably not wholly misdirected, have been made to the mask that is worn by the Klan in public parades and demonstrations. The objections would have all the more force if it were true that the membership of the Klan were concealed from public scrutiny; but this is not true. Every local Klan has the custody of its roster and the roster may be given to the public at the option of the local Klan. Besides, it is overlooked that the Ku Klux Klan is a chartered organization-in fact twice chartered under the laws of Georgia.

Its membership is subject to the scrutiny of the State at its will. In addition to all this, the leaders of the Ku Klux Klan in respective communities are well-known, responsible and representative men, and their connection with the Klan is generally known to the community at large. So influential and conspicuous are those men that their leadership is a guarantee of the worthy and orderly purposes of the Klan. However, the matter of removing the mask from the Klan whenever it appears in public is under consideration, and it is not improbable that the Klan will be authorized to remove the mask whenever a public demonstration is given.

Outrages and atrocities, expressing various forms of prejudice and hate, have broken out in some parts of the country during the past twelve months. Often they have been charged to the Ku Klux Klan. It is the same old story repeating itself. During Reconstruction days, crimes were perpetrated by men wearing regalia similar to that of the Ku Klux Klan. The government spent much time and money investigating these crimes, and compiled altogether forty-six volumes in reports, but wherever the perpetrators of an outrage against order and decency were uncovered, they were found to be not Klansmen but Scalawags and Carpet-Baggers who had used regalia like that of the Klan under which they might enact their dual purpose of committing a crime and blackening the reputation of the Klan. At the recent investigation in Washington numerous crimes were charged to the present-day order of the Ku Klux. These had been heralded in startling stories by the press throughout the land. I vigorously denied that a single crime had ever been committed by the authority of the Knights of the Ku Klux Klan. I repeat that it is not an order that can tolerate or condone disorder, violence or lawlessness. It pledges itself now and always, here and everywhere, to the protection of society under constituted authority. It holds itself in readiness to serve the best interests of society, not despite the law, but always under the law and through the law.

Symbolism teaches the great principles of life, and being, and destiny, better than any form of speech. There is in human nature an element of mysticism that responds to suggestion and intimation when no logic or philosophy could reach it. The mightiest movements in our human nature, those which transform the character and transfigure the spirit, have their seat in a realm deeper than where man does his thinking or even his willing. It is in that part of human nature where the loyalties and affections, the prejudices and the passions are kept, and it is only the mystical, the mysterious, the intangible that can reach these forces in human nature, arouse them, and put them into action. It is poetry and art and music that move and stir the best that is in us and make us conscious of what we may do and be.

It is not strange then that symbolism has been used by the church in order to stimulate reverence and devotion; that it has been used by lodges to awaken fraternalism and humanism; and that it has been used by every great patriotic organization to arouse passion for native land and freedom. Indeed, every cause that has ever lived and flourished in the world whether religious, fraternal, or patriotic, has been highly spiritualized and all the fiery forces of the inner man have been elicited and organized in its service. There must be in every real movement something of the fervor of the Crusaders. Without this every spiritual effort of man, whether great or small, has had its ardor grow cold and the bright light of its enthusiasm go out in darkness.

What, indeed, could be more appealing to the finer things in human nature than the fiery cross? "By that symbol we conquer." It carries the idea of illumination and sacrifice. It symbolizes a love that lights the way to the noblest service; it symbolizes a service that is impelled by a burning love.

Here lies the only way forward. The world's amelioration is proclaimed by the glowing cross. We sometimes think of the cross as remote, as belonging to the past, as an isolated event. The cross is now and here and it is an essential part in the advancements in the world's civilization. It means the highest sense, freedom-the freedom of all mankind.

But there is no emancipation in all the world that comes as a gratuity. Wherever human life is freed a ransom price must be paid. When it comes to the liberation of human thought and the breaking of chains from immortal souls, there is no ransom that will pay the price except that into which men mint their lives, and out of which they coin their higher selves.

All this and more the fiery cross of the Ku Klux Klan conveys to the Klansman. It means the supreme agony of love through the sacrifice of life, to the end that freedom and democracy may be secured to all mankind forever.

Copyright by Stephenson Studio

HIRAM WESLEY EVANS
Imperial Wizard and Emperor, Knights of the Ku Klux Klan

Reprinted from NORTH AMERICAN REVIEW, March-April-May 1926

# THE KLAN'S FIGHT FOR AMERICANISM

### by HIRAM WESLEY EVANS

Imperial Wizard and Emperor, Knights of the Ku Klux Klan

The Ku Klux Klan on last Thanksgiving Day passed its tenth anniversary. In one decade it has made a place and won a record for achievement which are almost, if not quite, unique in the history of great popular movements. It has not merely grown from a handful to a membership of millions, from poverty to riches, from obscurity to great influence, from fumbling impotence to the leadership in the greatest cause now before the American people. All these are important, but not vital.

What is vital is that in these years the Klan has shown a power to reform and cleanse itself from within, to formulate and vitalize fundamental instincts into concrete thought and purposeful action, to meet changing conditions with adaptability but without weakness, to speak for and to lead the common people of America and, finally, to operate through the application of practical patriotism to public life with increasing success, and along the only constructive lines to be found in the present welter of our national thought.

By these things the Klan has proved not only its ability to live, but its right to life and influence. It has already lasted longer than any similar movement; its tenth birthday finds it stronger than ever before, with its worst weaknesses conquered or being eliminated, and so well prepared for the future that it may fairly be said to stand merely on the threshold of its life and service.

The greatest achievement so far has been to formulate, focus, and gain recognition for an idea-the idea of preserving and developing America first and chiefly for the benefit of the children of the pioneers who made America, and only and definitely along the lines of the purpose and spirit of those pioneers. The Klan cannot claim to have created this idea: it has long been a vague stirring in the souls of the plain people. But the Klan can fairly claim to have given it purpose, method, direction and a vehicle. When the Klan first appeared the nation was in the confusion of sudden awakening from the lovely dream of the melting pot, disorganized and helpless before the invasion of aliens and alien ideas. After ten years of the Klan it is in arms for defense. This is our great achievement.

The second is more selfish; we have won the leadership in the movement for Americanism. Except for a few lonesome voices, almost drowned by the clamor of the alien and the alien-minded "Liberal", the Klan alone faces the invader. This is not to say that the Klan has gathered into its membership all who are ready to fight for America. The Klan is the champion, but it is not merely an organization. It is an idea, a faith, a purpose, an organized crusade. No recruit to the cause has ever been really lost. Though men and women drop from the ranks they remain with us in purpose, and can be depended on fully in any crisis. Also, there are many millions who have never joined, but who think and feel and-when called on-fight with us. This is our real strength, and no one who ignores it can hope to understand America today.

Other achievements of these ten years have been the education of the millions of our own membership in citizenship, the suppression of much lawlessness and increase of good government where ever we have become strong, the restriction of immigration, and the defeat of the Catholic attempt to seize the Democratic party. All these we have helped, and all are important.

The outstanding proof of both our influence and our service, however, has been in creating, outside our ranks as well as in them, not merely the growing national concentration on the problems of Americanism, but also a growing sentiment against radicalism, cosmopolitanism, and alienism of all kinds. We have produced instead a sane and progressive conservatism along national lines. We have enlisted our racial instincts for the work of preserving and developing our American traditions and customs. This was most strikingly shown in the elections last fall, when the conservative reaction amazed all politicians--especially the LaFollette rout in the Northwest. This reaction added enormously to the plurality of the President, the size of which was the great surprise of the election.

I wish it might fairly be claimed that the Klan from the beginning had this vision of its mission. Instead the beginnings were groping and futile, as well as feeble; they involved errors which long prevented any important achievement. The chief idea of the founders seems to have been merely to start a new fraternal society, based on rather vague sentiments of brotherhood among white Americans, and of loyalty to the nation and to Protestantism. There was also a sentimental reverence for the Klan of the Sixties which led to revival of the old name and some of the ritual. There was finally the basic idea of white supremacy, but this was also at the time a mere sentiment, except as it applied to some Negro unrest.

But along with these ideas there shortly appeared others far from laudable. The Klan had remained weak, gaining barely 10,000 members in the first few years. Then the possibility of profit, both in cash and in power, was seen, and soon resulted in a "selling plan" based partly on Southern affection for the old Klan, partly on social conditions in the South, but chiefly on the possibility of inflaming prejudices. They began to "sell hate at $10 a package."

To us who know the Klan today, its influence, purpose and future, the fact that it can have grown from such beginnings is nothing less than a miracle, possible only through one of those mysterious interventions in human affairs which are called Providence. The fact is, as we see now, that beneath the stupid or dangerous oratory of those early leaders lay certain fundamental truths, quite unseen by them, and then hardly bigger than the vital germ in a grain of corn, but which matured automatically.

The hate and invisible government ideas, however, were what gave the Klan its first great growth, enlisted some 100,000 members, provided wealth for a few leaders, and brought down upon the organization the condemnation of most of the country, leaving it a reputation from which it has not yet recovered. But even before outside indignation had appeared there began an inside reaction, caused by abuses and excesses and by the first stirrings of the purposes which now dominate. Thus began the reform of the Klan by itself, which gained steadily until it won full control in 1922. It laid the basis for the astounding growth of the last three years, and for the present immense influence.

This reform did more than merely rectify the old abuses; it developed into full life the hidden but vital germs, and released one of the most irresistible forces in human affairs, the fundamental instinct of race pride and loyalty-what Lothrop Stoddard calls "the imperious urge of superior heredity." Closely associated with it are two other instincts vital to success among the northern races: patriotism, stimulated to unusual activity by the hyphenism revealed in the World War; and spiritual independence, a revival of the individualism which sprang up just as the Nordic races began to assert themselves in their great blossoming of the last four centuries, and which found its chief expression in Protestantism. These ideas gave direction and guidance to the reforms demanded by the rank and file three years ago. They have been further developed, made more definite and more purposeful, and they are the soul of the Klan today.

The direct reforms brought about were several. First was the stopping of any exercise of "invisible government." This was reinforced by a change in the oath, by which all Klansmen are sworn to uphold legally constituted officers in enforcing the law at all times. One result of this is to be seen in the decrease of lawlessness in Klan territory. We can justly claim credit for the remarkable improvement as regards lynching in the last two years.

The elimination of private profit for officers of the Klan came next and with it went a democratizing of the order. The Klan, being chiefly an organized crusade, cannot operate efficiently on a purely democratic basis, but the autocracy of the early years has been replaced by a system approximating that of the American Government in its early years; final power in the hands of the rank and file, but full power of leadership in the officers they choose.

Another most important reform was a complete change in the method of "propagation"--of recruiting and spreading our gospel. In the early days this had been done very secretively, a high percentage of money had gone to the kleagles - the "sales agents "-there had been a high-pressure appeal to sentimentality, hatred and the invisible government idea- and a tendency to emphasize numbers rather than quality of recruits. Today, instead of the evangelistic emphasis is put on Americanism, Protestant Christianity, and action through government machinery; an increasing number of the field agents are on salary, lists of possible members are carefully weeded out before any are approached, and those found worthwhile are won by personal work, backed by open discussion. This has, to be sure, cut down the number of new members accepted, but has greatly increased quality and loyalty- and it has brought amazing gains in strength, particularly in the Mid-West and North.

Most important of all has been the formulation of the true Klan purposes into definite principles. This has been a gradual process. We in the lead found ourselves with a following inspired in many ways beyond our understanding, with beliefs and purposes which they themselves only vaguely understood and could not express, but for the fulfillment of which they depended on us. We found ourselves, too, at the head of an army with sable influence to produce results for which responsibility would rest on us- the leaders - but which we had not foreseen and for which we were not prepared. As the solemn responsibility to give right leadership to these millions, and to make right use of this influence, was brought home to us, we were compelled to analyze, put into definite words, and give purpose to these half conscious impulses.

The Klan, therefore, has now come to speak for the great mass Americans of the old pioneer stock. We believe that it does fairly dutifully represent them, and our proof lies in their support. To understand the Klan, then, it is necessary to understand the character and present mind of the mass of old-stock Americans. The mass, it must be remembered, as distinguished from the intellectually mongrelized "Liberals." These are, in the first place, a blend of various peoples of the so-called Nordic race, the race which, with all its faults, has given world almost the whole of modern civilization. The Klan does not try to represent any people but these.

There is no need to recount the virtues of the American pioneers: but it is too often forgotten that in the pioneer period a selected process of intense rigor went on. From the first only hardy, adventurous and strong men and women dared the pioneer dangers; from among these all but the best died swiftly, so that the new Nordic blend which became the American race was bred up to a point probably the highest in history. This remarkable race character, along with new-won continent and the new-nation, made the inheritance of the old-stock Americans the richest ever given to a generation of men.

In spite of it, however, these Nordic Americans for the last found themselves increasingly uncomfortable, and finally deeply distressed. There appeared first confusion in thought and opinion, a groping and hesitancy about national affairs and private life alike, in sharp contrast to the clear, straightforward purpose of our earlier years. There was futility in religion too, which was in many ways even more distressing. Presently we begin to find that we were dealing with strange ideas; policies that sounded well, but somehow always made us still more uncomfortable.

Finally, came the moral breakdown that has been going on for two decades. One by one all traditional moral standards went by the boards, or were so disregarded that they ceased to be binding. The sacredness of our Sabbath, of our homes, of even of our right to teach our own children in our own schools fundamental facts and truths were torn away from us. Those who maintained the old standards did so only in the face of constant ridicule.

Along with this went economic distress. The assurance for the future of our children dwindled. We found our great cities and the control of much of our industry and commerce taken over by strangers, who stacked the cards of success and prosperity against us. Shortly they came to dominate our government. The "bloc" system by which this was done is now familiar to all. Every kind of inhabitant except the Americans gathered in groups which operated as units in politics, under orders of corrupt, self-seeking and un-American leaders, who both by purchase and threat enforced their demands on politicians. Thus it came about that the interests of Americans were always the last to be considered by either national or city governments, and that the native Americans were constantly discriminated against, in business, in legislation and in administrative government.

So the Nordic American today is a stranger in large parts of the land his fathers gave him. Moreover, he is a most unwelcome stranger, one much spit upon, and one to whom even the right to have his own opinions and to work for his own interests is now denied with jeers and reviling. "We must Americanize the Americans," a distinguished immigrant said recently. Can anything more clearly show the state to which the real American has fallen in this country which was once his own?

Our falling birth rate, the result of all this, is proof of our distress. We no longer feel that we can be fair to children we bring into the world, unless we can make sure from the start that they shall have capital or education or both, so that they need never compete with those who now fill the lower rungs of the ladder of success. We dare no longer risk letting our youth "make its own way" in the conditions under which we live. So even our unborn children are being crowded out of their birthright!

All this has been true for years, but it was the World War that gave us our first hint of the real cause of our troubles, and began to crystallize our ideas. The war revealed that millions whom we had allowed to share our heritage and prosperity, and whom we had assumed had become part of us, were in fact not wholly so. The had other loyalties: each was anxious to the interests of the country that had given him shelter to the interests of the one he was supposed to have cast off; each in fact did use the freedom and political power we had given him ourselves whenever he could see any profit for his older loyalty.

This, of course, was chiefly in international affairs, and the excitement caused by the discovery of disloyalty subsided rapidly after the war ended. But it was not forgotten by the Nordic Americans. They had been awakened and alarmed; they began to suspect that the hyphenism which had been shown was only it part of what existed; their quiet was not that of renewed sleep, but of strong men waiting very watchfully. And presently they began to form decisions about all those aliens who were Americans profit only.

They decided that even the crossing of salt water did not dim a spot on a leopard; that an alien usually remains an alien no matter what is done to him, what veneer of education he gets, what oaths he takes, nor what public attitudes he adopts. They decided that the melting pot was a ghastly failure, and remembered that the very name was coined by a member of one of the races the Jews - which most determinedly refuses to melt.

They decided that in every way, as well as in politics, the alien in the vast majority of cases is unalterably fixed in his instincts, thought and interests by centuries of racial selection and development, that he thinks first for his own people, works only with and for them, cares entirely for their interests, considers himself one of them, and never an American. They decide in character, instincts, thought, and purposes-in his soul-an alien remains fixedly alien to America and all it means.

They saw, too, that the alien was tearing down the American standard of living, especially in the lower walks. It become clear that while Americans can out-work the alien, the alien can so far under-live the American as to force him out of all competitive labor. So they came to realize that the Nordic can easily survive and rule and increase if he holds for himself the advantages won by strength and daring of his ancestors in times of stress and peril, but that if he surrenders those advantages to the peoples who could not share the stress, he will soon be driven below the level at which he can exist by their low standards, low living and fast breeding. And they saw that the low standard aliens of Eastern and

Southern Europe were doing just that thing to us.

They learned, though more slowly, that alien ideas are just as dangerous to us as the aliens themselves, no matter how plausible such ideas may sound. With most of the plain people this conclusion is based simply on the fact that the alien ideas do not work well for them. Others went deeper and came to understand that the differences in racial background, in breeding, instinct, character and emotional point of view are more important than logic. So ideas which may be perfectly healthy for an alien may also be poisonous for Americans.

Finally they learned the great secret of the propagandists; that success in corrupting public opinion depends on putting out the subversive ideas without revealing their source. They came to suspect that "prejudice" against foreign ideas is really a protective device of nature against mental food that may be indigestible. They saw, finally, that the alien leaders in America act on this theory, and that there is a steady flood of alien ideas being spread over the country, always carefully disguised as American.

As they learned all this the Nordic Americans have been gradually arousing themselves to defend their homes and their own kind of civilization. They have not known just how to go about it; the idealist philanthropy and good-natured generosity which led to the philosophy of the melting pot have died hard. Resistance to the peaceful invasion of the immigrant is no such simple matter as snatching up weapons and defending frontiers, nor has it much spectacular emotionalism to draw men to the colors.

The old-stock Americans are learning, however. They have begun to arm themselves for this new type of warfare. Most important, they have broken away from the fetters of the false ideals and philanthropy which put aliens ahead of their own children and their own race.

To do this they have had to reject completely-and perhaps for the moment the rejection is a bit too complete--the whole body of "Liberal" ideas which they had followed with such simple, unquestioning faith.

The first and immediate cause of the break with Liberalism was that it had provided no defense against the alien invasion, but instead had excused it--even defended it against Americanism. Liberalism is today charged in the mind of most Americans with nothing less than national, racial and spiritual treason.

But this is only the last of many causes of distrust. The plain people now see that Liberalism has come completely under the dominance of weaklings and parasites whose alien "idealism"reaches its logical peak in the Bolshevist platform of "produce as little as you can, beg or steal from those who do produce, and kill the producer for thinking he is better than you." Not that all Liberalism goes so far, but it all seems to be on that road. The average Liberal idea is apparently that those who can produce should carry the unfit, and let the unfit rule them.

This aberration would have been impossible, of course, if American Liberalism had kept its feet on the ground. Instead it became wholly academic, lost all touch with the plain people, disowned its instincts and common sense, and lived in a world of pure, high, groundless logic.

Worse yet, this became a world without moral standards. Our forefathers had standards--the Liberals today say they were narrow and they had consciences and knew that Liberalism plus kept within fixed bounds. They knew that tolerance of things that touch the foundations of the home, of decency, of patriotism or of race loyalty is not lovely but deadly. Modern American Liberalism has no such bounds. If it has a conscience it hides it shamefacedly; if it has any standards it conceals them well. If it has any convictions-but why be absurd? Its boast is that it has none except conviction in its own decadent religion of Liberalism toward everything the right of every man to make a fool or degenerate of himself and to try to corrupt others; in the right of anyone to pull the foundations from under the house or poison themselves; in the right of children to play with matches in a powder mill!

The old stock Americans believe in Liberalism, but not in this thing. It has undermined their Constitution and their national customs and institutions, it has corrupted the morals of their children, it has vitiated their thought, it has degenerated and perverted their education, it has tried to destroy their God. They want no more of it. They are trying to get back to decency and common sense.

The old stock "plain people" are no longer alone in their belief as to the nature of the dangers, their causes, and the folly of Liberal thought. Recently men of great education and mind, students of wide reputation, have come to see all this as the plain Americans saw it years before. This was stated by Madison Grant:

"The Nordic race ... if it takes warning in time, may face the future with assurance. Fight it must, but let the fight be not a civil war against its own blood kindred but against the dangerous foreign races, whether they advance sword in hand or in the more insidious guise of beggars at our gates, pleading for admittance to share our prosperity. If we continue to allow them to enter they will in time drive us out of our own land by the mere force of breeding."

"The great hope of the future here in America lies in the realization of the working classes that competition of the Nordic with the alien is fatal, whether the latter be the lowly immigrant from Southern or Eastern Europe, or the more obviously dangerous Oriental, against whose standards of living the white man cannot compete. In this country we must look to such of our people--our farmers and artisans--as are still of American blood, to recognize and meet this danger."

"Our present condition is the result of following the leadership of idealists and philanthropic doctrinaire."

The chief of Mr. Grant's demands, that the un-American alien be barred out, has already been partly accomplished. It is established as our national policy by overwhelming vote of Congress, after years of delay won by the aliens already here through the political power we gave them. The Klan is proud that it was able to aid this work, which was vital.

But the plain people realize also that merely stopping the alien flood does not restore Americanism, nor even secure us against final utter defeat. America must also defend herself against the enemy within, or we shall be corrupted and conquered by those to whom we have already given shelter.

The first danger is that we shall be overwhelmed, as Mr. Grant forecasts, by the aliens' "mere force of breeding". With the present birthrate, the Nordic stock will have become a hopeless minority within fifty years, and will within two hundred have been choked to death, like grain among weeds. Unless some means is found of making the Nordic feel safe in having children, we are already doomed.

An equal danger is from disunity, so strikingly shown during the war and from a mongrelization of thought and purpose. It is not merely foreign policy that is involved; it is all our thought at home, our morals, education, social conduct--everything. We have already confused and disunited in every way; the alien groups themselves, and the skillful alien propaganda, are both tearing steadily at all that makes for unity in nationhood, or for the soul of Americanism. If the word " integrity" can still be used in its original meaning of singleness of purpose or thought, then we as a nation have lost all integrity. Yet our old American motto includes the words "... divided we fall!"

One more point about the present attitude of the old stock American: he has revived and increased his long-standing distrust of the Roman Catholic Church. It is for this that the native Americans, and the Klan as their leader, are most often denounced as intolerant and prejudiced. This is not because we oppose the Catholic more than we do the alien, but because our enemies recognize that patriotism and race loyalty cannot safely be denounced while our own tradition of religious freedom gives them an opening here, if they can sufficiently confuse the issue.

The fact is of course, that our quarrel with the Catholics is not religious but political The Nordic race is, as is well known, almost entirely Protestant, and there remains in its mental heritage an anti-Catholic attitude based on lack of sympathy with the Catholic psychology, on the historic opposition of the Roman Church to the Nordics' struggle for freedom and achievement, and on the memories of persecutions. But this strictly religious prejudice is not now active in America, and so far as I can learn. never has been. I do not know of a single manifestation in recent times of hostility to any Catholic because of his religion, nor to the Catholic Church because of its beliefs. Certainly the American has always granted to the Catholic not only full religious liberty, without interference or abuse either public or private. but also every civil, social and political equality.

Neither the present day Protestant nor the Klan wishes to change this in any degree. The only possible exception to this statement is worth mentioning only because some people give it far too much importance. This has been in the publication of vicious and ignorant anti-Catholic papers, with small circulation and minute influence. These publications, by the way, the Klan has denounced and helped suppress. If the Catholic Church would do as much by Tolerance and some of the equally vicious and ignorant sheets published under its aegis, it could come into court against the American people with cleaner hands.

The real indictment against the Roman Church is that it is, fundamentally and irredeemably, in its leadership, in politics, in thought, and largely in membership, actually and actively alien, un-American and usually anti-American. The old stock Americans, with the exception of the few such of Catholic faith- who are in a class by themselves, standing tragically torn between their faith and their racial and national patriotism- see in the Roman Church today the chief leader of alienism, and the most dangerous alien power with a foothold inside our boundaries.

It is this and nothing else that has revived hostility to Catholicism. By no stretch of the imagination can it fairly be called religious prejudice, though, now that the hostility has become active, it does derive some strength from the religious schism. We Americans see many evidences of Catholic alienism. We believe that its official position and its dogma, its theocratic autocracy and its claim to full authority in temporal as well as spiritual matters, all make it impossible for it as a church, or for its members if they obey it, to cooperate in a free democracy in which Church and State have been separated. It is true that in this country the Roman Church speaks very softly on these points, so that many Catholics do not know them. It is also true that the Roman priests preach Americanism, subject to their own conception of Americanism, of course. But the Roman Church itself makes a point of the divine and unalterable character of its dogma, it has never seen fit to abandon officially any of these un-American attitudes, and it still teaches them in other countries. Until it does renounce them, we cannot believe anything except that they all remain in force, ready to be called into action whenever feasible, and temporarily hushed up only for expediency.

The hierarchical government of the Roman Church is equally at odds with Americanism. The Pope and the whole hierarchy have been for centuries almost wholly Italian. It is nonsense to suppose that a man, by entering a church, loses his race or national loyalties. The Roman Church today, therefore, is just what its name says-Roman; and it is impossible for its hierarchy or the policies they dictate to be in real sympathy with Americanism. Worse, the Italians have proven to be one of the least assimilable of people. The autocratic nature of the Catholic Church organization, and its suppression of free conscience or free decision, need not be discussed; they are unquestioned. Thus it is fundamental to the Roman Church to demand a supreme loyalty, overshadowing national or race loyalty, to a power that is inevitably alien, and which at the best must inevitably inculcate ideals un-American if not actively anti-American.

We find, too, that even in America, the majority of the leaders and of the priests of the Roman Church are either foreign born, or of foreign parentage and training. They, like other aliens, are unable to teach Americanism if they wish, because both race and education prevent their understanding what it is. The service they give it, even if sincere, can at best produce only confusion of thought. Who would ask an American, for instance, to try to teach Italians their own language, history, and patriotism, even without the complication of religion?

Another difficulty is that the Catholic Church here constantly represents, speaks for and cares for the interests of a large body of alien peoples. Most immigration of recent years, so un-assimilable and fundamentally un-American, has been Catholic. The Catholics of American stock have been submerged and almost lost; the aliens and their interests dictate all policies of the Roman Church which are not dictated from Rome itself. Also, the Roman Church seems to take pains to prevent the assimilation of these people. Its parochial schools, its foreign born priests, the obstacles it places in the way of marriage with Protestants unless the children are bound in advance to Romanism, its persistent use of the foreign languages in church and school, its habit of grouping aliens together and thus creating insoluble alien masses - all these things strongly impede Americanization. Of course they also strengthen and solidify the Catholic Church, and make its work easier, and so are very natural, but the fact remains that they are hostile to Americanism.

Finally, there is the undeniable fact that the Roman Church takes an active part in American politics. It has not been content to accept in good faith the separation of Church and State, and constantly tries through political means to win advantages for itself and its people--in other words, to be a political power in America, as well as a spiritual power. Denials of Catholic activity in politics are too absurd to need discussion. The "Catholic vote" is as well recognized a factor as the "dry vote."

All politicians take it for granted.

The facts are that almost everywhere, and especially in the great industrial centers where the Catholics are strongest, they vote almost as a unit, under control of leaders of their own faith, always in support of the interests- of the Catholic Church and of Catholic candidates without regard to other interests, and always also in support of alienism whenever there is an issue raised.

They vote, in short, not as American citizens, but as aliens and Catholics! They form the biggest, strongest, most cohesive of all the alien "blocs." On many occasions they form alliances with other alien blocs against American interests, as with the Jews in New York today, and with others in the case of the recent opposition to immigration restriction. Incidentally they have been responsible for some of the worst abuses in American politics, and today are the chief support of such machines as that of Brennan in Chicago, Curley in Boston and Tammany in New York.

All this might occur without direct sanction from the Roman Church, though that would not make it less a "Catholic" menace. But the evidence is that the Church acts directly and often controls these activities. The appearance of Roman clergy in "inside" political councils, the occasional necessity of "seeing" a prelate to accomplish political results, and above all the fact that during the fight in the Democratic National Convention of 1924 the hotel lobbies and the corridors of Madison Square Garden were suddenly black with priests, all seem to prove that the Catholic Church acts in politics as a church, and that it must bear responsibility for these evils.

This is the indictment of the old-stock Americans against the Roman Church. If at any time it should clear its skirts, should prove its willingness to become American in America, and to be politically an equal among equals with other religious bodies, then Americans would make no indictment of it whatever. But until it does these things it must be opposed as must all other agencies which stand against America's destiny.

Just a word about the American Catholics, of whom there are a few hundred thousand only. From the time of the Reformation on there have always been Catholics (like Lord Howard, who commanded the English fleet against the Armada) despite the Pope's bulls who have put race and national patriotism ahead of loyalty, not to their faith, but to the self-created Roman hierarchy. There are such in America today, and always have been. With these the American people have no quarrel whatever. They, even the Klan, have supported some of them at the polls, and will continue to do so.

But these people are not "good Catholics" in the eyes of the hierarchy. They are really in a tragic situation. They are pulled on one side by their faith and on the other by the deepest racial and patriotic instincts. If there should be a crisis they would he torn between them. They are put into this position not by their religion but by the autocratic hierarchy which uses their faith as a weapon to enforce its own power; which demands not only truth and piety, but subservience, as the price of salvation. What they may do in a crisis no man can forecast, but whatever it may be, they will deserve nothing but the deepest sympathy. This is the general state of mind of the Nordic Americans of the pioneer stock today. Many of them do not understand the reasons for their beliefs so fully as I have stated them, but the state of mind is there beyond doubt, and the reasons are true at for all vital points. It is inevitable that these people are now in revolt.

This is the movement to which the Klan, not through Providence than its own wisdom, has begun to give leadership. The Ku Klux Klan, in short, is an organization which gives expression, direction and purpose to the most vital instincts, hopes and resentments of the old stock Americans, provides them with leadership, and is enlisting and preparing them for militant, constructive action toward fulfilling their racial and national destiny. Madison Grant summed up in a single sentence the grievances, purpose and type of membership of the Klan:

"Our farmers and artisans... of American blood, to recognize and meet this danger." The Klan literally is once more the embattled American farmer and artisan, coordinated into a disciplined and growing army, and launched upon a definite crusade for Americanism!

This Providential history of the Klan, and the Providential place it has come to hold, give it certain definite characteristics. The disadvantages that go with them, as well as the advantages, may as well be admitted at once. We are a movement of the plain people, very weak in the matter of culture, intellectual support, and trained leadership. We are demanding, and we expect to win, a return of power into the hands of the everyday, not highly cultured, not overly intellectualized, but entirely unspoiled and not de-Americanized, average citizen of the old stock. Our members and leaders are all of this class - the opposition of the intellectuals and liberals who held the leadership, betrayed Americanism, and from whom we expect to wrest control, is almost automatic.

This is undoubtedly a weakness. It lays us open to the charge of being "hicks" and "rubes" and "drivers of second hand Fords". We admit it. Far worse, it makes it hard for us to state our case and advocate our crusade in the most effective way, for most of us lack skill in language. Worst of all, the need of trained leaders constantly hampers our progress and leads to serious blunders and internal troubles. If the Klan ever should fail it would be from this cause. All this we on the inside know far better than our critics, and regret more. Our leadership improving, but for many years the Klan will be seeking better leaders, and the leaders praying for greater wisdom.

Serious as this is, and strange though our attitude may seem to the intellectuals, it does not worry us greatly. Every popular movement has suffered from just this handicap, yet the popular movements have been the mainsprings of progress, and have usually had to win against the "best people" of their time. Moreover, we can depend on getting this intellectual backing shortly. It is notable that when the plain people begin to win with one of their movements, such as the Klan, the very intellectuals who have scoffed and fought most bitterly presently begin to dig up sound - at least well-sounding logic in support of the success. The movement, so far as can be judged, is neither hurt nor helped by this process.

Another weakness is that we have not been able, as yet, to bring home to the whole membership the need of continuous work on organization programs both local and national. They are too prone to work only at times of crisis and excitement, and then to feel they can let down. Partly, of course, this is inherent in the evangelistic quality of our crusade. It is "strong medicine", highly emotional, and presently brings on a period of reaction and lethargy. All crusaders and evangelists know this; the whole country saw it after the war. The Klan will not be fully entrenched till it has passed this reaction period, and steadied down for the long pull. That time is only beginning for most of the Klan, which really is hardly three years old.

But we have no fear of the outcome. Since we indulge ourselves in convictions, we are not frightened by our weaknesses. We hold the conviction that right will win if backed with vigor and consecration. We are increasing our consecration and learning to make better use of our vigor. We are sure of the fundamental rightness of our cause, as it concerns both ourselves and the progress of the world.

We believe that there can be no question of the right of the children of the men who made America to own and control America. We believe that when we allowed others to share our heritage, it was by our own generosity and by no right of theirs. We believe that therefore we have every right to protect ourselves when we find that they are betraying our trust and endangering us. We believe, in short, that we have the right to make America American and for Americans.

We believe also that only through this kind of a nation, and through development along these lines, can we best serve America, the whole world today, and the greater world yet unborn. We believe the hand of God was in the creation of the American stock and nation. We believe, too, in the right and duty of every man to fight for himself, his own children, his own nation and race. We believe in the parable of the talents, and mean to keep and use those entrusted to us-the race, spirit and nationhood of America!

Finally we believe in the vitality and driving power of our race; a faith based on the record of the Nordics throughout all history, and especially in America. J.P. Morgan had a motto which said, in effect, "Never bet against the future of America."

We believe it is equally unsafe to bet against the future of any stock of the Nordic race, especially so finely blended and highly bred a stock as that of the sons of the pioneers. Handicaps, weaknesses, enemies and all, we will win!

Our critics have accused us of being merely a "protest movement," of being frightened; they say we fear alien competition, are in a panic because we cannot hold our own against the foreigners. That is partly true. We are a protest movement- protesting against being robbed. We are afraid of competition with peoples who would destroy our standard of living. We are suffering in many ways, we have been betrayed by our trusted leaders, we are half beaten already. But we are not frightened nor in a panic. We have merely awakened to the fact that we must fight for our own. We are going to fight-and win!

The Klan does not believe that the fact that it is emotional and instinctive, rather than coldly intellectual, is a weakness. All action comes from emotion, rather than from ratiocination. Our emotions and the instincts on which they are based have been bred into us for thousands of years; far longer than reason has had a place in the human brain. They are the many-times distilled product of experience; they still operate much more surely and promptly than reason can. For centuries those who obeyed them have lived and carried on the race; those who were weak, or who failed to obey, have died. They are the foundations of our American civilization, even more than our great historic documents; they can be trusted where the fine-haired reasoning of the denatured intellectuals cannot.

Thus the Klan goes back to the American racial instincts, and to the common sense which is their first product, as the basis of its beliefs and methods. The fundamentals of our thought are convictions, not mere opinions. We are pleased that modern research is finding scientific backing for these convictions. We do not need them ourselves; we know that we are right in the same sense that a good Christian knows that he has been saved and that Christ lives-a thing which the intellectual can never understand. These convictions are no more to be argued about than is our love for our children; we are merely willing to state them for the enlightenment and conversion of others.

There are three of these great racial instincts, vital elements in both the historic and the present attempts to build an America which shall fulfill the aspirations and justify the heroism of the men who made the nation. These are the instincts of loyalty to the white race, to the traditions of America, and to the spirit of Protestantism, which has been an essential part of Americanism ever since the days of Roanoke and Plymouth Rock.

They are condensed into the Klan slogan: "Native, white, Protestant supremacy."

First in the Klansman's mind is patriotism--America for Americans. He believes religiously that a betrayal of Americanism or the American race is treason to the most sacred of trusts, a trust from his fathers and a trust from God. He believes, too, that Americanism can only be achieved if the pioneer stock is kept pure. There is more than race pride in this. Mongrelization has been proven bad. It is only between closely related stocks of the same race that interbreeding has improved men; the kind of interbreeding that went on in the early days of America between the English, Dutch, German, Hugenot, Irish and Scotch.

Racial integrity is a very definite thing to the Klansman. It means even more than more than good citizenship, for man may be in all ways a good citizen and yet a poor American, unless he has racial understanding of Americanism, and instinctive loyalty to it. It is in no way a reflection on any man to say he is un-American; it is merely a statement that he is not one of us. It is often not even wise to try to make an American of the best of aliens. What he is may be spoiled without his becoming American.

The races and stocks of men are as distinct as breeds of animals, and every boy knows that if one tries to train a bulldog to herd sheep, he has in the end neither a good bulldog nor a good collie.

Americanism, to the Klansman, is a thing of the spirit, a purpose and a point of view, that can only come through instinctive racial understanding. It has, to be sure, certain defined principles, but he does not believe that many aliens understand those principles, even when they use our words in talking about them. Democracy is one, fair-dealing, impartial justice, equal opportunity, religious liberty, independence, self-reliance, courage, endurance, acceptance of individual responsibility as well as individual rewards for effort, willingness to sacrifice for the good of his family, his nation and his race before anything else but God, dependence on enlightened conscience for guidance, the right to unhampered development-these are fundamental. But within the bounds they fix there must be the utmost freedom, tolerance, liberalism. In short, the Klansman believes in the greatest possible diversity and individualism within the limits of the American spirit. But he believes also that few aliens can understand that spirit, that fewer try to, and that there must be resistance, intolerance even, toward anything that threatens it, or the fundamental national unity based upon it.

The second word in the Klansman's trilogy is "white." The white race must be supreme, not only in America but in the world. This is equally undebatable, except on the ground that the races might live together, each with full regard for the rights and interests of others, and that those rights and interests would never conflict. Such an idea, of course, is absurd; the colored races today, such as Japan, are clamoring not for equality but for their supremacy. The whole history of the world, on its broader lines, has been one of race conflicts, wars, subjugation or extinction. This is not pretty, and certainly disagrees with the maudlin theories of cosmopolitanism, but it is truth. The world has been so made that each race must fight for its life, must conquer, accept slavery or die. The Klansman believes that the whites will not become slaves, and he does not intend to die before his time.

Moreover, the future of progress and civilization depends on the continued supremacy of the white race. The forward movement of the world for centuries has come entirely from it. Other races each has had its chance and either failed or stuck fast, while white civilization shows no sign of having reached its limit. Until the whites faltered or some colored civilization has a miracle of awakening, there is not a single colored stock that can claim even equality with the white; much less supremacy.

The third of the Klan principles is that Protestantism must be supreme; that Rome shall not rule America. The Klansman believes this not merely because he is a Protestant, nor even because the Colonies that are now our nation were settled for the purpose of wresting America from the control of Rome and establishing a land of free conscience. He believes it also because Protestantism is an essential part of Americanism; without it

America could never have been created and without it she cannot go forward. Roman rule would kill it.

Protestantism contains more than religion. It is the expression in religion of the same spirit of independence, self-reliance and freedom which are the highest achievements of the Nordic race. It sprang into being automatically at the time of the "great up-surgence" of strength in the Nordic peoples that opened the spirit of civilization in the fifteenth century. It has been a distinctly Nordic religion, and it has been through this religion that the Nordics have found strength to take leadership of all white, and the supremacy of the earth. Its destruction is the deepest purpose of all other peoples, as that would mean the end of Nordic rule.

It is the only religion that permits the unhampered individual development and the unhampered conscience and action which were necessary in the settling of America. Our pioneers were all Protestants, except for an occasional Irishman-Protetants by nature if not by religion-for though French and Spanish dared and explored and showed great heroism, they made little of the land they owned. America was Protestant from birth.

She must remain Protestant, if the Nordic stock is to finish its destiny. We of the old stock Americans could not work-and the work is mostly ours to do, if the record of the past proves anything ---if we become priest-ridden, if we had to submit our consciences and limits our activities and suppress our thoughts at the command of any man, much less of a man sitting upon Seven Hills thousands of miles away. This we will not permit. Rome shall not rule us. Protestantism must be supreme.

Let it be clear what is meant by "supremacy." It is nothing more than power of control, under just laws. It is not imperialism, far less is it autocracy or even aristocracy of a race or stock of men. What it does mean is that we insist on our inherited right to insure our own safety, individually and as a race, to secure the future of our children, to maintain and develop our racial heritage in our own, white, Protestant, American way, without interference.

Just how we of the Klan will accomplish this we do not yet know. Our first task has been to organize and this is not yet quite accomplished. But already we are beginning our second stage, which is to meet, stop and remove the invader and leave ourselves free once more. In the strict sense we have no program. We are not ready for one and have not put our minds to it. No such popular movement ever springs full-panoplied from the head of any man or group. For some time we must be opportunists, meeting the enemy wherever he attacks and attacking where we can. This course, so far, has accomplished much more than could have been done by a hard and fast program. We expect to continue it.

There are, however, certain general principles and purposes which are always kept in view. Enough has been said about pioneer Americanism. Another constant aim is better citizenship. The Klan holds that no man can be either a good Klansman or a good American without being a good citizen. A large part of our work is to preach this, and no man can be a Klansman long without feeling it.

Another constant objective is good government, locally and nationally. The Klansman is pledged to support law and order, and it is also a part of his duty to see that both law and officers are as good as possible. We believe that every man and woman should keep well-informed on all public matters, and take an active and direct part in all public affairs. There is nothing spectacular about this; it is merely good citizenship on the job.

The Klan, however, never attempts to dictate the votes of its members, but does furnish information about men and measures. In the National Government our interest is along the same lines, with special emphasis on anti-alien and pro-American legislation. Also far more than local in affairs we take pains to support men who understand and are loyal to the best American traditions. Apart from that the Klan takes no interest in any government matters except those having a direct hearing on decency and honesty.

We take great pains in all the matters never to be made use of at least not twice by and man, party or faction. We have no political interests except Americanism and do not belong in or with any party or faction. We do support a certain American type of man, and will support and group which draws the right kind of an issue. If there is no such issue, and no choice between candidates from the American point of view, we keep out. It is true that some men have been able to make use of the Klan once, but it has always reacted against them.

It is inevitable that most of the active work of the Klan, outside our own ranks, should be in public affairs. By no other means can most of our demands be accomplished. And it is against this patriotic activity that the most violent criticisms have been made. We are accused of injecting old prejudices, hatred, race and religion into politics, of creating an un-American class division, of trying to profit by race and religious enmities, of violating the principle of equality, and of ruining the Democratic party.

Most of these charges are not worth answering. So long as politicians cater to alien racial and religious groups it is the merest self defense to have also a Protestant and an American vote and to make it respected. The hatred and prejudice are as has been evident to every candid person, displayed by our enemies and not by us.

As to the charge that the Klan brought race and religion into politics, that simply is not true. That was done by the very people who are now accusing us, because we are cutting into the profits they had been making in politics out of their races and their religions. Race and religion have for years been used by the aliens as political platforms. The Klan is in no way responsible for this condition. We merely recognized it when others dared not, and we fight it in the open. Our belief is that any man who runs for office or asks political favors or advocates policies or carries on any other political activity, either as a member of any racial or religious group, or in the interests of or under orders from such a group or of any non-American interest whatever, should be opposed for that very reason. The Klan's ambition is to get race and religion out of politics, and that cannot be done so long as there is any profit in exploiting them. It therefore fights every attempt to use them.

This vicious kind of politics has mostly been more or less secret. We of the Klan wish we could claim credit for bringing the scandal into the open, but we cannot even do that. The open issue was raised for the first time on a national scale at the Democratic National Convention of 1924. This was the doing of the Catholic politicians, who seized upon Catholicism as a cement for holding the anti-McAdoo forces together. The bitter cleavage that followed was inevitable, and it was they- the Catholic leaders- who so nearly wrecked the party and were quite ready to wreck it completely if that would have helped their local Catholic machines.

One of the Klan's chief interests is in education. We believe that it is the duty of government to insure to every child opportunity to develop its natural abilities to their utmost. We wish to go to the very limit in the improvement of the public schools; so far that there will be no excuse except snobbery for the private schools.

Further, the Klan wishes to restore the Bible to the school, not only because it is part of the world's great heritage in literature and philosophy and has profoundly influenced all white civilization, but because it is the basis on which all Christian religions are built, and to which they must look for their authority. The Klan believes in the right of each child to pass for itself on the ultimate authority behind the creed he is asked to adopt; it believes in preserving to all children their right to religious volition, to full freedom of choice. This is impossible if they are barred from the Bible. We oppose any means by which any priesthood keeps its hold on power by suppressing, hiding or garbling the fundamental Christian revelation.

This is one of the reasons for the Klan's objection to parochial schools of the any church. They very readily become more mere agencies of propaganda. Another reason is that in many the teaching is in the hands of aliens who cannot possibly understand Americanism or train Americans for citizenship. In many even, the textbooks have been so perverted this Americanism is falsified, distorted and betrayed. The Klan would like to see all such schools closed. If they cannot be abolished, the Klan aims to bring them under control of the state, so as to eliminate these evils, ensure religious volition, and enforce the teaching of true Americanism.

This, then, is the mental attitude, the purpose and the plan of the Klan today, and it is against this position of ours and against nothing else, that charges of bigotry, narrowness, intolerance and prejudice can be brought. Changes made on other grounds need not be discussed, but we of the Klan are prepared to admit that some of these charges are at least partly justified.

This does not mean that there are "bigots and fanatics" among us. There certainly are; we are weeding them out, but we have some left, and some will join in spite of our utmost care. The fault is serious, but not fatal. Every such movement has then, as Roosevelt found when he dubbed the similar nuisances in his own movement "the lunatic fringe."

Nor does this mean, either, and admission of the charges of those who deny to Americans the right which every alien claims and uses-to speak his mind freely and criticize things about him. Jews or Catholics are lavish with their caustic criticism of anything American. Nothing is immune; our great men, our historic struggles, and sacrifices, our customs and personal traits, our Puritan consciences -all have been sacrificed without mercy. Yet the least criticism of these same vitriolic critics or their people bring howls of "anti-Semitic" or "anti-Catholic." We of the Klan pay no attention to those who argue with epithets only. They thereby admit their weakness. And are still waiting for someone to answer us with facts and reasons.

Aside from these things, however, we of the Klan admit that we are intolerant and narrow in a certain sense. We do not think our intolerance is so serious as that of our enemies. It is not an intolerance that tries to prevent free speech or free assembly. The Klan has never broken up a meeting, nor tried to drive a speaker to cover, nor started a riot, nor attacked a procession or parade, nor murdered men for belonging to the Knights of Columbus or the B'nai B'rith.

And we deny that either bigotry or prejudice enters into our intolerance or our narrowness. We are intolerant of everything that strikes at the foundations of our race, our country or our freedom of worship. We are narrowly opposed to the use of anything alien-race, loyalty to any foreign power or to any religion whatever---as a means to win political power. We are prejudiced against any attempt to use the privileges and opportunities which aliens hold only through our generosity as levers to force us to change our civilization, to wrest from us control of our own country, to exploit us for the benefit of any foreign power--religious or secular-- and especially to use America as a tool or cat's-paw for the advantage of any side in the hatreds and quarrels of the Old World. This is our intolerance; based on the sound instincts which have saved us many times from the follies of the intellectuals. We admit it. More and worse, we are proud of it.

But this is all of our intolerance. We do not wish harm to any man, even to those we fight. We have no desire to abuse, enslave, exploit, or deny any legal, political or social right to any man of any religion, race or color. We grant them full freedom- except freedom to destroy our own freedom and ourselves. In many ways we honor and respect them. Every race has many fine and admirable traits, each has made notable achievements.

There is much for us to learn from each of them. But we do insist that we may learn what we choose, and what will best fit the peculiar genius of our own race, rather than have them choose our lessons for us, and then ram them down our throats.

The attitude of the Klan toward outsiders is derived logically from these beliefs. From all Americans except the racial and spiritual expatriates we expect eventual support. Of the expatriates nothing can be hoped. They are men without a country and proud of it.

The Negro, the Klan considers a special duty and problem of the white American. He is among us through no wish of his; we owe it to him and to ourselves to give him full protection and opportunity. But his limitations are evident; we will not permit him to gain sufficient power to control our civilization. Neither will we delude him with promises of social equality which we know call never be realized. The Klan looks forward to the day when the Negro problem will have been solved on some much saner basis than miscegenation, and when every State will enforce laws making any sex relations between a white and a colored person a crime.

For the alien in general we have sympathy, opportunity, justice, but no permanent welcome unless he becomes truly American. It is our duty to see that he has every chance for this, and we shall gladly accept him if he does. We hold no rancor again him; his race, instincts, training, mentality and whole outlook of life are usually widely different from ours. We cannot blame him if he adheres to them and attempts to convert us to them, even by force. But we must see that he can never succeed.

The Jew is a more complex problem. His abilities are great, he contributes much to any country where be lives. This is particularly true of the Western Jew, those of the stocks we have known so long. Their separation from us is more religious than racial. When freed from persecution these Jews have shown a tendency to disintegrate and amalgamate. We may hope that shortly in the free atmosphere of America, Jews of this class will cease to be a problem. Quite different are the Eastern Jews of recent immigration; the Jews known as the Askhenasim. It is interesting to note that the anthropologists now tell us that these are not true Jews, but only Judaized Mongols-Chazars. These, unlike the true Hebrew, show a divergence from the American type so great that there seems little hope of their assimilation.

The most menacing and the most difficult problem facing America today is this of the permanently un-assimilable alien. The only solution so far offered is of Dr. Eliot, president emeritus of Harvard. After admitting that the melting pot has failed-thus supporting the primary position of the Klan -he adds that there is no hope of creating here a single homogeneous race-stock of the kind necessary for national unity. He then suggests that, instead, there shall be a congeries of diverse peoples, living together in sweet harmony, and all working for the good of all and of the nation! This solution is on a par with the optimism which foisted the melting pot on us. Diverse races never have lived together in such harmony; race antipathies are too deep and strong. If such a state were possible, the nation would be too disunited for progress. One race always ruled, one always must, and there will be struggle and reprisals till the mastery is established-and bitterness afterwards. And, speaking for us Americans, we have come to realize that if all this could possibly be done, still within a few years we should be supplanted by the "mere force of breeding" of the low standard peoples. We intend to see that the American stock remains supreme.

This is a problem which must shortly engage the best American minds. We can neither expel, exterminate nor enslave these low-standard aliens, yet their continued presence on the present basis means our doom. Those who know the American character know that if the problem is not soon solved by wisdom, it will be solved by one of those cataclysmic outbursts which have so often disgraced-and saved the race! Our attempt to find a sane solution is one of the best justifications of the Klan's existence.

Toward the Catholic as an individual the Klan has no "attitude" whatever. His religion is none of our business. But toward the Catholic Church as a political organization and toward the individual Catholic who serves it as such, we have a definite intolerance. We are intolerant of the refusal of the Roman Church to accept equality in a democracy, and resent its attempts to use clerical power in our politics. We resent, too, the subservience of members who follow clerical commands in politics. We are intolerant, also, of the efforts of the Roman Church to prevent the assimilation of immigrant members. We demand that in politics and in education the Roman Church abandon its clutching after special and un-American privileges, and that it become content to depend for its strength on the truth of its teachings and the spiritual power of its leaders. Further than this we ask nothing. We admit that this is intolerant; we deny that it is either bigoted or unjust.

The Klan today, because of the position it has come to fill, is by far the strongest movement recorded for the defense and fulfillment of

Americanism. It has a membership of millions, the support of millions more. If there be any truth in the statement that the voice of the people is the voice of God, then we hold a Divine commission. Our finances are sound as they have been for years; we permit no great accumulation, but have reduced our fees when we found them producing more than enough to carry on our crusade.

Our ritual is still incomplete. We have been too busy getting our army into shape and our crusade started, to perfect the higher degrees, but this is being done. Our first, and so far only largely used degree, inculcates and symbolizes loyalty - to America, to Protestantism, to law and order and to the Klan. The second, just coming into use, emphasizes patriotism. The third will center around Protestantism, and the fourth and last around pride, loyalty and responsibility. It may be added that members of other orders who have seen such ritualism as we already use, agree that it is unexcelled in solemnity, dignity and beauty.

One of the outstanding principles of the Klan is secrecy. We have been much criticized for it, and accused of cowardice, though how any sane person can allege cowardice against men who stood unarmed while rioters beat and shot them down, as Klansmen were beaten and shot at Carnegie and other places, we cannot understand. Our secrecy is, in fact, necessary for our protection so long as the bitter intolerance and fanatic persecution lasts. Until the Klan becomes strong in a community, individual members have often found themselves in danger of loss of work, business, property and even life. There is also the advantage in secrecy that it gives us greater driving force since our enemies are handicapped in not knowing just what, where or how great is the strength we can exert.

Both these reasons for secrecy will grow less in time, but it can safely be predicted that the Klan will never officially abandon its secrecy. The mask by the way, is not a part of our secrecy at all. but of our ritual, and can never he abandoned. The personal secrecy occasionally disappears, as the Klan gains strength, from the zeal of members who wish to work openly, whereby the Klan can be seen emerging as Masonry did a century ago.

One more charge against the Klan is worth noting: that we are trying to cure prejudice by using new and stronger prejudice, to end disunity by setting up new barriers, to speed Americanization by discriminations and issues which are un-American. This is a plausible charge, if the facts alleged were true, for it is certain that prejudice is no cure for prejudice, nor can we hope to promote Americanism by violating its principles.

But the Klan does not stimulate prejudice, nor has it raised race or religious issues, nor violated the spirit of Americanism in any way. We simply recognize facts, and meet the situation they reveal, as it must be met. Non-resistance to the alien invasion, and ostrich-like optimism have already brought us to the verge of ruin. The time has come for positive action. The Klan is open to the same charge of creating discord that lies against any people who, under outside attack, finally begin resistance when injuries have become intolerable---it is blameable to that extent, but no more. There can he no hope of curing our evils so long as it is possible for leaders of alien groups to profit by them, and by preventing assimilation. Our first duty is to see to it that no man may grow rich or powerful by breeding and exploiting disloyalty.

The future of the Klan we believe in, though it is still in the hands of God and of our own abilities and consecration as individuals and as a race. Previous movements of the kind have been short-lived, killed by internal jealousies and personal ambitions, and partly, too, by partial accomplishment of their purposes. If the Klan falls away from its mission, or fails in it, perhaps even if it succeeds - certainly whenever the time comes that it is not doing needed work - it will become a mere derelict, without purpose or force. If it fulfills its mission, its future power and service are beyond calculation so long as America has any part of her destiny unfulfilled. Meantime we of the Klan will continue, as best we know and as best we can, the crusade for Americanism to which we have been providentially called.

# III

**KU KLUX KLAN-**
SECRETS EXPOSED!
&
**IS THE KU KLUX KLAN CONSTRUCTIVE OR DESTRUCTIVE?**
A Debate Between
Imperial Wizard Evans,
Israel Zangwill and Others

Illustration by William Fisher from Thomas Dixon's THE BLACK HOOD (1924)

# KU KLUX KLAN

# SECRETS EXPOSED!

## CHAPTER 1

### THE OLD KU KLUX KLAN

To the old Ku-Klux Klan which rode through the south in the days following the civil war the new Ku-Klux Klan is a relative only in name.

It is not tied by blood. It holds the same position to its Southern aristocratic forbear as an imposter in social life does to some illustrious gentleman of the same name of whom he claims to be a descendant.

The old Ku-Klux Klan was a historical development. The new is a man's contrivance. The old Ku-Klux Klan movement was an outcome of conditions that prevailed in the southern states after the war. The present Klan, apparently, is an outcome of a group of men's desire to make money.

Widespread, spontaneous, popular, the movement of 1866 grew out of a disordered society, not as a "movement" at all at first, but as a scheme for having fun, a source of amusement among a group of young, full-blooded southern men to puzzle outsiders. Its use as a weapon against the stranger in the old south came later.

The "stranger" was a northern carpetbagger. To the south he was the pestilence that follows war. He was the blunderer who entered the land whose social customs were unknown to him, in a year when the fabric by those social customs was in need of mending.

## NO RELIGIOUS TEST

When southern society seized the Ku-Klux Klan as an instrument with which to resist there were only two classes, carpet-bagger and unruly negro, against which it operated. To join the ranks of the white-robed horsemen, there were no qualifications of religion. The Klan made no mention of Jew or Catholic. Its purpose was to restore order, not to fan prejudice, and therein lies the difference between the old Klan and the present Klan which makes the latter a maverick.

The first unit of the horseback riding knights was founded in the village of Pulaski, Tenn., with the same motive for its organization as the old-time college hazing society. Its members were young men who had come back from the war, poor, exhausted, discouraged, and bored with the tameness of a country town.

## HOW IT STARTED

According to the story which has lived south of the Mason and Dixon line since those post-bellum days, a group of youths cooling their heels in a law office one May evening in 1866 organized a society for a good time. If anyone had suggested to them at that time that five years later a committee of congress would devote thirteen volumes to a history of their "movement" and pass a law to suppress it, or that before the child of their wits was fully grown it would have developed into a terrorizing "hobgoblin" sheeted for lawlessness, they would have thought it a jest.

When their mere joke had become a grim joke, neighbors who feared it found in its name "Ku-Klux" the suggestion of a clicking rifle. But the name itself was proposed by its charter members in Tennessee as a derivative of the Greek word "Kuklos," meaning a circle. From "Kuklos" to "Ku-Klux" was an easy transition. The "Klan" followed because these youthful students of Greek had an ear for the alliterative.

From the Pulaski law office the society migrated to a haunted house on the outskirts of the village. Its members found their first source of amusement in initiation rites. They named their chief officer a Grand Cyclops and their vice president a Grand Magi. Other officers were the Grand Turk, or marshal; a Grand Exchequer or treasurer, and two Lictors.

## WORE WHITE MASKS

The only germ in their constitution from which the "Imperial Wizard" Simmons of the twentieth century Klan could breed his present organization was the promise of absolute secrecy. For his copying years later, the first Klan also contrived a disguise. It consisted of a white, mask, a tall cardboard hat, a gown or robe, and for the night riding excursions, a cover for the horses' bodies and mufflers for their feet.

Only after the Pulaski organization had entertained itself for many nights did the phenomenon present itself which was to make the Klan a weapon in the progress of post-war reconstruction. It was the discovery that the African negro was twice as fearful of mysticism and mystery as the white man. It taught the white men of Tennessee and neighboring states that they had a means of their own of preventing what they considered political mismanagement and social insolence in the control by northerners and freedmen of the state government.

## BECOMES A MILITARY ORGANIZATION

The Pulaski riders made themselves popular. Young men of neighboring towns organized brother Klans. When southern society found itself a Humpty Dumpty fallen from the wall, it grasped the Pulaski idea as the means for pulling itself up again. The Klan became a military organization, with the purpose of keeping order among the negroes by intimidating them. Mysticism in the order grew. Humor grew with it, and by the time the states of the north discovered that the south had an organization which was in purpose a society of regulators, the young southern war veterans were donning their white robes and cardboard hats with a human skull and two thigh bones as the symbols of allegiance.

The oath which the grand cyclops administered has been preserved in southern diaries and documents. It was taken in a solemn manner as the knights were grouped amid the bones. The oath follows.

"We (or I, as the case might be) do solemnly swear before Almighty God and these witnesses, and looking upon these human bones, that I will obey and carry into effect every order made by any cyclops or assistant cyclops, and if I fail strictly to conform and execute every order made, as above required of me, unless I am prevented from some cause which shall be no fault of mine, or if I shall give any information to any person or persons except members of this order, that the doom of all traitors shall be meted out to me, and that my bones may become as naked and dry as the bones I am looking upon. And I take this oath voluntarily, without any mental reservation or evasion whatever, for the causes set out in said order, so help me God."

Ku-Klux horsemen who rode white-sheeted through the south in the nights of 1866 regarded themselves as upholders of sectional patriotism. They considered themselves the spiritual descendants of the New Englanders who threw the English tea overboard into Boston harbor nearly 100 years before. Their protests, and the acts of intimidation by which they enforced their protests were against the white "carpetbagger" from the north, the negro freedman to whom liberty meant arrogant office-holding, and the "scalawag," by which terms they designated those deserters from the southern aristocracy who had joined the ranks of the northern stranger.

The second stage came within a year after the secret body had its birth, when the band of burlesquers became a band of regulators. To the south, the reconstruction acts which congress passed in 1867 were pernicious. The one-time white confederate soldier believed that the congressional legislation made official mismanagement permanent. He saw negroes organized into the militia. He saw his former slaves voting twice and thrice at elections where he himself had to pass, literally, under bayonets to reach the polls. He disliked the Freedman's Bureau, which substituted northern alien machinery for the old patriarchal relation between white employer and black employee. He heard drunken negroes at his gates in the night. He saw the "carpetbagger" urging upon the freedman civic rights which he knew the latter was not educated enough to perform.

## FIRST OBJECTS POLITICAL

These were the prejudices against which the original Ku-Klux Klan threw itself. They were surface indications of an historical development. They had nothing to do with the racial and religious biases which the present Klan attempted to propagate. To the present Klan, the old Klan, in its first stage, was unrelated. In its second stage it was related only in its methods of terrorism and its removal of justice from the courts to the masques until its own leaders were powerless to check it.

The Klan early fell a victim to the abuses inseparable from secrecy. It happened that Tennessee, the birthplace of the hooded institution, was also the first southern state to find itself turned upside down in reconstruction. "Dem Ku-Kluxes," as the negro called the mysterious union, became a band of regulators. Their first official convention was held in Nashville early in 1867.

The Klan, which, until then, had been bound together only by the deference which priority rights gave to the grand cyclops of the parental Pulaski "den," was organized into the "Invisible Empire of the South." It was ruled by a grand wizard of the whole empire, a grand dragon of each realm, or state, a grand titan of each dominion, or county, a grand cyclops of each den, and staff officers with names as equally suggestive of Arabian Nights.

## LAWS DEFINE OBJECTS

For the first time its laws defined serious objects. First was the duty of protecting people, presumably white southerners, from indignities and wrongs; second was the duty of succoring the suffering, particularly among the families of dead confederate soldiers; finally was the oath to defend "the Constitution of the United States and all laws passed in conformity thereto," and of the states also, to aid in executing all constitutional laws, and to protect the people from unlawful seizures and from trial otherwise than by jury.

It is these purposes which Imperial Wizard Simmons of the modern clan pretends to perpetuate, plus persecutions of Jews, Catholics and negroes, while denying charges of terrorizing outbreaks.

The Nashville convention chose Gen. Nathan B. Forrest, the confederate cavalry leader, as its supreme ruler. He is known to have increased the membership of the hooded horsemen in the old south to 550,000. Among his aids were Generals John B. Gordon, A.H. Colquitt, G.T. Anderson, A.B. Lawton, W.J. Hardee, John C. Brown, George W. Gordon and Albert Pike. The latter became one of the foremost authorities of Masonry.

Terrorism spread, until during the political campaign which preceded the 1868 presidential election, 2,000 persons were killed and injured in Louisiana by Ku-Klux Klansmen, who rode at night, disguised as freebooters, and according to James G. Blaine, defeated candidate for the presidency at a later date, hesitated at no cruelty.

In the north, in the years immediately after the civil war, the original Ku-Klux Klan was called a conspiracy.

In the south, where society was being ground in the mills of reconstruction, the Klan started its midnight "rovings" as an instrument of moral force. But within three years its period of usefulness, as the white southerner saw it useful, was over.

Its founders had played with it as with an exciting bonfire. During the months, however, when former confederate soldiers used it to frighten away northern officeholders with oppressive tactics, it had leaped in size until when the moment came for smothering it out its leaders discovered it beyond control.

Not until the full fire department of federal and state law had been called out did the Invisible Empire cease to operate.

## TENNESSEE ACTS AGAINST IT

By 1872 the white-robed knights of midnight, whose purpose to enforce law had in itself yielded to lawlessness, were for the most part disappeared. But so, in one state after another, had the northern carpetbagger and the southern scalawag.

Tennessee, where the Klan was founded, was the first to take legislative action against it. In September, 1868, its legislature passed a statute making membership in the Klan punishable by a fine of $500 and imprisonment for not less than five years.

As a result, in February, 1869, Gen. Nathan B. Forrest, former cavalry officer of the confederate army, who was grand wizard of the order, officially proclaimed the Ku-Klux Klan and Invisible Empire dissolved and disbanded forever.

But members of the adventurous law-assuming organization were reluctant to yield their mysterious power.

The Wizard's order went into effect. Klan regalia was burned.

## NEW BANDS SPRING UP

Immediately in southern states, as far west as Arkansas, there sprang up disguised bands, some of them who traveled in the night to win personal ends, still others founded new orders in imitation of the Ku-Klux and using similar methods.

Of the last, the Knights of the White Camellia was the largest. In some private notebooks of the south, its membership was said to be even larger than the parent Klan.

From New Orleans early in 1868, it spread across to Texas and back to the Carolinas. Racial supremacy was its purpose.

Only white men 18 years or older were invited to the secrets of its initiation, and in their oath they promised not only to be obedient and secret, but to "maintain and defend the social and political superiority of the white race on this continent."

Initiates were enjoined, notwithstanding, to show fairness to the negroes and to concede to them in the fullest measure "those rights which we recognize as theirs."

## "PALE FACES" AND OTHERS

Other bands of nightriders responded to the names of "Pale Faces," "White Leaguers," the "White Brotherhood" and the "Constitutional Union Guards."

Surviving members are hazy as to their aims and methods, the character of their membership, their members, and the connection between them.

Federal recognition that the Invisible Empire, whether it was the original Klan or not, was everywhere a real empire came in the spring of 1871, when a Senate Committee presented majority and minority reports on the result of its investigations of the white man's will to rule against the freedmen's militia in the south.

The majority report found that the Ku-Klux Klan was a criminal conspiracy of a distinctly political nature against the laws and against the colored citizens.

The minority found that Ku-Klux disorder and violence was due to misgovernment and an exploitation of the States below the Mason and Dixon line by radicals.

The first Ku-Klux bill was passed in April, 1871, "to enforce the fourteenth amendment." Power of the President to use troops to put down the white-hooded riders was hinted at.

In the next month the second Ku-Klux bill was passed to enforce "the right of citizens in the United States to vote."

In 1872 federal troops were sent into the south to back up his anti-Ku-Klux proclamation. By the end of 1872 the "conspiracy" was thought to be overthrown.

At various times individuals in the south and elsewhere have tried to put breath into the Klan's dead body.

It was left for "Grand Wizard" Simmons of Atlanta to accomplish it. His new organization, he explains, is imbued with the Ku-Klux "spirit."

"That this spirit may live always to warm the hearts of many men," he says, "is the paramount ideal of the Knights of the Ku-Klux Klan."

President Grant answered: "Thou shalt not" to the Ku-Klux Klan in 1871. He backed up his word with armed troops.

During the whole of one session of Congress, Senators and Representatives serving in Washington in the years just after the civil war occupied themselves in stripping the masques off the southern night-riders.

Into the country south of the Mason and Dixon line they dispatched Congressional investigators, whose duty it was to enter the "portals of the invisible empire" and discover what was hiding behind them. When they reported that the Ku-Klux Klan, decked out in the uniform of ghosts, was waging midnight warfare on the negro and carpetbagger congress passed legislation which suppressed the order.

## PUTS ROBES OUT OF FASHION

The committee recorded the results of their investigation.

Action was quick. Almost before the government printing presses had finished turning out ten volumes in which the white robes and hoods of the Ku-Kluxes had gone out of fashion in the old south.

President Grant in 1871 was without precedent. His law enforcers, just getting acquainted with the amendment which freed the slaves, were without a statute to deal with the armed clique, which proposed to keep the negro down in the day by frightening him in the night. The emergency bill which congress passed at that period empowers the regular army or the navy to put down any unlawful combination which is doing domestic violence.

When Congress met for its forty-second session in 1871, the cross bones and skull and coffin with which the Ku-Klux were marking their threats had become the symbols of terrorism in the south. So grave was the situation that speakers on the floor of the house, when the session opened, classed the conspiracy of the Klan "less formidable, but not less dangerous to American liberty" than the just-ended war of the rebellion. They charged that as well as binding its members to execute crimes against its opponents in the social-political life of the south, it protected them against conviction and punishment by perjury on the witness stand and in the jury box. Representatives asked why, of all offenders, not one had been convicted.

## PRESIDENT URGES ACTION

On March 23, 1871, President Grant sent a message to both houses in which he recommended that all other business be postponed until the Klan was made subservient to the flag.

"A condition of affairs now exists in some of the states of the Union rendering life and property insecure and the carrying of the mails and the collection of revenue dangerous," his message said. "The proof that such a condition of affairs exists in some localities is now before the senate. That the power to correct these evils is beyond the control of the senate authorities I do not doubt; that the power of the executive of the United States, acting within the limits of existing laws is sufficient for present emergencies, is not clear. Therefore, I urgently recommend such legislation as in the judgment of Congress shall effectually secure, life, liberty and property and the enforcement of law in all parts of the United States. It may be expedient to provide that such law as shall be passed in pursuance of this recommendation shall expire at the end of the next session of Congress. There is no other subject on which I would recommend legislation during the present session."

## "FORCE BILL AT DISPOSAL"

The law which was at the disposal of President Harding was popularly known as "the Force bill." Under congressional passage it was entitled "An act to enforce the Fourteenth amendment of the constitution of the United States and for other purposes." President Grant approved it April 20, 1871.

It is aimed at two or more persons who conspire to use force and intimidation "outside the law." It forbids them to go in disguise along a public highway or upon the premises of another person for the purpose, either directly or indirectly, of depriving that person of equal privileges under the law. Punishment for the offense may be imprisonment from six months to six years, a fine not less than $500, nor more than $5,000, or both.

The act took particular action against the practice of the Klanists of protecting each other in court. It provides that every man called for service on a jury in a Klan case shall take oath in open court that he is not a member of nor has ever aided or advised any such "unlawful, combination or conspiracy."

## DISGUISE IS BARRED

That individual was declared a violator of the law who shall "go in disguise upon the public highway or upon the premises of another for the purpose, either directly or indirectly, of depriving any person or class of persons of the equal protection of the laws, or of equal privileges or immunities under the laws, or by force, intimidation or threat to prevent any citizen lawfully entitled to vote from giving his support or advocacy in a lawful manner toward the election of any lawfully qualified person for office."

The act states further: "That in all cases where insurrection, domestic violence, unlawful combinations or conspiracies in any state shall so obstruct or hinder the execution of the laws thereof, and of the United States, as to deprive any portion or class of the people of any rights, privileges or immunities or protection, and the constituted authorities of such state shall either be unable to protect, or shall fail in or refuse protection, it shall be unlawful for the president, and it shall be his duty, to take such measures by the employment of the militia or the land and naval forces of the United States for the suppression of such insurrection."

## "KU-KLUX" FILLS RECORDS

Pages of the Congressional Globe, as the present Congressional Record was then called, were filled during the months before the passage of this act with the word "Ku-Klux."

The verb "Kukluxed" became in the mouths of Senators and Representatives arguing over the bill a synonym for "intimidated." Friends of the nightriders termed them "modern knights of the Round Table," and "conservators of law and order." Opponents on the floor of the house advocated a policy of "amnesty for every rebel, hanging for every Ku-Klux."

Black and white victims of the gun-toting ghosts were brought from Tennessee, Georgia, Louisiana, Texas and other states where the Klan rode to recount before the Congressional Committee the details of their persecutions. Their accounts as the government documents preserve them might well have been a primer, it has been said, for the acts of later Lenines and Trotzkys.

## REPORT OF OFFENSES VARIES

The report of the Congressional Committee is a recital varying from mirth to murder. In one county the victim of the hooded Klan might be an itinerant minister who had offended by teaching a negro mammy to pray. Next door a Ku-Klux sign, with a coffin painted in blood, might be hung over the dead body of a "bad" negro whose freedom had made him officious.

One negro was whipped for stealing beef. Another was tarred and feathered because his daughter ran away from the white man who had employed her. Colored cooks were beaten for talking saucily to their southern mistresses. Northern white women were threatened for hiring colored cooks.

## IGNORES NOTE, DIES

When a negro ignored a note carrying the Ku-Klux skull and cross bones and voted "republican" instead of "conservative," his body, ornamented with skull and bones in blood, might be found the next morning in the middle of the road - lifeless.

The Congressional minutes report a bold, public display of the Klan's official orders. They might appear in a whisk of the wind on the post office window. They might be pinned on a tree or pole or building. On one occasion, when a member of the Klan was on trial in a county court, a band of white masqueraders, riding through the courtyard on horse, dropped a note addressed to the court, grand jury and sheriff.

"Go slow," it commanded. At the bottom was a drawing of a coffin and on each side a rope. The signature was "K.K.K."

Ku-Klux rule in the south half a century ago was an attempt to govern by masque.

Secret covenants arrived at by a sheeted brotherhood veiled signs, orders written in blood and posted at midnight on the victim's door - by such means did the Klan substitute the masque for the ballot.

Congressional Investigating Committees who stripped the night-riding organization of secrecy during the administration of President Grant, were entertained during a session of Congress by tales of lares and lemurs howling at night in fields or on crossroads, bad luck omens for the negroes.

### UNDER MARTIAL LAW

In organization the Klan was military, and its town, county and state rule, as recorded in the Congressional Globe, operated as under martial law.

As the revolt of the white southerner to colored and northern domination reared itself into giant-size, towns under Klan domination came to take their rule and law from the K. K. K. note, flapping in the wind on a tree or fencepost, with the coffin on its signature, urging that it be obeyed.

### WARN CARPET BAGGERS

In South Carolina, according to the report of the Federal Committee, townsfolk journeyed to the post office, not to get their mail, but to read the daily Ku-Klux bulletin. One such, reprinted in the ten-volume report of the committee which examined southern outrages, was a warning against further "carpet bagger" administration.

It is as follows:

Headquarters, Ninth Division, S. C.

Special Orders, No. 3, K. K. K.

Ignorance is the curse of God.

For that reason we are determined that members of the legislature, the school committee and the county commissioners of Union county shall no longer officiate.

Fifteen days' notice from this date is given, and if they, and all, do not at once and forever resign their present inhuman, disgraceful and outrageous rule, then retributive justice will as surely be used as night follows day.

By order of the Grand Chief,

A. O., Grand Secretary.

## THREATEN NEGROES FOR FIRES

Another "special order," this one warning that the colored race in general would be punished for all malicious fires in particular, was made public in the Charleston News, Jan. 31, 1871.

Headquarters, K.K.K.

January 22, 1871.

Resolved: That in all cases of incendiarism, ten of the leading colored people and two white sympathizers shall be executed.

That if any armed bands of colored people are found hereafter picketing the roads, the officers of the company to which the pickets belong shall be executed.

Southern speakers on the floor of the house in the debates which preceded the passage of "the act to enforce the fourteenth amendment," traced the origin of the Ku-Klux to the Union league, an association in the south composed chiefly of northerners. Charges were also made by statesmen once in the confederate army that "Tammany Hall" in New York furnished arms to the Klanists, in order that they might murder southern republicans.

## SUPPRESSED IN 1871

When the act suppressing the Klan was approved by President Grant on April 20, 1871, it was estimated that the night riders were operating in eleven states of the south. Six months later, in October, President Grant issued a proclamation calling on members of illegal associations in nine counties in South Carolina to disperse and surrender their arms and disguises in five days.

Five days afterwards, another proclamation was issued suspending the privileges of the writ of habeas corpus in the counties named. More than 200 persons were arrested within a few days. It is believed that the Ku Klux Klan was practically overthrown by the middle of the following January.

**CHAPTER II**

**THE NEW KU KLUX KLAN**

*Must every citizen be a slave of Fear spread by masked night-riders, or will he live under the protection of the Constitution of the United States?*

Are you a citizen of the United States? If you are it is to your interest to inform yourself about the Ku Klux Klan. As a citizen you are under the protection of the constitution of the United States. The Ku Klux Klan has set itself above the constitution. It has made laws of its own. Its members have inaugurated a reign of lawlessness that may drag you out of your bed at midnight and submit you to a coat of tar and feathers through the whims of some neighbor who does not like the country in which you were born, or who objects to your religion, your color, your opinions, your personal habits or anything else about you that does not suit his fancy.

The constitution guarantees that your house, your person, your papers and effects are free from unlawful search and seizure; that you cannot be deprived of life, liberty or property without due process of law, which law must be publicly enforced in God's sunshine by persons legally chosen; that when you are accused of any delinquency or crime you shall have a speedy, public trial before a judge and an impartial jury; that you may be a member of any religious denomination or sect with whom you may worship as you please; that you have the right of free speech; that you cannot be held in involuntary servitude except as a punishment for crime, for which you have been found guilty in a legal way; that you cannot be denied the right to vote on account of your color.

## MASKED MEN DEFY CONSTITUTION

Masked riders of the night disagree with these guarantees of freedom. They break into your house under cover of darkness unlawfully seize your person and ride away with you, depriving you of liberty without due process of law. They accuse you of charges that may or may not be true, without giving you the opportunity of knowing the identity of your accusers, because they are masked. They try you without giving you a chance to defend yourself. They make themselves accuser, judge, jury and executioner. They deny that you have the right to worship God as you please. They deny your right to free speech, because they forbid you to criticize what they do.

The Ku Klux Klan clamps involuntary servitude on its own members by making them take oaths to uphold their leaders, even when they violate the constitution. It aims to place those whom it opposes under its heel. It openly defies the article of the constitution that guarantees race equality, by binding its members to put the black race under the supremacy of the white.

The American constitution says that if you were born abroad, but have become a naturalized citizen of the United States, you have as many rights here as though you were actually born here. The Ku Klux Klan is against the constitution on that point. The Ku Klux Klan wants to make the foreigner a serf.

The Ku Klux Klan has set itself up as a regulator of morals. Persons against whom there has been neighborhood gossip have been tarred and feathered. Thanks to the New York World, court records have been published showing that some of the highest persons in the Ku Klux have been involved in proceedings as disgraceful as those for which tar and feather parties have been organized by the Klan or persons masquerading as Ku Klux.

## MISTREAT WHITES AND BLACKS

Men and women, white and black - have been mistreated by masked men. The number of these attacks grows as the Klan increases in size. At present the Klan has branches in all states of the union except three -New Hampshire, Montana and Utah. In each state the law would be enforced by legal officials against any persons guilty of crime if public spirited citizens would make it their business to assist public officials to round up law breakers. The Klan, however, believes in its own method of punishment against those whom it opposes. It protects its own members and there is no case on record where a Klansman has been outraged. The Klan has one law for itself and another for its victims. The revelations of scandal among its leaders have not resulted in any movement on the part of its members to "clean house." Its motto seems to be "A Klansman can do no wrong." The lesson to be drawn from the revelations is that those in high places in the Klan have played on the gullibility of tens of thousands of otherwise sensible Americans. These leaders have become rich by dealing in the hocus-pocus of mysticism, secret rites and high sounding phrases and by inflaming the passions of dupes by false stories involving religions and races.

In the south they have preached and conspired against the negroes. This hatred also has been carried into certain sections of large cities of the north where there are large negro populations. In some states they have played upon the feelings of those who might be drawn into the Klan by a crusade against Catholics. They have made use of counterfeit documents in secret bids for membership on this score. In cities like New York and Chicago, where the populations are largely Jewish, they have fanned the flames of religious hatred by propaganda against the Jews. Where foreign-born residents are living in large numbers the Klan has secretly intrigued against them. On the Pacific coast this propaganda is made against the Japanese; on the eastern seaboard it has been against persons born in European and Asiatic countries.

### A GOLD MINE FOR PROMOTERS

Those who have investigated the Klan are convinced that its principal promoters are not inspired by a zeal for the welfare of the United States, but on the other hand they are certain that the promoters are in the Ku Klux Klan business to make money out of it; that they have profited by millions of dollars and that for this filthy money they have spread loose seeds of discontent and disorder that must be raked out of the body politic by the united action of all patriotic organizations and individuals. As far as its chief protagonists are concerned the Ku Klux is a huge money-making hoax-a gold mine. The poor dupes who have been "soaked" for regalia and dues will wake up sometime and discover how they have been deluded and misled. In the meantime, however, it is the duty of every true American to inform himself about the Klan so that in whatever way may come to his lot he may counteract the terrible consequences of its teachings and practices.

## CHAPTER III

## HOW THE MODERN KU KLUX KLAN WAS ORGANIZED

*Something about those who sit in judgment on the affairs of the "Invisible Empire"; their troubles in court.*

William J. Simmons (who carries a bogus title as "colonel") is the "Imperial Wizard" of the "Invisible Empire, Knights of the Ku Klux Klan." He organized the masked men on Thanksgiving night in 1915. Some of the organizers associated with him had belonged to the original Ku Klux Klan which rampaged in the southern states after the Civil War, killing hundreds of negroes and whites, and which was put out of business by President U.S. Grant after the states had failed to do so.

Simmons and thirty-four others secured a charter from the state of Georgia on December 4, 1915. It is signed by Philip Cook, who was then secretary of state of that commonwealth. Later, on July 1, 1916, a special charter was issued by the Supreme Court of Fulton county, Ga. The granting of the charters followed the organization of the Klan which occurred with midnight ceremonies on the top of Stone Mountain, near Atlanta, Thanksgiving night.

## THAT COLD WINTER NIGHT

In referring to the first ceremonies, Simmons has written as follows in the official records of the Ku Klux:

"On Thanksgiving night, 1915, men were seen emerging from the shadows and gathering round the spring at the base of Stone Mountain, the world's greatest rock, near Atlanta, Ga., and from thence repaired to the mountain top, and there under a blazing fiery cross they took the oath of allegiance to the Invisible Empire, Knights of the Ku Klux Klan."

"And thus on the mountain top that night at the midnight hour, while men braved the surging blasts of wild wintry mountain winds and endured a temperature far below freezing, bathed in the sacred glow of the fiery cross, the Invisible Empire was called from its slumber of half a century to take up a new task and fulfill a new mission for humanity's good, and to call back to mortal habitation the good angel of practical fraternity among men."

It will be noticed that Simmons refers to "a temperature far below freezing." The official weather reports of the region for that night show that the temperature was thirty degrees above the freezing point.

Simmons had a fraternal order in mind when he organized the Ku Klux. He had been an itinerant Methodist preacher and organizer for the Modern Woodmen of the World and had not met with success in either capacity. He was a good talker but lacked the "punch" to put things over. The Ku Klux Klan did not prosper under his direction. Then he met Edward Y. Clarke and Mrs. Elizabeth Tyler. Clarke and Mrs. Tyler were the owners of the Southern Publicity Association of Atlanta. During the war they had been publicity agents for various "drives," managed for the Y.M.C.A., such Y.W.C.A., the Salvation Army and such enterprises. Clarke saw the value of the publicity that could be coined from the old name of the Ku Klux Klan and entered into an arrangement with Simmons to promote the Klan. He agreed to give Simmons $100 a week if Simmons would follow his directions. Simmons was to brush up on delivering speeches and writing articles for The Searchlight, a magazine which Clarke founded as the official organ of the Ku Klux.

From this joining of forces Simmons, Clarke and Mrs. Tyler have become rich. The Klan has extended its membership to all except three states and it claims that 500,000 to 700,000 Klansmen are in its ranks. Clarke is the "Imperial Kleagle," or boss salesman of memberships. Mrs. Tyler is Grand Chief of Staff in charge of the woman's division of the Klan.

## WHAT POLICE RECORDS SHOW

Investigation of the police and court records of Atlanta disclosed that Clarke and Mrs. Tyler were arrested in their night clothes in a house that Mrs. Tyler owned at No. 185 South Pryor Street, Atlanta. This occurred in October, 1919. Clarke gave the name of "Jim Slaton" and Mrs. Tyler gave the name of "Mrs. Elizabeth Carroll."

The cases were on the book of the Recorder's court as City of Atlanta versus E. Y. Clarke and City of Atlanta versus Mrs. Elizabeth Tyler, page 305 of the docket of 1919, case numbers 17,005 and 17,006. The police were put on the trail of Clarke and Mrs. Tyler by Clarke's wife.

In addition to the charge of disorderly conduct, a charge of possessing whisky illegally was placed against Mrs. Tyler and Clarke. This was an amazing charge against Clarke because he had been known as one of the leaders of the anti-saloon movement in Georgia. The whisky charge was dropped when J.Q. Jett, son-in-law of Mrs. Tyler, claimed ownership of the whisky and was fined $25.

The Klan is supposed to stand for respect of women and children. The records of the Atlanta courts still contain charges against Clarke that he deserted and abandoned his wife and child. He never has denied the charges. Mrs. Clarke went to work to support herself and her little son. A suit for divorce was filed in October, 1919, by Mrs. Clarke, who charged that her husband had deserted her three years previously. After his arrest with Mrs. Tyler Clarke agreed to pay his wife $75 a month. Since Clarke has become prosperous in the Ku Klux Klan he has bought his wife a $10,000 house.

## RECORDS ARE STOLEN

When newspaper men began to investigate Mrs. Tyler and Clarke, they discovered that the official records of the Atlanta police department and the Recorder's office had been mutilated. Somebody had stolen the pages from the books containing the records of the cases. Members of the Ku Klux Klan are numbered among the police and official attaches of the city and newspaper comment indicates that they helped smother the case in behalf of their leaders.

## SCANDAL OF "CHAPLAIN" RIDLEY

Another leader of the Ku Klux Klan is "Rev." Caleb A. Ridley, who is the "Imperial Chaplain" of the order. He is a right-hand assistant of Mrs. Tyler and helps her to edit The Searchlight.

Ridley also has had an experience in the recorder's court. He was arrested on complaint of the husband of Mrs. J.B. Hamilton, who lives on Cooper Street, Atlanta, not a great distance from the Central Baptist church, where Ridley preaches. Recorder Johnson dismissed the case against Ridley.

Mrs. Hamilton testified that Ridley used to walk past her house when she sat on the porch and smile up at her. One day, without being invited and with no encouragement from her, he walked up on the porch and sat next to her on a swing. She said he chatted with her about church questions, although she was not a member of his church. Then he placed his arm around her, tried to embrace her and said something that she thought was not proper.

One witness testified that he had seen Ridley go on the porch and sit on the swing. He had seen Mrs. Hamilton push Ridley away from her. Ridley was supported by his flock. Several women testified in behalf of his character. He said he visited Mrs. Hamilton because she looked lonely.

**CHAPTER IV**

**HOW THE KU KLUX KLAN GETS MEMBERS**

*First Approached by Mysterious Notes, the Candidate is Soaked for a "Donation" and Money for His Robes.*

The man who is invited to join the Ku Klux Klan is kidded into the belief that he is one of the chosen of God's beings and that he is being honored because his presence in the ranks is an honor to himself as well as to the Klan. A kleagle is a common salesman. He has charge of a small district. He works under a king kleagle, who has charge of a state. He is the state sales manager. A cyclops is in charge of the king kleagles and the kleagles in several states.

Here is the way one group of kleagles work. They are given the name of a person who is eligible. One kleagle is assigned to catch him. The kleagle sends the sucker the following message:

"Sir (or Brother) - Six thousand men who are preparing for eventualities have their eyes on you. You are being weighed in the balance!"

"The Call is coming! Are you able and qualified to respond?"

"Discuss this matter with no one."

"Yu-Bu-Tu"

A few days later this card is sent:

"Sir-You have heard from us because we believe in you. We are for you and Need you!"

"The impenetrable Veil of Mystery is drawing aside. Soon you will appear exactly as you are."

"Are you a Real Man?"

"Lift your eyes to the Fiery Cross and falter not, but go forward to the Light."

"Discuss this matter with no one."

"Yu-Bu-Tu"

After another short wait this third message is sent:

"Sir:"

"You have been weighed in the balance and found not wanting!"

"Strong Men - Brave Men - Real Men. We need such Men. We know you are one."

"The Goblins of the Invisible Empire will shortly issue their Call. Be discreet, preserve silence and bide its coming."

"Discuss this matter with no one.

"Yu-Bu-Tu"

By this time the candidate is supposed to be in a mood to fall, and the kleagle calls on him personally.

## QUESTIONS FOR THE CANDIDATE

The kleagle presents the prospective initiate with the following list of questions to be answered (note the questions marked with stars - they are used to bar out Jews, Catholics, negroes and foreign born):

1. Is the motive prompting your inquiry serious?
2. What is you age?
3. What is your occupation?
4. Where were you born?
5. How long have you resided in your present locality?
6. Are you married, single or widower?
* 7. Were your parents born in the United States of America?
* 8. Are you a gentile or Jew?
* 9. Are you of the white race or of a colored race?
10. What educational advantages have you?
11. Color of eyes? Hair? Weight? Height?
*12. Do you believe in the principles of Pure Americanism?
*13. Do you believe in white supremacy?
14. What is your politics?
*15. What is your religious faith?
*16. Of what church are you a member (if any)?
*17. Of what religious faith are your parents?
18. What secret, fraternal orders are you a member of (if any)?
19 Do you honestly believe in the practice of Real fraternity?
*20. Do you owe any kind of allegiance to any foreign nation, government, institution, sect, people, ruler or person?

I most solemnly assert and affirm that each question above is truthfully answered by me and in my own handwriting and that below is my real signature.

Signed………………......................… Inquirer.

Business Address ............................................................
Telephone No…………………………………………….
Date………………………………………………...........19…..
Residence Address………………………………………….
………………………………………………………………
Telephone No…………………………………………….....

N.B. - If space above is not sufficient to answer questions, then make your answer on the other side of this sheet. Number the answer to correspond with the question.

If the candidate answers the question satisfactorily, he must pay his initiation fees, called "donation" and provide money to pay for his mask, robe, etc. This will be explained later. With his money affairs settled, he is ready for the initiation, together with whatever other candidates there are in the vicinity. The initiation services are held at midnight, with a flaming cross, an American flag, a sword or dagger, and a Bible as the chief outward signs of the order. There is also a bottle of water on the "altar."

## CHAPTER V

## OATH OF THE KU KLUX KLAN

*Those who join the order must pledge blind allegiance to Constitution. They do not see.*

Blind and unconditional obedience to the "constitution, laws, regulations usages and requirements" of the Ku Klux Klan, even to the extent of endorsing the principle of secret mob violence, is accepted by every person who takes the oath of Grand Wizard Simmons' Invisible Empire.

That every Klansman, under penalty of death, also agrees to carry out the mandates, degrees, edicts, rulings and "instructions" of Emperor Simmons also is shown in a reproduction of the oath as supplied by Klan organizer and officials.

The first section of this oath that carries veiled hints a violence to back it binds the members to unconditional obedience to a constitution he has never seen. Not only that, but it binds him to obey any laws that may be enacted in the future, whether or not he approves of them. When he takes this obligation he gives a lease on his life to Simmons.

## SWEARS TO ABSOLUTE SECRECY

Absolute secrecy even in the face of death is his second obligation and he promises that he "will pay promptly all just and legal demands made upon me to defray the expenses of my Klan when same are due or called for."

Then, with his left hand over his heart and his right hand raised to heaven and with the promise that "this oath I will seal with my blood," the candidate takes oath that he "will most zealously and valiantly shield and preserve by any and all JUSTIFIABLE means and methods (not legal means and methods) the sacred constitutional rights and privileges of free public schools, free speech, free press, separation of church and state, liberty, white supremacy, just laws and the pursuit of happiness, against any encroachment of any nature by any person or persons, political party or parties, religious sect or people, native, naturalized or foreign, of any race, color, creed, lineage or tongue whatsoever."

## MYSTERY IN AUTHORITY

Who defines the permissible limits of zeal and valor is not stated. Neither is it stated who decides when schools are free, speech and press free, nor when church and state are sufficiently separated. It is not stated whether it is the individual Klansman, the local Klan, the supreme council or the Imperial Wizard.

It has been revealed, however, that this phase of the Klan movement has been much fathered by the sales crew selling subscriptions at $10 each under the direction of Wizard Simmons and Imperial Kleagle Clarke.

The exact text of the oath of allegiance administered to new members of the Ku Klux Klan is given herewith. The asterisks are printed to take place of the Ku Klux Klan and also the officers of the order. These places are left blank in the printed oath because it is carried by Klan officials and might be lost, revealing their secret.

The oath:

You will place your left hand over your heart and raise your right hand to heaven.

### SEC. I. - OBEDIENCE

(You will say) "I" _____ (pronounce your full name - and repeat after me) "In the presence of God and Man - most solemnly pledge, promise and swear - unconditionally - that I will faithfully obey - the constitution and laws - and will willingly conform to all regulations, usages and requirements - of the [KKK]*** - which do now exist - or which may be hereafter enacted - and will render at all times loyal respect and steadfast support - to the Imperial Authority of same - and will heartily heed - all official mandates - decrees - edicts - rulings and instructions - of the [Imperial Wizard] *** thereof. I will yield prompt response - to all summonses - I having knowledge of same - Providence alone preventing.

### SEC. II.- SECRECY

I most solemnly swear - that I will forever - keep sacredly secret - the signs, words and grip - and any and all other - matters and knowledge - of the [KKK]***- regarding which a most rigid secrecy - must be maintained - which may at any time - be communicated to me - and will never divulge same - nor even cause the same to be divulged - to any person in the whole world - unless I know positively - that such person is a member of this Order in good and regular standing - and not even then - unless it be - for the best interest of this Order.

I most sacredly vow - and most positively swear - that I will not yield to bribe - flattery - threats - passion - punishment - persecution - persuasion - nor any enticements whatever - coming from or offered by - any person or persons - male or female - for the purpose of _ obtaining from me - a secret or secret information - of the [KKK]*** - I will die rather than divulge same - so help me God - AMEN!

You will drop your hands.

GENTLEMEN (or SIR):

You will wait in patience and peace until you are informed of the decision of the [Exalted Cyclops]E*C* and his klonklave assembled.

You will place your left hand over your heart and raise your right hand to heaven.

## SEC. III.-FIDELITY

(You will say) "I" _____ (pronounce your full name and repeat after me) "Before God - and in the presence of - these mysterious Klansmen - on my sacred honor - do most solemnly and sincerely pledge - promise and swear - that I will diligently guard and faithfully foster - every interest of the [KKK]*** - and will maintain - its social cast and dignity.

I swear that I will not recommend - any person for membership in this Order - whose mind is unsound - or whose reputation I know to be bad - or whose character is doubtful - or whose loyalty to our country - is in any way questionable.

I swear that I will pay promptly - all just and legal demands - made upon me to defray the expenses - of my and this Order - when same are due or called for.

I swear that I will protect the property - of the [KKK]*** - of any nature whatsoever - and if any should be entrusted to my keeping - I will properly keep - or rightly use same - and will freely and promptly surrender same - on official demand - or if ever I am banished from - or voluntarily discontinue - my membership in this Order.

I swear that I will most determinedly - maintain peace and harmony - in all the deliberations - of the gatherings or assemblies -- of the [Invisible Empire]I*E* - and of any subordinate jurisdiction - or thereof.

I swear that I will most strenuously - discourage selfishness - and selfish political ambition - on the part of myself or any Klansman.

I swear that I will never allow - personal friendship - blood or family relationship - nor personal political - or professional prejudice - malice nor ill-will - to influence me in casting my vote - for the election or rejection - of an applicant - for membership in this Order - God being my helper -

AMEN!

You will drop your hands.

You will place your left hand over your heart and raise your right hand to heaven.

### SEC. IV.-KLANISHNESS

(You will say) "I" - (Pronounce your full name - and repeat after me) "Most solemnly pledge, promise and swear - that I will never slander - defraud receive - or in any manner wrong - the*** [KKK] - a Klansman - nor a Klansman's family - nor will I suffer the same to be done - if I can prevent it.

I swear that I will be faithful - in defending and protecting - the home - reputation - and physical and business interest - of a Klansman - and that of a Klansman's family.

I swear that I will at any time - without hesitating -- go to the assistance or rescue - of a Klansman in any way - at his call I will answer - I will be truly Klanish toward Klansmen - in all things honorable.

I swear that I will not allow - any animosity friction nor ill-will- to arise and remain - between myself and a Klansman - but will be constant in my efforts - to promote real Klanishness - among the members of this Order.

I swear that I will keep secure to myself - a secret of a Klansman - when same is committed to me - in the sacred bond of Klansmanship - the crime of violating THIS solemn oath - treason against the United States of America - rape - and malicious murder - alone excepted.

I most solemnly assert and affirm - that to the Government of the United States of America and any State thereof of which I may become a resident - I sacredly swear - an unqualified allegiance - above any other and every kind of government - in the whole world - I here and now - pledge my life - my property - my vote - and my sacred honor - to uphold its flag - its Constitution - and Constitutional laws - and will protect - defend - and enforce same unto death.

I swear that I will most zealously - and valiantly - shield and preserve - by any and all - justifiable means and methods - the sacred constitutional rights - and privileges of - free public schools - free speech - free press - separation of church and state - liberty - white supremacy - just laws - and the pursuit of happiness - against any encroachment - of any nature - by any person or persons - political party or parties - religious sect or people - native, naturalized or foreign - of any race - color - creed - lineage or tongue whatsoever.

All to which I have sworn by THIS oath - I will seal with my blood - be Thou my witness - Almighty God - AMEN!

You will drop your hands.

## OLD PLEDGE OF LOYALTY

### APPELLATION

This Organization shall be styled and denominated, The Order of the (then follows three stars; no other name given).

### CREED

We, the Order of the ***[KKK], reverentially acknowledge the majesty and supremacy of the Divine Being, and recognize the goodness and providence of the same. And we recognize our relation to the United States Government, the supremacy of the Constitution, the Constitutional Laws thereof, and the Union of States there under.

### OBJECTS OF THE ORDER

This is an institution of Chivalry, Humanity, Mercy, and Patriotism; embodying in its genius and its principles all that is chivalric in conduct, noble in sentiment, generous in manhood, and patriotic in purpose; its peculiar object being:

First: To protect the weak, the innocent, and the defenseless, from the indignities, wrongs, and outrages, of the lawless, the violent, and the brutal; to relieve the injured and oppressed; to succor the suffering and unfortunate, and especially the widows and orphans of Confederate soldiers.

Second: To protect and defend the Constitution of the United States, and all laws passed in conformity thereto, and to protect the States and the people thereof from all invasion from any source whatever.

Third: To aid and assist in the execution of all constitutional laws, and to protect the people from unlawful seizure, and from trial except by their peers in conformity to the laws of the land.

Note the vast difference between this and the following page. One, the pledge to all that is right and uplifting - the other to a single autocrat. The above was formed for the protection and enforcement of law - the Kleagle's pledge, merely a vow to do anything that the Imperial Wizard Simmons might see fit.

## MODERN KLEAGLE'S PLEDGE OF LOYALTY

I, the undersigned, in order to be a regular appointed Kleagle of the Invisible Empire, Knights of the Ku Klux Klan (Incorporated), do freely and voluntarily promise, pledge and fully guarantee a lofty respect, whole-hearted loyalty and an unwavering devotion at all times and under any and all circumstances and conditions from this day and date forward to William Joseph Simmons as Imperial Wizard and Emperor of the Invisible Empire, Knights of the Ku Klux Klan (Incorporated). I shall work in all respects in perfect harmony with him and under his authority and directions, in all his plans for the extension and government of the Society, and under his directions, with any and all of my officially superior officers duly appointed by him.

I shall at any and all times be faithful and true in all things, and most especially in preventing and suppressing any factions, cisms or conspiracies against him or his plans and purposes or the peace and harmony of the Society which may arise or attempt to arise. I shall discourage and strenuously oppose any degree of disloyalty or disrespect on the part of myself or any klansman, any where and at any time or place, towards him as the founder and as the supreme chief governing head of the Society above named.

This pledge, promise and guarantee I make is a condition precedent to my appointment stated above, and the continuity of my appointment as a Kleagle, and it is fully agreed that any deviation by me from this pledge will instantly automatically cancel and completely void my appointment together with all its prerogatives, my membership in the Society, and I shall forfeit all remunerations which may be then due me.

I make this solemn pledge on my Oath of Allegiance and on my integrity and honor as a man and as a klansman, with serious purpose to keep same inviolate.

Done in the city of…………….……………,
State of ………………………………on this the…….
day of ……………......………..…….A. D.19……
Signed……………..………......……
Address……………..…………….
Witness……………………………………..………
Address………………………………..……………

This is the oath taken by Kleagles in the Ku Klux Klan. It binds the Kleagle to "Imperial Wizard" Simmons personally in an almost slavish fashion. The oath is taken as a pledge of loyalty to Simmons and not to the order.

## CHAPTER VI

## HOW THE DOLLARS ROLL IN

*The Klan Claims to have 500,000 to 700,000 Members and Plans to get College Boys.*

The Ku Klux Klan claims to have 500,000 to 700,000 members. As a matter of fact it is generally believed that this number is a hot air figure. It offers a basis for some interesting figures on the money that has changed hands, however.

Every person initiated must pay $10 as an initiation fee. Kleagles who have left the order say that the "initiation" fee is called a "donation" so that the Klan can escape paying income tax to the government, because dues in clubs and societies are taxable.

Of the $10, the kleagle who enrolls the member gets $4. The king kleagle, or state sales manager, gets $1. The cyclops, or division manager, gets 50 cents. Clarke, the Imperial Kleagle, gets $3 and the office of Imperial Wizard Simmons gets $1.50. On this basis of 700,000 members, Clarke has collected more than $2,000,000. So far as known no public accounting ever has been made.

In addition the person initiated pays $6.50 for a mask, or helmet, and a robe. This he must purchase from the Gate City Manufacturing Company of Atlanta, owned by Clarke. Clarke's fortune grows every time a new member is taken in. If the Klansmen rides a horse in ceremonies he must buy a horse robe for $14 - also from Clarke's company.

### WATER AT $10 A QUART

Another source of revenue to Clarke is the water used in initiations. It comes from the Chattahoochee river (Indian for "muddy water") near Atlanta. It is sent around around the country as special Ku Klux Klan liquid without which an initiation cannot be held. It costs $10 a quart, money to be paid to Clarke.

Simmons and Clarke live in costly houses on Peachtree Road, outside of Atlanta. It is explained that their homes were presented to them by the Klan. It also is explained that some of the money of the Klan goes to Lanier University, near Atlanta, where young students are to be trained to spread the Ku Klux Klan to every village of the country.

### AFTER THE COLLEGE BOYS

In addition to the general membership, Simmons started a plan to get college boys into the Ku Klux Klan at $1 a head and with a charge of $5 for masks and regalia. The watchword for the college boys was to be "Kuno." Simmons, according to kleagles who deserted him, explained that he got the college idea from the German militarism system, which started to train boys for the army when they were in school. Simmons wrote this inspiration to attract college boys:

"Klannishners is your creed and faith; therefore, let no angel, man or devil break you from its glorious anchorage. Then when the end of your initiation shall have been reached in this life and you have been summoned to take your place as an inhabitant of the Invisible Empire, as you pass through the veil you can say to the world in tones of truth triumphant: 'I have kept the Faith! Thus preserving your honor by a faithful allegiance your life shall not have been lived in vain.'"

## THE BOOK OF "KLORAN"

The ceremony of initiation is contained in a copyrighted book called the Kloran written by Imperial Wizard Simmons. The Bible is opened at the 12th Chapter of Romans.

These songs are sung:

"We meet in cordial greetings
In this Our sacred cave
To pledge anew our compact
With hearts sincere and brave;
A band of faithful Klansmen
Knights of the K.K.K.
We all will stand together
Forever and for aye."

Chorus:

"Home, home, country and home;
Klansmen, we'll live and die
For our country and home."

"Her honor, love and justice

Must actuate us all,

Before our sturdy phalanx

All hate and strife shall fall.

In union we'll labor

Wherever we may roam,

To shield a Klansman's welfare,

His country, name and home."

### KLEXOLOGY

(Tune-America)

"God of Eternity,

Guide, guard our great country.

Our homes and store.

Keep our great state to Thee;

Its people right and free

In us Thy glory be

Forevermore."

## CHAPTER VII

## KU KLUX KLAN AND THE JEWS

*"Drive them out of the United States" are the words that are used to enlist Jew-haters into the ranks.*

In spite of the fact that ever since the beginning of the American colonies, in the war of the revolution and in other national crises, great Jews have helped to make the United States what it is today, the Ku Klux Klan recruits misguided members on the representation that it has found a scheme to drive the Jews out of the country. Anti-Jewish propaganda is used particularly in large cities and in smaller communities where racial and religious flames may be fanned in order to win members and money for the Ku Klux.

The Searchlight, the official paper of the Klan, teems with anti-Jewish literature. Secret documents and stories are passed around privately among the organizers and used in gaining recruits.

"Chaplain" Ridley is one of the most rabid of the campaigners against the Jews. He never lets an opportunity go by to ridicule Jews and stir up prejudice.

In the first place, Jews are barred from the Ku Klux Klan. In a questionnaire that must be filled in by those who are initiated these questions are asked:

"Are you a gentile or a Jew? What is your religious faith? Of what church are you a member (if any)? Of what religious faith are your parents?"

### CHAPLAIN ATTACKS JEWS

"Chaplain" Ridley in The Searchlight, writes:

"I cannot help being what I am racially. I am not a Jew, nor a negro nor a foreigner. I am an Anglo-Saxon white man, so ordained by the hand and will of God, and so constituted and trained that I cannot conscientiously take either my politics or my religion from some secluded ass on the other side of the world."

"Now, if somebody else happens to be a Jew, I can't help it any more than he can. Or if he happens to be black, I can't help that, either. If he were born under a foreign flag, I couldn't help it - but there is one thing I can do. I can object to his un-American propaganda being preached in my home or practiced in the solemn assembly of real Americans."

The Searchlight constantly mixes Jews and negroes in ridiculous "movements." For instance, one writer in the issue of July 30, 1921, declares that his investigations have demonstrated that Jewish plotters are stirring up the negroes to make a race war so that the government will be destroyed.

The writer goes on:

"For the same reason, the Jew is interested in overthrowing Christian Russia. But remember, he does not intend to stop at Russia. Through his Third Internationale of Moscow he is working to overthrow all the Gentile Governments of the world. I am enclosing an editorial clipped from The New York World of Saturday, July 23. You will keep in mind that The World is Jew-owned, as is every other newspaper in New York City except the Tribune. — In all my twenty-five years traveling about over this continent I have never met a disloyal American who failed to be either foreign-born or a Semite. With the best wishes for the success of the Ku Klux Klan."

## VOW TO THROW JEWS OUT

In the instructions to kleagles, who sell memberships in the Klan, the anti-Jewish feeling in some communities is appealed to in this manner:

"The Jew patronizes only the Jew unless it is impossible to do so. Therefore, we klansmen, the only real Americans must, by the same methods, protect ourselves, and practice by actual application the teachings of klannishness. With this policy faithfully adhered to, it will not be long before the Jew will be forced out of business by our practice of his own business methods, for when the time comes when klansmen trade only with klansmen then the days of the Jews' success in business will be numbered and the Invisible Empire can drive them from the shores of our own America."

Another favorite way to create interest in the anti-Jewish movement is to represent that Imperial Kleagle Clarke has in hand the organization of a nation-wide Jewish society to oppose the Sons of Israel. This society is to be created by Jews who are in the pay of Kleagle Clarke and who are really traitors to their own co-religionists. Spies working in the ranks of the Sons of Israel will keep the Ku Klux Klan informed of what the Sons of Israel are doing and finally a clash between the two organizations is to be engineered, to the destruction of both. Of course this is the wildest sort of propaganda, but it demonstrates how the agents play with fire in order to get members.

## "SEARCHLIGHT" AND THE JEWS

Among the articles in The Searchlight there are those headed, "A Message from Jerusalem - Esau the Wanderer must Pay for His Pottage - the Mightiest Weapons for the Jews are Pounds and Pence."

"Doesn't Think Much of the Jews."

"Jewish Rabbi Gets Rabid."

A paragraph from "Doesn't Think Much of the Jews," published Feb. 12,

1921, contains this passage:

"Their religion is to control wealth and thereby control all nations. And you cannot deny but they are doing so under false names. Jews are entering into every Government, every nation on earth except China and Japan, where their heavenly God received little recognition. They spread their ingenious religion that strangled the ignorant and credulous by causing dissension to their advantage."

## CHAPTER VIII

## KU KLUX KLAN AND THE CATHOLICS

*Misrepresentation of Oath of Knights of Columbus is Used to excite Religious Hatred in order to get money.*

Just as the organizers of the Ku Klux Klan misrepresent the Jews in order to get members and money for their order, they go to great lengths to create prejudice against Catholics. In some communities anti-Catholic arguments are thought to be those that will bring the most members into the fold. Fake documents and false statements on printed cards that can be slyly passed from hand to hand are used for this purpose. Anti-Catholic lies that can be hurled at Klansmen at meetings to inspire them to get in more members and increase the incomes of the "imperial wizard," the kleagles and other officers are spread around.

One of these documents is a card entitled "Do You Know?" A kleagle of the Klan asked the King Kleagle of his state for some literature that he could employ to stir up interest in the Klan. In a short time the kleagle received the literature from the Gate City Manufacturing Company of Atlanta, Ga., a company promoted by "Imperial Kleagle" Clarke. The supply of literature contained 100 copies of a card bearing the heading "Do You Know?"

Another document that is sent broadcast to foment religious unrest and hatred is a fake oath ascribed to the Knights of Columbus, which is composed of Catholics and which has published the oath that its members take. Before reading the fake oath, it will be well to examine the real oath.

### REAL K. OF C. OATH

The bona fide oath that is taken by men initiated into the Knights of Columbus, and which, it has been proven, is the correct oath follows:

"I swear to support the Constitution of the United States. I pledge myself, as a Catholic citizen and Knight of Columbus, to enlighten myself fully upon my duties as a citizen and to conscientiously perform such duties entirely in the interest of my country and regardless of all personal consequences. I pledge myself to do all in my power to preserve the integrity and purity of the ballot, and to promote reverence and respect for law and order. I promise to practice my religion openly and consistently, but without ostentation, and to so conduct myself in public affairs, and in the exercise of public virtue as to reflect nothing but credit upon our Holy Church, to the end that she may flourish and our country prosper to the greater honor and glory of God."

### BOGUS K. OF C. OATH

We can now appreciate the animus behind the bogus oath that is ascribed to the Knights of Columbus by the Ku Klux Klan. This fraudulent oath, as used by the recruiting organization of kleagles of Ku Klux follows:

"I, _____, now in the presence of Almighty God, the blessed Virgin Mary, the blessed St. John the Baptist, the Holy Apostles, St. Peter and St. Paul, and all the saints, sacred host of Heaven, and to you, my Ghostly Father, the Superior General of the Society of Jesus, founded by St. Ignatius Loyola, in the pontificating of Paul the III, and continued to the present, do by the womb of the Virgin, the matrix of God, and the rod of Jesus Christ, declare and swear that His Holiness the Pope is Christ's viceregent and is the true and only head of the Catholic or Universal Church throughout the earth; and that by virtue of the keys of binding and losing given His Holiness by my Savior, Jesus Christ, he hath power to depose heretical Kings, Princes, states, Commonwealths and Governments and they may be safely destroyed. Therefore to the utmost of my power I will defend this doctrine and His Holiness's right and custom against all usurpers of the heretical or Protestant authority whatever, especially the Lutheran Church of Germany, Holland, Denmark, Sweden and Norway, and the now pretended authority and Churches of England and Scotland, and the branches of same now established in Ireland and on the Continent of America and elsewhere, and all adherents in regard that they may be usurped and heretical opposing the sacred Mother Church of Rome."

"I do now denounce and disown any allegiance as due to any heretical King, Prince, or state, named Protestant or liberals, or obedience to any of their laws, Magistrates, or officers."

"I do further declare that the doctrine of the Churches of England and Scotland, of the Calvinists, Huguenots and others of the name of Protestants or Masons to be damnable, and they themselves to be damned who will not forsake the same."

"I do further declare that I will help, assist and advise all or any of His Holiness' agents, in any place where I should be, in Switzerland, Holland, Ireland or America, or in any other kingdom or territory I shall come to, and do my utmost to extirpate the heretical Protestant or Masonic doctrines and to destroy all their pretended powers, legal or otherwise. "

## MORE OF IT

"I do further promise and declare that, notwithstanding that I am dispensed with to assume any religion heretical for the propaganda of the Mother Church's interest, to keep secret and private all her agents' counsels from time to time, as they instruct me, and not divulge, directly or indirectly, by word, writing or circumstances whatever, but to execute all that should be proposed, given in charge or, discovered unto me by you, my Ghostly Father, or any of this sacred order."

"I do further promise and declare that I will have no opinion or will of my own or any mental reservation whatsoever, even as a corpse or cadaver (perinde ac cadaver), but will unhesitatingly obey each and every command that I may receive from my superiors in the militia of the Pope and of Jesus Christ."

"That I will go to any part of the world whithersoever I may be sent, to the frozen regions north, jungles of India, to the centers of civilization of Europe or to the wild haunts of the barbarous savages of America without murmuring or repining, and will be submissive in all things whatsoever is communicated to me."

## AND STILL MORE

"I do further promise and declare that I will, when opportunity presents, make and wage relentless war, secretly and openly, against all heretics, Protestants and Masons, as I am directed to do, to extirpate them from the face of the whole earth; and that I will spare neither age, sex or condition, and that I will hang, burn, waste, boil, flay, strangle, and bury alive these infamous heretics; rip up the stomachs and wombs of their women and crush their infants' heads against the walls in order to annihilate their execrable race. That when the same cannot be done openly, I will secretly use the poisonous cup, strangulation cord, the steel of the poniard or the leaden bullet, regardless of the honor, rank, dignity or authority of the persons, whatever may be their condition in life, either public or private, as I at any time may be directed so to do by any agents of the Pope or superior of the Brotherhood of the Holy Father of the Society of Jesus."

"In confirmation of which I hereby dedicate my life, soul and all corporate powers, and with the dagger which I now receive I will subscribe my name written in my blood in testimony thereof; and should I prove false or weaken in my determination, may my brethren and fellow soldiers of the militia of the Pope cut off my hands and feet and my throat from ear to ear, my belly opened and sulphur burned therein with all the punishment that can be inflicted upon me on earth and my soul shall be tortured by demons in eternal hell forever."

### NEARING THE END NOW

"That I will in voting always vote for a K. of C. in preference to a Protestant, especially a Mason, and that I will leave my party so to do; that if two Catholics are on the ticket I will satisfy myself which is the better supporter of Mother Church and vote accordingly "

"That I will not deal with or employ a Protestant if in my power to deal with or employ a Catholic. That I will place Catholic girls in Protestant families, that a weekly report may be made of the inner movements of the heretics."

"That I will provide myself with arms and ammunition that I may be in readiness when the word is passed or I am commanded to defend the church, either as an individual or with the militia of the Pope."

"All of which I, _____, do swear by the blessed Trinity and blessed sacrament which I am now to receive to perform and on my part to keep this, my oath. "

"In testimony whereof, I take this most holy and blessed sacrament of the Eucharist and witness the same further with my name written with the point of this dagger dipped in my own blood and seal it in the face of this holy sacrament." (Excerpts from "Contested election case of Eugene C. Bonniwell against Thomas S. Butler," as appears in the Congressional Record - House, Feb. 15, 1913, at pages

3215, & c., and ordered printed therein "by unanimous consent." Attached thereto and printed {on page 3216} as a part of said report as above.)

The above spurious oath, and others like it, have been found to be fraudulent, both by the courts and by an investigation made by Masonic bodies. The above oath made its appearance according to a book published by Maurice Francis Egan, for eleven years United States Minister to Denmark, and John B. Kennedy, in 1912. Messrs. Egan and Kennedy explain it as follows:

"It was filed by Mr. Eugene C. Bonniwell of Pennsylvania in his charge against Thomas S. Butler before the Committee of Elections No.1, in Congress, when Mr. Bonniwell stated that it had been used against him as a Fourth Degree Knight of Columbus in an election contest. Mr. Butler, in his defense, stated that he had refrained from condemning the 'oath,' until election day, although he did not believe it to be genuine, because he feared to give it notoriety."

"Far from being disconcerted by the airing of this delectable document in Congress, those profiting by its circulation seized upon its inclusion in the Congressional Record to give it an air of authority by printing on future copies the annotation 'Copied from the Congressional Record,' not pausing, however, to explain the circumstances under which it was allowed to appear in that official journal."

### EDITORS ARE CONVICTED

A. M. Morrison and Garfield E. Morrison, editors of the Morning Journal of Mankato, Minn., charged E. M. Lawless, editor of the Waterville, Minn., Sentinel with having taken the bogus oath. Lawless took the case to court and the two Morrisons were convicted. The foreman of the jury was a Methodist minister.

In 1914 the bogus oath came to light in California. The Knights of Columbus asked a committee of two, 32nd and 33rd degree, Masons, Past or Past Grand Masters of Masonry of that state, to make an investigation of all the rituals, pledges and oaths used by the Knights of Columbus. The Masonic committee gave out a report saying that they had made such an investigation. They found that the ceremonies of the Knights of Columbus were embodied in four degrees "intended to teach and inculcate principles that lie at the foundations of every great religion and every great state."

## WHAT MASONS REPORTED

Their report continued:

"Our examination was made primarily to ascertain whether or not a certain alleged oath which has been printed and widely circulated was in fact used by the Order and whether any oath, obligation or pledge was used which was or would be offensive to Protestants or Masons. We find that neither the alleged oath nor any such oath or pledge bearing the remotest resemblance thereto in matter, manner, spirit or purpose is used or forms a part of the ceremonies of any degree of the Knights of Columbus. The alleged oath is scurrilous, wicked and libelous and must be the invention of an impious and venomous mind. There is no propaganda proposed or taught against Protestants or Masons or persons not of Catholic faith. We can find nothing in the entire ceremonials of the Order that to our minds could be objected to by any person."

The Searchlight, official organ of the Ku Klux, contains many articles that misrepresent the Catholics. For instance, of Feb. 26, 1921, The Searchlight had an article which was captioned: "Facts Gathered by the Knights of Luther from the Washington Bureau of Statistics"

## CHARGES OF "KNIGHTS OF LUTHER"

Without one word to support them, the following were printed as "facts": "The National Democratic Committee is by majority a Roman Catholic body. It usually has a Roman Catholic President and secretary."

"Catholics influenced the national campaign which elected Wilson."

"The President's private secretary is a Roman Catholic. Over 70 per cent of all appointments made by President Wilson are Catholics. Their influence is so powerful it compels the homage of those in authority."

"Five States now have Catholic Administrations."

"Thirty-one States have Roman Catholic Democratic Central Committees."

"Twenty thousand public schools have one-half Catholic teachers."

"Over 100,000 public schools now contribute a part or all of the school tax to Catholic Churches and schools."

"Six hundred public schools use Catholic readers and teach from them the Roman Catholic catechism."

"Sixty-two per cent of all offices of the United States, both elective and appointive, are now held by Roman Catholics."

"New York, Chicago, Baltimore, Philadelphia, Buffalo, Cleveland, Toledo, St. Louis, Los Angeles, San Francisco and Boston now have 75 per cent Catholic teachers in their public schools."

"In all the cities and towns of the United States of 10,000 or more inhabitants an average of over 90 per cent of the police force are Roman Catholics."

"Roman Catholics are in the majority of the City Council of 10,000 cities and towns of the United States."

## MORE OF THE SAME STUFF

The Searchlight continues:

"We will now look at the results of Catholic teaching on vice and virtue. The history of assassins of heads of Governments in the past is a history of murderous Roman Catholics. In 90 per cent of the cases where criminals are executed for crimes committed, the victims of the execution have a priest at their elbow to administer the last sacrament."

"The man who shot Roosevelt was a Roman Catholic."

"The man who shot President Garfield was a Roman Catholic."

"The man who shot President Lincoln was a Roman Catholic."

"The plot that took the life of Lincoln emanated from Roman Catholic influence in the house of a Roman Catholic."

"Abraham Lincoln said, 'I do not pretend to be a prophet but, though not a prophet, I see a very dark cloud on our horizon, and that cloud is coming from Rome. It is filled with tears and blood. The true motive power is secreted behind the walls of the Vatican, the colleges and schools of the Jesuits, the convents of the nuns, and the confessional boxes of Rome, and such opinions cost the Nation his life."

"Over 65 per cent of prison convicts of all grades and of all kinds of prisoners are Roman Catholics, while less than 5 percent are graduates of our public schools."

"These statements are astounding when we remember that only about 12 ½ percent of the entire population of the United States are Roman Catholics, while the other 87 ½ per cent are not."

## CHAPTER IX

## KU KLUX KLAN AND THE MASONS

*Iowa and the Missouri Jurisdiction Grand Masters Issue Public Denunciations Against the Klan.*

Promoters of the Ku Klux Klan brag that most of its members are Masons. Whether this is true no one on the outside can tell. It is known, however, that the kleagles or salesmen, who solicit members in a community try to play upon the Masonic spirit to help along their game. That this is done with the disapproval of the leading Masonic bodies of the country is shown by the action of the grand commanders of the Iowa and Missouri jurisdictions. They have issued public denunciations of the operations and purposes of the Klan, especially that feature that resorts to the masking of members when they are taking part in Klan rites. The examples of Iowa and Missouri are being followed by Masons in other states.

## IOWA GRAND MASTER'S STATEMENT

Amos N. Alberson of Washington, Iowa, grand master of that state, has directed a communication to all Masonic lodges under his jurisdiction as follows:

"Whereas, It has become known to your grand master that a certain 'Ku Klux Klan' has been and is now organizing within this jurisdiction an alleged 'secret and invisible empire'; and,"

"Whereas, It is reported that its organizers and agents have stated and intimated to members of our craft that the said 'Ku Klux Klan' is in effect an adjunct of Free-masonry and in accord with its principles and purposes; and,"

"Whereas Any such statement or intimation is absolutely false and untrue, in that Masonry can not and does not approve of or ally itself with any organization or movement, secret or public, that proposes to subvert or supersede the processes of orderly representative government 'of the people, for the people, and by the people'; nor one that appeals to bigotry and endeavors to foster hatred of any nationality, class, religious faith or sect, as such."

## THE SOLEMN CHARGE

"Therefore, I, Amos N. Alberson, grand master of Masons in Iowa, do solemnly charge each and all of the regular Masons in Iowa, now as heretofore when you were made a Mason, that in the state you are to be a quiet and peaceable subject, true to your government and just to your country; you are not to countenance disloyalty or rebellion, but patiently submit to legal authority, and conform with cheerfulness to the government of the country in which you live."

## CITES MASONIC OBLIGATION

"Furthermore, I charge each and all, that as our fathers have framed the truly Masonic principles of liberty and conscience, equality before the law, and fraternity among men into the constitutions of this nation and state, we as Free Masons and citizens of this republic are obligated to perform our full moral and civic duty, to promote and enforce an orderly administration of justice and equity, acting openly that it may be known of all men."

Grand Master Alberson further orders and directs "that this letter to the craft be read aloud at the next meeting, whether regular or special, of each lodge throughout this jurisdiction; that it shall be made of record, and due notice of the same circulated among the brethren, that it may come to the knowledge of all Masons in Iowa."

## MISSOURI'S ACTION ON KLAN

William F. Johnson, grand master of the Carterlin Grand Lodge of Missouri Ancient Free and Accepted Masons made this statement at the annual meeting of the grand lodge, which indorsed it:

"As the impression seems to prevail in some sections, that the Masonic fraternity is directly or indirectly associated with or furthering this secret organization (Ku Klux Klan), and as I have been asked on numerous occasions what relations, if any, our fraternity bears to such secret society or order, it is well that the seal of disapproval be positively placed by this grand lodge upon this secret organization, which assumes to itself the right and authority to administer law and punish crimes."

"Nothing is more destructive of free government than secret control. The arraying of race against race, color against color, sect against sect is destructive of peace and harmony, which is the great end we, as Free Masons, have in view. We profess and boast that we are true to our government and just to our country."

### IS SUBVERSIVE OF THE REPUBLIC

"We can not, as Free Masons and good citizens, recognize the right of any secret society or combination of men to assume unto themselves the right to administer law and to inflict punishment upon their fellow men. Such an assumption is subversive of our republican institutions, contrary to the great principles of Free Masonry."

"An organization that practices censorship of private conduct behind the midnight anonymity of mask and robe, and enforces its secret decrees with the weapons of whips and tar and feathers must ultimately merit and receive the condemnation of those who believe in courts, open justice and good citizenship."

## CHAPTER X

## KU KLUX KLAN AND THE NEGRO

*Members of the Klan take an oath to bring about White Supremacy, notwithstanding the Constitution, which guarantees the Negro Equal Rights.*

Under the Constitution of the United States, the negro is guaranteed equal rights with all other citizens. When the President of the United States is sworn into office he takes an oath to uphold the Constitution and the laws passed under it. Every senator, congressman, governor and other important officer in the United States and in each of the states is sworn to uphold the Constitution.

But the members of the Ku Klux Klan take an oath that puts the Constitution at naught. They swear to bring about "white supremacy." Taken in conjunction with the speeches and writings of their leader, this oath shows that the Klansmen intend to work together to create strife against the negro, to belittle him and his family, his churches, his business, his social societies and other things that are dear to him. The Klan is determined to put the negro out of business in the

United States and to drive him back to Africa.

As is all other main objects - the warfare on Jews, Catholics and foreign born - the Klan intends to follow its own laws in dealing with the negro. The writings of its leaders are very plain on that point.

In his oath the Klansman swears:

"I swear that I will most zealously and valiantly shield and preserve by any and all justifiable means and methods White Supremacy."

"All to which I have sworn by this oath. I will seal with my blood by Thou my witness, Almighty God. Amen."

Prominent lawyers who have examined this oath declare that it really is an oath upholding mob rule and that any time the Klansman is given orders he will follow his leaders in a crusade outside the Constitution of the United States that might lead to serious trouble and bloodshed.

Chaplain Ridley of the Ku Klux Klan has written in The Searchlight on white supremacy as follows:

"Back in the days of the reconstruction the fathers gathered at the call of the low, shrill whistle and rode into immortal fame, rescuing a threatened civilization and making real once more the White Man's Supremacy. Klansmen of today, whether they assemble in the mountains of Maine, or 'neath the shadows of the great Rockies, or on the plains of the Wonderful West, or amid the trailing vines and wild flowers of Dixie, meet to keep alive the memory of these men and preserve the traditions of those days when the souls of men were tried as if by fire."

In Texas a white man who testified in behalf of an accused negro - he merely told the truth under oath as he knew it - was tarred and feathered by masked men.

The Searchlight has printed column after column of anti-negro stuff, mostly under anonymous names or under the titles of organizations whose addresses are not given. One such resolution adopted by the "Patriotic Societies of Atlanta" condemns Rev. Ashby Jones, a minister, for inviting an honorable negro to an interracial meeting and for addressing the negro as "mister."

Here are some of the titles of articles in The Searchlight, showing its evident purpose of stirring up racial feelings:

"Social Equality Put Under Ban."

"Negroes Must Serve on Chain Gangs Now."

"Separate Cars for Negroes!"

"White Woman Marries a Negro."

The Searchlight condemned President Harding for appointing Henry Lincoln Johnson, a negro, as register of deeds.

**CHAPTER XI**

**KU KLUX KLAN AND WOMEN**

Here is the proclamation issued by Imperial Wizard Simmons, making Mrs. Elizabeth Tyler his "grand chief of staff" to have charge of the women's organization to be affiliated with the Ku Klux Klan:

"To all Genii, Grand Dragons and Hydras of Realms, Grand Goblins and Kleagles of Domains, Grand Titans and Furies of Provinces, Giants, Exalted Cyclops and Terrors of Cantons, and to all citizens of the Invisible Empire, Knights of the Ku Klux Klan, in the name of our valiant and venerated dead, I affectionately greet you."

"In view of our Nation's need and as an additional force in helping on the great work of conserving, protecting and making effective the great principles of our Anglo-Saxon civilization and American ideals and institutions, the Imperial Kloncilium, in regular session assembled, after deliberate care and earnest prayer, decided that there shall be established within the bounds and under the supreme authority and government of the Invisible Empire an organization that will admit the splendid women of our great national commonwealth, who are now citizens with us in directing the affairs of the Nation. Which decision of the Imperial

Kloncilium I have officially ratified after serious, careful and devoted consideration of all matters and things involved by this move."

"In view of the foregoing, I hereby officially declare and proclaim that such organization does now exist in prospect. Plans, methods, ritualism and regulations of same are now in process of formation and will be perfected at an early date and officially announced."

"I do further proclaim that in order to have the proper assistance in the formation and perfecting of this organization, I have this day and date selected and officially appointed Mary Elizabeth Tyler of Atlanta, Fulton county, Ga., to be my grand chief of staff, to have immediate charge of work pertaining to said woman's organization under my authority and direction."

"Further information will be duly and officially communicated from time to time."

"Done in the Aulic of His Majesty, Imperial Wizard, Emperor of the Invisible Empire, Knights of the Ku Klux Klan, in the Imperial City of Atlanta, Commonwealth of Georgia, United States of America, on this, the ninth day of the ninth month of the year of our Lord, 1921."

"Duly signed and sealed by His Majesty,
William Joseph Simmons,
Imperial Wizard."

## CHAPTER XII

## ATROCITIES COMMITTED IN THE NAME OF THE KU KLUX KLAN

*Ku Klux Klan Knights of Beaumont, Texas, issue a justification for taking the law into their own hands.*

Confession that the Ku Klux Klan uses tar and feathers and the lash to punish persons whose actions it condemns is made by the Klansmen of Beaumont, Tex. The Beaumont Ku Klux Klan organization tarred and feathered Dr. J.S. Paul and R.F. Scott and later acknowledged, under its official seal, that its members did the job.

"Knights of the Ku Klux Klan, No.7, Beaumont, Texas," admitted taking the law into their own hands in a statement dated July 21, 1921. This statement was made to the editors of two newspapers of Beaumont. It sought to justify the "tar and feather party" and gave warning that the "heavy hand of the Ku Klux Klan" was waiting to yank other persons from their beds in case they came into its displeasure.

## SHOW SIMMONS MISREPRESENTS

Grand Wizard William J. Simmons has declared publicly that the Ku Klux did not indulge in midnight raids on defenseless victims whom it tarred and feathered. He has defended the Ku Klux Klan by ascribing these unlawful actions to imposters who use the regalia of the Ku Klux. The Beaumont incident proves that the Ku Klux not only was responsible for assaults on Dr. Paul and Scott, but that it boasted of its exploits with them.

## LETTER ADMITS USE OF TAR

The Paul-Scott "party" occurred on May 8. Its details were telegraphed all over the country. The letter to the two Beaumont newspapers the following July read:

"Your publication since the organization of the Ku Klux Klan in the city of Beaumont has on various occasions published information concerning and pertaining to the affairs of this organization. We believe, as you do, that a newspaper should serve the best interests of its constituency and that all legitimate news should be given the public through its columns. During the past two months items have appeared in your paper relative to the case of the Ku Klux Klan and its connection with Dr. J. S. Paul."

"Now, that you and the public may be fully informed of the true facts in the case, the Klan has assembled and here - and hands you an intelligent, true and correct history of the entire matter. The Klan suggests that this summary of facts be published in the columns of your paper not later than Sunday, July 24, 1921, and that it be published verbatim, according to the enclosed copy, typographical errors excepted."

"Knights of the Ku Klux Klan."

## PHYSICIAN IS ACCUSED

The intelligent, true and correct history of the entire matter was a lengthy statement. It accused Dr. Paul of being a physician who for years had sold whisky and narcotic drugs and had performed illegal operations on women. Because he had political and financial backing grand jury proceedings against him had been squelched.

About the middle of December, 1920, R.F. Scott, who lived in Deweyville, Texas (Scott was a former member of the United States Marine corps), consulted Dr. Paul and arranged for an illegal operation. The statement declares the girl became seriously ill as a result of malpractice on Dr. Paul's part and was taken from her residence to a hospital, where a serious operation was performed.

After this occurrence the girl demanded that Dr. Paul assist her in defraying the extra expense due to his negligence, and he offered her $500 to leave Beaumont. This bargain he broke and is accused of having threatened to cause her arrest for attempted blackmail, or with death if she exposed him.

## MORAL LAW ABOVE WRITTEN

Her predicament was reported to the Klan and the statement says her cry was heard by men who respect the "great moral law, more than the technicalities of the legal code."

The statement goes on:

"The eyes of the unknown had seen and had observed the wrong to be redressed. Dr. Paul was wealthy. His victim was a poor girl. Between the two stood the majesty of the law, draped in technicalities of changes of venue, mistrials, appeals, postponements, eminent counsel skilled in the esoteric art of protecting crime and interpreting laws involved in a mass of legal verbiage, the winding and unwinding of red tape, instead of the sinewy arm of justice, wielding the unerring sword. The law of the Klan is JUSTICE."

"Dr. Paul was approached in his office by three men on the night of May 7 and instructed to go with them. He was placed in a waiting automobile and escorted a few miles out of town. The judgment of the Klan was read to him and charges were related to him, none of which he would deny."

### "LASHED, TARRED AND FEATHERED"

"In a cowardly, whimpering plea, he pleaded that others were as guilty as he. The lash was laid on his back and the tar and feathers applied to his body. He was then informed of the will of the Klan that he should leave the city within forty-eight hours. Upon the return of the party to Beaumont, Dr. Paul was discharged from an automobile at the intersection of two of the main streets of the city, that he might be a warning to all of his ilk that decent men and women no longer wanted him in the community."

"Dr. Paul complied with the instructions of the Klan that he leave the city and returned for a few days to his former home at Lufkin. During this time he was constantly under the surveillance of the Klan. Within a few days he had surrounded himself with relatives and hired henchmen of his own tribe and character and returned to Beaumont."

### SCOTT ALSO TARRED AND FEATHERED

"Scott, who had been constantly watched by the Klan, whose number is legion and whose eye is all-seeing and whose methods of gathering information are not known to the alien world, was apprehended and punished in the same manner Dr. Paul had been dealt with. He was taken to the woods and guarded until nightfall. His captors during this time treated him with kindness and consideration. They provided him with food and fruit to eat and ice water to drink. During the day he was questioned and admitted all the charges the Klan had accused him of. The judgment of the Klan was that he was to be given ten lashes across the bare back and that he was to be tarred and feathered. "

## EYES OF "THE UNKNOWN" ARE ON HIM

"Scott left Beaumont on Monday, July 18, and spent the major portion of the day in Orange parading the streets and proclaimed the diabolical lie that he had been subjected to the tortures of the inquisition. He posed to the gullible public and sensational newspapers as a patriot and a hero. All these things the eyes of the unknown have seen and their ears have heard. We can not be deceived and JUSTICE will no longer be mocked."

The seal of the Beaumont Klan was attached to the end of the statement.

Rev. Caleb Ridley, known as the imperial chaplain of the order, acknowledged that the Klan's purpose was to set itself up as prosecutor, jury, judge and sheriff.

## PASTOR GIVES WARNING

On Aug. 26, 1921, he issued to the citizens of Dallas County, Texas, the following warning:

"To the Citizens of Dallas County, Greetings: This organization has caused to be posted the following proclamation:"

"Be it known and hereby proclaimed-"

"That this organization is composed of native-born Americans and none other."

"That its purpose is to uphold the dignity and the authority of the law."

"That this organization recognizes that situations frequently arise where no existing law offers a remedy."

"That this organization does not countenance and will not stand for social parasites remaining in this city. It is equally opposed to the gambler, the trickster, the moral degenerate and the man who lives by his wits and is without visible means of support."

"The eye of the unknown hath seen and doth constantly observe all, white or black, who disregard this warning. 'Whatsoever thou sowest that shall you also reap.' Regardless of official, social or financial position, this warning applies to all living within the jurisdiction of this Klan."

"This warning will not be repeated. Mene, Mene, Tekel, Upharsin."

"Hereafter all communications from us will bear the official seal of the Klan."

"KNIGHTS OF THE KU KLUX KLAN."

## KU KLUX KLAN SHOOTS SHERIFF

The attitude of members of the Ku Klux Klan toward officers of the law was demonstrated on October 1, 1921, in Lorena, Tex., when the Ku Klux Klan shot Sheriff Bob Buchanan of McLennan County, when he attempted to stop a parade of Masked Knights.

Without getting an official permit to hold the parade, the Ku Klux Klan announced that it would be held at 8:30 p.m. The sheriff notified the community that the parade was against the law and that he would not allow it. The word was carried to the Ku Klux Klan leaders. Messages were sent back and forth, and the Ku Kluxers tried to scare the sheriff into a retreat. He refused to back down, however, and ended the negotiations by telling the Klansmen that they had to obey the law as well as other citizens.

The sheriff said there was a law against uncertain masked men who refused to divulge their identity. He would agree to the parade if the names of the masked men were furnished to him. This the Klan leaders refused to do.

The Klansmen held a council of war at which the sheriff was denounced for daring to give them orders. They decided to show the people of Lorena that they were bigger than the sheriff or the law that he represented. The chief of the Klansmen gave the order for the parade to start.

With a posse of citizens and deputies, Sheriff Buchanan met the parade at the intersection of the main streets. Thousands of persons were out to witness the test of strength between the law and the Ku Klux Klan. The sheriff approached a masked Klansman who carried a fiery cross. He attempted to seize the cross. There was a shot. A bullet hit the sheriff in the right arm. A general gun fight followed and ten persons were injured. The Masked Knights hurriedly departed, carrying one of their number who was wounded.

Sheriff Buchanan is hailed as a hero in Texas by the law-abiding element. The United States needs more public officials like him - men with the courage to stand by their oaths of office.

## OTHER OUTRAGES

Since the Ku Klux Klan was organized night outrages in which masked men are involved have increased to a frequency not known in the United States since the years just following the Civil War, when the original Ku Klux Klan was active in the southern states against "carpet baggers" and Negroes.

A murder was committed on June 9, 1921, at Sea Breeze, Fla., by masked men who said they were Ku Klux Klan. They took Thomas L. Reynolds from his bed and punched and kicked him. Then one of the masked men shot him. He died later.

Official investigation failed to involve the Ku Klux Klan.

## WIZARD SIMMONS DENIES

In the case of Paul and Scott in Beaumont, Tex., an organization claiming to be the Ku Klux Klan admitted under a seal that it was responsible. In many other instances the masked riders have openly boasted that they were Ku Kluxers. In other cases they have worn regalia like that of the Ku Klux. Imperial Wizard

Simmons has denied that the Ku Klux is responsible for any outrages. Whether he knows what he is talking about probably will be determined only by a Congressional investigation.

Meanwhile the people of the country have the big fact on which to form their judgment - namely, that since the Ku Klux has extended its membership and influence by influencing hundreds of thousands to get down on their knees and take the oath of "white supremacy," bands of night riders who take the law into their own hands have been carrying on these disgraceful marauding "parties" with a boldness that challenges public attention.

In Daytona, Fla., H. C. Sparkman, an editor, carried on a campaign against the Ku Klux Klan. On June 12, 1921, Sparkman received by mail a threat warning him that if he did not let the Ku Klux alone the Klan would take up his case and that he might be killed. In Pensacola, Fla., on July 8, 1921, a band of men wearing white robes like those of the Ku Klux Klan in their initiation ceremonies appeared at the store of Chris Lochas, a restaurant keeper, and while the chief of police was looking on gave him a written order to leave town because of certain charges. The warning was signed "K. K. K."

## KU KLUX KLANSMAN KILLED

In the city of Atlanta, Ga., where the Ku Klux Klan is strongest a killing resulted from a raid by masked men on J.C. Thomas, who had a lunch room at 280 ½ Decatur Street. Thomas had received letters threatening him with violence unless he "let alone" a certain woman in his employ. On March 12, 1920, four men got Thomas to enter an automobile and drove him to a spot in a lonely neighborhood. There they took him from the car and told him that he was to be punished because he had not observed their warnings. When they started to strike Thomas, he took a knife from his pocket and killed Fred Thompson who was later identified as a member of the Ku Klux Klan.

The case of killing against Thomas was put before a grand jury but the jury refused to indict him. At the inquest into the death of Thompson, Homer Pitts was identified as the driver of the car in which Thomas had been kidnapped. Pitts was represented in the proceedings by Attorney W. S. Coburn. In the official list of Ku Kluxers there is a H. R. Pitts who is a kleagle at Fresno, Cal., and a W. S. Coburn who is a grand goblin with headquarters at Los Angeles, Cal.

## 100 OUTRAGES IN TEXAS

Texas, where the Ku Klux Klan is strong, has been the scene of nearly 100 unlawful punishments by masked men. In one case the initials "K.K.K." were branded on the forehead of a negro who was who was horsewhipped on the charge of having been found in a white woman's room.

Something the same treatment that was given Dr. Paul was handed out to J.S. Allen, an attorney of Houston, Tex., who on April 10, 1921, was whisked from a downtown street, driven to the country and tarred and feathered. The masked men then took him back to the city and threw him out of the automobile into a crowd. He was nude except for his coat of tar and feathers.

[Ezra A. Cook was born on November 5, 1841 in Windsor, Connecticut, a son of Methodist minister. He enlisted in the Union Army, the 39th Illinois Volunteer Infantry, during the Civil War because of his loathing of the institutions slavery. After which, his moral convictions led him and his wife, Maria Elizabeth Blanchard, to Washington-- to work for improvements in both immigration and labor rights for individuals of Asian descent.
    In 1867, Ezra established the printing company (Ezra A. Cook & Co.) on LaSalle Street in Chicago. Initially, bank documentation was the mainstay of the company.
    In time, Ezra became a founding member of the National Christian Association. The primary endeavor of this group was to organize opposition against all secret societies, especially the Freemason. He decides to help the cause by publishing books describing the "secret society rituals" of these groups in an attempt to "de-mistify" them.
    Ezra A. Cook died in 1911. The publishing company which he founded carried on his work and in 1922, at the height of the Klan's power and influence, published KU KLUX KLAN SECRETS EXPOSED.]

Reprinted from LITTLE BLUE BOOK #652 published in 1924, Haldeman-Julius Co., Kansas

# IS THE KU KLUX KLAN CONSTRUCTIVE OR DESTRUCTIVE?

A Debate Between Imperial Wizard Evans, Israel Zangwill and Others - Edited by E. Haldeman-Julius

*At the Hotel Lincoln in Indianapolis recently Edward Price Bell of The Daily News staff, under dramatic circumstances, obtained the first authorized interview with the Imperial Wizard of the Ku Klux Klan, Dr. H. W. Evans. This interview, given in the presence of some of his principal advisers, has been read and approved by Dr. Evans and it therefore stands as his own official statement of the views and purposes of the organization of which he is the head.*

Part I - An Interview with Dr. Evans

**CREED OF THE KLAN AND THOSE WHO DEBATE IT**

Indianapolis has become, under the direction of Dr. Evans, the chief publication center of the Ku Klux Klan. Its official newspaper, the Fiery Cross, which not very long ago published nine editions to be circulated in as many different parts of the country, added two further editions before the end of 1923 and has announced that beginning with January, 1924, it will publish twenty-three editions. It claims a circulation of about 400,000 weekly and asserts that with the establishment of the new editions it will have a circulation of 700,000. The organization maintains a Washington bureau, from which much of its material for circulation among Klansmen is sent out, and it also has a sort of "court circular," the Night Hawk, which is published in Atlanta, Ga. Atlanta remains the chief governmental city of the organization and Dallas, Tex., also is a center from which is sent out literature for a considerable part of the country.

In view of the extraordinary claims and the manifest growth of the Ku Klux Klan, The Daily News thought it well to obtain and set forth the views of the Imperial Wizard. Mr. Bell presented these views to the criticism of the eminent author, Israel Agnail, who is one of the most widely known representatives of the Jewish race. Herewith appear the Imperial Wizard's interview and an interview with Mr. Agnail given in the presence of a number of leading and representative Jewish citizens of Chicago.

Because the Klansmen's activities are a leading political issue in Indiana, Mr. Bell obtained interviews with one of the chief representatives of the Klan in that state, and also an interview with Mayor Davis of Terre Haute, an anti-Klan candidate for the Republican nomination for governor. These interviews also appear in this little book, as well as an interview with Edward H. Morris, colored, a prominent member of the Chicago bar.

Thus is presented more clearly and forcefully than they have been presented elsewhere the two sides of the serious issue which the Ku Klux Klan has raised in this country. That issue challenges the earnest attention of the American people.

### DR. EVANS ANSWERS QUESTIONS

"What roots, if any, has the Klan in history?"

"Strictly speaking, the Ku Klux Klan of today is a new organization to meet a new problem. When it was started, some seven years ago, certain grandiloquent words were used. Formally associating it with the old Klan of the southern states. But, really, the old Klan was antiquated when its work was finished, and the new Klan has no essential connection with it. Post-Civil War Klansmen fought to destroy a bad local government; Klansmen of today are fighting to preserve a good national one."

## IS THE KU KLUX KLAN CONSTRUCTIVE OR DESTRUCTIVE?

### THE METHOD EXPLAINED

"And how do you think this can be done?"

"By maintaining a Christian civilization in America. This we can maintain if we will. We can reach a higher level than mankind ever has reached hitherto if we will. All the materials, natural and human, for this achievement -we have. Preeminence belongs to us. Preeminence is enjoined upon us by God and by our obligations to the world. If the Klan aspires to purify America and make her impregnable, it is not for any selfish reason; selfishness corrodes and destroys the soul; it is in order that America, pure and impregnable may extend a giant's helping hand to people less fortunate."

### KLAN TURNS TO THE PEOPLE

"How are purity and impregnability to be realized?"

"By conservation and stimulation of the best qualities of the commonwealth. Our mental, moral and physical heritage is menaced; indeed, is in process of overthrow. It must be consolidated. It must be re-energized. It must go into action against the forces that are crowding it to the wall. Great leaders, dazzling minds, super-personalities cannot save us; we survive or perish according to the strength or the infirmity of our people in the mass. It is the mass of which the Klan is thinking. It is the standard of this mass which we purpose to defend and lift up. Enlightened statecraft is all right, great and honest leadership is a precious and beautiful thing, but the potter's skill is useless without the proper clay. Our people must be of the right composition, the stuff of which they are made must be sound, or they cannot vindicate the American political and social experiment."

## REGULATION OF IMMIGRATION

"How is this soundness to be insured?"

"First of all, in my judgment, with exceptions applying only to separated families, we temporarily should stop immigration absolutely. Then we should collect the information indispensable to a wise immigration policy. Such information would contain full knowledge of the causes and the effects of the foreign influx, the facts relative to our needs for rural and urban labor, and scientific counsel concerning how these needs can be met without injury to the all-important principle of ultimate amalgamation into our political and social structure. We can tolerate no immigration policy that militates against our private and public standards of life. Ellis Island horrors should go forever. Examination of emigrants should take place abroad. Every newcomer we are to have in the future should make the voyage to America knowing he will be admitted and will be welcomed and looked after when he is here."

"How grave is the immigration peril one scarcely need point out any longer. Ku Klux Klansmen have been underlining it for some years, and now many leading American journals and publicists are sounding a deep and loud alarm. Action cannot be too quick. Something has been done, but not enough; the quota law is but a step in the right direction. Illiteracy, disease, insanity and mental deficiency are still pouring in upon us. Immigrants are streaming into cities to make modern Sodoms and Gomorrahs. Up to 1850, 95 per cent of our immigration was of the Nordic types-kindred desirable, easily assailable people. By 1910 it was a Mississippi of inferior foreign elements, mostly utterly and eternally hopeless from the American point of view. What Nordic greatness has wrought in this country, if the Ku Klux Klan has anything to say-and it is going to have something to say-neither shall be torn down by political madness nor shall be dragged down by disease and imbecility."

## DENIES CHARGES OF INTOLERANCE

"Ku Kluxism generally is regarded as religiously and racially intolerant."

"Ignorance of its nature, prejudice and calumny explain this view. Our entire fundamental concern is with the question of what permanent policy best will promote civilization ours and that of others-for civilization is one and indivisible. This wide conception of our order I cannot too sharply accent. Klanism is altruistic or it is nothing. Every benefit we seek we seek not to monopolize, but to diffuse throughout our own citizenship and to place, so far as may be, at the service of mankind."

"Catholics, Roman and Greek, make themselves ineligible to membership in the Klan by their predilection for churchly chief ship in human affairs. We separate church and state unconditionally and inexorably. We do so for the sake of both the church and the state, remembering history's lesson of the evils that attend each in any attempt to merge them. We wholly distrust and forever will oppose the parochial school as an institution in American life. It seems to us a dangerous civic and social lisintegrant, inspired with the very essence of intolerance and un-Americanism. Catholics cannot be Klansmen while to them the presidency at Washington is subordinate to the priesthood at Rome. We make no war upon their religion. Freedom of thought, liberty of conscience, the right to worship how one will -the Klan not only concedes them all, but will fight for them all, as it will fight for every guaranty in the American constitution, its political bible. Catholics cannot be Klansmen not because of their particular form of worship, but because their theory of education and of government seems to the Klan incompatible with the organic scheme of Americanism."

## DECLARES JEW UNASSIMILABLE

"How about our Jewish population?"

"Of the good qualities of the Jewish character I am as well aware as is any man. Wandering ever since his ejection from Judea, nearly everywhere persecuted, the Jew, I am happy to say, has had a better home in America than almost any other land in which he has lived. One-fifth of his race is here. By deliberate selection he is unassailable. He rejects intermarriage. His religious and social rites and customs are inflexibly segregate. Law-abiding healthy, moral, mentally alert, energetic, loyal and reverent in his home life, the Jew is yet by primal instinct a Jew, indelibly marked by persecution, with no deep national attachment a stranger to the emotion of patriotism as the Anglo-Saxon feels it. Klansmen have no quarrel with him, no hatred of him, no thought of persecuting him. As Protestants are unavailable for membership in all-Jewish societies so Jews are unavailable for membership in an all Protestant society like the Klan. Moreever their jealousy guarded separatism unfits them for co-operation in a movement dedicated to the thorough unification of the dominant strains in American life."

## ATTITUDE TOWARD COLORED RACES

"Your attitude to the colored races?"

"Our attitude to every race, as I have tried to show, is one of sympathy, not of antipathy. My heart is not only devoid of racial hate but full of compassion for my fellow men of every creed and color. It is just this love for humanity that excites me to action to aid in rescuing America from a destructive inundation. I would save America if I could for her own sake. I am infinitely happier to work for her salvation for the glory of God and the general human good. When we shut out the Chinese and the Japanese from our shores we seemed to them harsh. We were not. They would have ruined us and by ruining us ruined our power to be of assistance to them in the passing years. I suspect all enlightened Chinese and Japanese see this now.

"We of the Klan are supposed to hate the negro. Nothing could be further from the truth. The negro was brought to America. He came as a slave. We are in honor and duty bound to promote his health and happiness. But he cannot be assimilated. Intermarriage with him on a wholesale scale is unthinkable. There are more than 10,000,000 of him-about a tenth of our population. He cannot attain the Anglo-Saxon level. Rushing into the cities, he is retrograding rather than advancing and his rate of mortality is shockingly high. It is not in his interests any more than in the interests of our white population that he should seek to assume the burdens of modern government. These are almost too heavy for the strongest shoulders and their weight is increasing. However much we may regret to state the truth when the truth is otherwise than pleasant, it is better that it be stated and faced. I am sure the interests of all are served thereby."

### POTENTIAL KLANSMEN

"Are all who fight for sound principles, cleanliness and courage in public life virtually Klansmen?"

"Not exactly Klansmen, but men marching toward the Klansmen's goal. Americanism ought to be understandable by this time to all who read and think. Americanism is the Klan's supreme objective. Whoever knows what it is, and whoever fights for it-no matter what his origin or other non-psychic characteristics-is among the forces upon which the Klan depends for the success of its precepts."

## DEFENSE OF THE MASK

"Will you explain the dress and the strange sounding names of the Klan?"

"What government, what church, what secret order, what fraternity of any kind is without its characterizing forms? Surely pomp and circumstance, ceremonial, ritual, formulary were not unknown in the world prior to the organization of native-born white American protestants, bent upon saving American traditions from the mongrelized and criminalized foreign deluge. Our mask, about which so many persons appear to vex their wits barrenly, has two substantial functions-it protects scores of thousands of our members from intimidation, sabotage and worse, and it screens our leaders from the temptation to forget the general interest in the pursuit of particular whims or ambitions. Self-esteem is eliminated. There is no lure of personal vanity nor of demagogy. Out of Klansmen's mouths issue only those things which in their hearts they feel are true, unselfish and patriotic. How many of the popular statesmen of the day would like to pour forth their messages from behind masks? It is labor with only one reward, though, as true values go, the best reward-the solace of duty done."

## MUST MAKE A CHOICE

"What is the answer to the argument that the nation cannot exist half Klan and half anti-Klan?"

"It is never going to be half Klan and half anti-Klan. It will be either predominantly Klan or the victim of those heterogeneous un-American elements which neither understand nor are able to execute the characteristic political and social inspiration of the founders of this country. Ku Kluxism, by whatever name it may be called, is the *sine qua non* of the fruition of the American principle of organized society."

## EXPLANATION OF THE OATH

"Are the theory and the oath of the Klan the same in all parts of America?"

"Precisely. It is a national organization."

"Do you mind explaining the oath?"

"Certainly not. It is as categorical and solemn as the English language can make it. It enjoins obedience to the order's constitution, laws, usages and requirements, and prescribes the strictest secrecy regarding its internal affairs. Each member swears he 'never will recommend for membership any person whose mind is unsound, whose reputation is bad, whose character is doubtful, or whose loyalty to the United States of America is in any way questionable.' Selfishness in every form is interdicted. Social loyalty is elevated above personal friendship, blood relationship, family interest and every other relatively narrow tie. Klansmanship is stringently enjoined, but only 'in all things honorable.' To the government of the United States and to the governments of the states of the union we 'sacredly swear unqualified allegiance,' pledging our property, our votes, our honor and our lives. Free education, free speech, free press, separation of church and state, white supremacy, just laws, the pursuit of happiness-all these each Klansman swears to seal with his blood, be Thou my witness, Almighty God."

## SAYS KLAN OPPOSES MOB

"Then the Klan is oath-bound to refrain from and to oppose mob violence?"

"Yes. Every Klansman who commits a lawless act, or who withholds his influence against such an act, at the same time commits perjury. Uninformed and malicious critics have accused us of being a whipping organization. Many crimes and cruelties abhorrent to our every feeling, conviction and purpose have been charged against our order calumniously. If we were a whipping organization, with our hundreds of thousands of ardent members spread throughout the country, and with insolent breakers of every law, human and divine, abounding, we should be whipping thousands of culprits every night. They deserve it. But that is not the Klan way. Our way is to put the right men into office and to build up a public sentiment that will not only encourage but compel them to do their duty in conformity with their oaths. Far from instigating mob violence, the Klan is reducing it. Lynchings are much fewer than they were before the Klan became powerful. Statistics this year will prove this and will show the areas of great Klan strength as freest from anarchic outbreaks of every kind. Klan power means power of law enforcement. I invite you to point out a single bootlegger, hi-jacker, black-leg gambler, den-keeper, rogue, crook, Bolshevist, anarchist, demagogue, political hypocrite or scoundrel who likes the klan. All this mottled horde is against us and will be against us to the finish. Is it not about time our decent critics began to love us for some of the enemies we have made?"

## SOLDIER NOT NECESSARILY A LEADER

"Returning to the Catholics, Jews and colored peoples, it has been remarked that if they are good enough to die for America they are good enough to live for it."

"Pure sophistry. Excellent demagogy, but pure sophistry. Any one of us may be able usefully to die for America without being able usefully to live for America. We had in France -there are in every army-many strong, intrepid and noble men who could not be trusted at the helm of a nation. Soldering is not statesmanship. In democratic countries the civilian, not the soldier, is supreme. And it is the Klan's object to create and sustain a civilian authority incomparably equipped by heredity, by experience, by the sum of its qualities, to see America through to the goal that stood out so brightly in the clairvoyance of our fathers."

## HE WELCOMES CRITICISM

"Do you think Klansmen and anti-Klansmen, on the principle of governments and oppositions in parliamentary countries, will tend to keep each other up to the mark?"

"I do. Any man, any organization, is better for criticism. The Klan welcomes it. Let those who can designate our shortcomings. Of all men in the world Klansmen are most concerned about the shortcomings of the Klan. At the same time I can assure those opposed to us that we shall not be found niggardly in critical reciprocity."

## EXPLAINS KLAN IDEALS

"Your Christianity has been impugned because of your exclusivism."

"Klansmen stand on the Holy Bible. Upon the Holy Bible rest the American constitution and American civilization. Klansmen are wholeheartedly Christian, implacably opposed to atheistic intellectualism and to all the amatory and erotic tendencies of modern degeneracy. We are Christian, but we have no monopoly of Christianity. God is love. Would that all men knew Him! In the whole structure of its thought and policy Klan quality is Christian quality. Its opposition, wherever it opposes, is for the purpose, not of injuring, but of helping. Education (I am in favor of a cabinet department of education second to none in its public importance), health (here we need another cabinet department, bent upon the greatest health crusade the world has known), home building-general intelligence, general health, the home the keystone of the American arch-these are Klan objectives, and certainly they are Christian. As education should be free, so health ministry should be free. Hospitals, nurses and doctors should be available to all, rich and poor, in the interests of the commonwealth. For the eternal good of the country the first three ranking places in the federal government should be budget, education and health."

### NO POLITICAL AFFILIATION

"What do you mean when you say the Klan, as such, will take no part in politics?"

"I mean that the Klan is not a political party. Klansmen may belong and do belong to all parties and to no party. Every Klansmen knows his principles and he votes for the candidate or the party in whose hands he regards his principles as safe or comparatively safe. To be sure, Klansmen, like other men, will use their influence to have parties and candidates further their objects; and, equally to be sure, if a candidate appears in the political arena blatantly proclaiming his hostility to our order and his purpose to destroy it if he can, Klansmen are likely to vote against him."

### PEACE THE SUPREME END

"What is your idea of American foreign policy?"

"It should be, in my judgment, a policy of the greatest energy, sympathy and courage - a Christian policy, sagacious and self-respecting, but not too self-regarding, and certainly not sordid. What the world needs above all else is the measureless boon of peace. No national government is worth its salt unless it not only piously favors, but patiently fights for peace. Aloofness as a barrier against war we have tried. It broke down. It probably will break down again. We should try a barrier of a different type. Our whole moral weight should be constantly - not desultorily, but constantly - in the scale for peace. We are told domestic problems are our most important problems. So they are. But what is of supreme importance to us domestically? Our manhood and womanhood and wealth, are they not?"

"And what becomes of these, what happens to these, if we have war? Our recent war, not to mention its horrible consequences to others and through them to ourselves, cost us primarily nearly $50,000,000,000 and will cost us four times that amount before it is liquidated. Thinking women and men throughout Christendom know that another great war would ruin civilization beyond repair. Militant spirituality is required in our leaders and in our citizens. We are a people of undoubted physical courage. But physical courage will not bring peace. Peace will come only through a resolute exercise of mental and moral force through clear thinking and vigorous pleading. Our voice should be heard in the council rooms of humanity. That we shall keep our independence inviolate need not be said to anyone outside a lunatic asylum. But inviolate independence does not imply, except in weak and befuddled intellects, a renunciation of fellowship with peace-loving mankind."

## Part II

### MR. ZANGWILL CRITICIZES THE KLAN

"One can feel the magnetism of Dr. Evans in his interview," said Mr. Zangwill, a British-born Jew and successful playwright, after a careful study of the remarks of the Imperial Wizard of the Ku Klux Klan. "His interview, indeed is a vividly-revealing portrait of himself-an honest man of force, with whom, I am sure, I could agree on many things, if we could sit down together and really come to understand each other."

"In a word, I have a great respect for Dr. Evans' character, but I have no respect for his knowledge. He is one of those men who make history; but history, unfortunately, very often is made by men like Torquemada, without either knowledge or philosophical inspiration. Dr. Evans, with all his good intention, talks a great deal of sheer nonsense and dangerous nonsense. Let him beware, lest, despite his good will he unleash the dogs of religious and racial war in America."

## NORDICISM AND CHRISTIANITY

"His conception is full of predominance and megalomania. He envisages a Nordic God-not a Universal God, but a Nordic God. Now all this Nordic idea is rubbish, as I shall show later. Dr. Evans would nationalize God, or naturalize Him-not, indeed, as an American God, but as a Nordic God omnipotent in America. As to this notion of naturalizing God as an American, I know of no adequate proof that He has lived in this country for the last 500 years. America was not discovered until 1492, and God had a home somehow before that."

"Dr. Evans' 'Christian civilization' and his ignorant Nordicism really will not do for America. Christianity always has been a minority religion. It is a religious rebellion. When the rebellion succeeded and Constantine established Christianity as a state religion, it turned into paganism, plus certain dogmas. Neither with his religious nor with his racial idea has Dr. Evans started soon enough. He might be able to carry out his program in Alaska; he cannot carry it out in America. Events in America have anticipated him. He also is too late in the Ku Klux movement. Romantic hooligans who started the movement may prove uncontrollable, and my advice to him is to resign from a position that no 'wizardry' can make possible. He commits the error of thinking of America as a country when he ought to think of it as a continent. Realities here, irreducible realities, religious and racial, hold the field against him. He could clear the ground for his proposed experiment only by smashing a large part of American civilization and removing it from the scene."

## WARNS OF REVERSION TO MEDIEVALISM

"This gigantic piece of sabotage, with its concomitant bloodshed, we must assume that Dr. Evans, with his genuine humanitarianism, would not wish to see. It was a Balkan patriot's lamentation that there was no chance for his Christian country, unless its Jews and Moslems could be killed off. Ku Kluxism, with all its falsification of American history, its bigotry, and its menace to the America of Washington and Lincoln-its threatened reversion to the medievalism which Europe has never really shaken off-has not yet arrived at the bloodthirstiness of this Balkan patriot and of millions of other Europeans."

"But its course sets in the same direction."

"Despite Dr. Evans' reassuring words, it is inimical to Catholics, of whom there are 18,260,000 in America; to Jews, of whom this country has 3,600,000, and to negroes, numbering some 11,999,000-in fine, to practically one third of the population of the United States. Even if there were such a thing as the Nordic homogeneity, the Nordic solidarity, of Dr. Evans' imagination -an uninstructed imagination- only a moment's consideration of these statistics, with the great and awesome facts they reflect, would suffice to show the reasoning mind that Dr. Evans is a dangerous dreamer."

"Scarcely a line of Dr. Evans' discussion is logic-proof. For example, he hyphenates 'purity' and 'impregnability.' They are incompatible teammates. Purity is moral, impregnability military. Purity implies 'God's fool,' the sheer beauty of holiness, a spiritual conception. Impregnability is a pagan ideal, implying, storming troops and fortresses. Everyone will agree with Dr. Evans in wanting to purify the masses of the people, but few will discern how this can be done by involving the masses in a quarrel pregnant with civil war. It is, of course, true that the potter's skill is wasted unless the potter have proper clay. Dr. Evans' error consists in his notion that there is no good clay except Nordic clay."

"A Jewish rabbi told me that Dr. Evans, himself inducted him into the 32nd degree of the Masonic order. It is questionable, therefore, whether the Ku Klux oath does not negate the oath that Dr. Evans himself takes at Masonic lodges to treat all other members as brothers, for these members include Jews and negroes."

"At this point let us look at this Nordic figment for a moment. In Dr. Evans' thinking, Nordicism is the sum of the essential components of the theory and the practice that alone can preserve 'Americanism.' Parenthetically, I would say that American ideals are not Christian ideals, but Jewish ideals -for the Puritan founders of your commonwealth were essentially Old Testament men- and that the destruction of these ideals would be more tragic for the world than even the destruction of the Jews, whose faith and literature have nourished continents."

## NORDICISM UNDER SCRUTINY

"Nordicists, in Dr. Evans' interpretation, stand on the Holy Bible. Their feet are planted upon it as upon a Gibraltar -a thing unchanging- though scholarship's reading of the Bible is changing. It is viewed from different and irreconcilable angles. Fundamentalists and modernists have their say about it. But let that pass. Dr. Evans, contemptuous of the Asiatics, stands upon the Holy Bible, which was written from cover to cover by Asiatics and first circulated exclusively by Asiatics. Dr. Evans is scornful of the Mediterraneans, though the savage north always has gone to the sunny south for its wealth of the mind-to Rome for its law, to Greece for its art and thought, and to Judea for its religion."

"Nordics of the Ku Klux type do not know their own history or blood. They forget that the Napoleonic code of Nordic France was created by a Corsican. They forget that Nordic mentality, if not Nordic physique, too, was made in Asia. They forget that all the great religions were made in Asia-those of Confucius, Buddha, Mohammed, Moses and Jesus. Ku Kluxers of the Dr. Evans school at least would reinstate the great German race-a bit of gold in their mass of base metal. Englishmen, if any men, should be sound Nordics. But how are they made? Blended of bloods innumerable. England, like every other country, has been a melting pot."

## ENGLAND AS A MELTING POT

"Recall Tennyson's lines in welcome of Princess Alexandra - 'Normans and Saxons and Danes are we, but all of us Danes in our welcome of thee.' Only three of the constituents. Everyone remembers the Huguenots. Near the British museum, London, is a church all of whose services are still in French, and the village children of Essex still ask for 'largesse.' When I called your country 'The Melting Pot,' I meant only that it was the most gigantic example of a universal process. Roman garrisons left their blood in our island. It often is forgotten that these occupations, with the many strange tribes of that great empire, are curiously analogous to the colonial troops of the French now in Germany."

"Roman tribes have left us Sarmatians in Essex, Tungerians at Dover, Spaniards at Pevensey, Belgians at Reculver, Stablesians (from Germany) at Burgh Castle, Dalmatians in Lincolnshire, Pannonians at Doncaster, an African tribe at Moresby, the Nervii at Ambleside, Cilicians at Greta Bridge, Portuguese at Pierce Bridge, more Belgians at Wallsend, Asturians at Benwell, Quadi, Marcomanni and Dacians, Moors and Thracians elsewhere. All these and many other elements have gone to the making of Dr. Evans' Nordics from England. And, I daresay, the Imperial Wizard of the Ku Klux Klan would be surprised to learn that Slavic Jews are objected to in Palestine on the ground that they are converted Nordics-Nordics that have converted to Judaism. You will observe that the whole Nordic mist vanishes before the sun of a little history and a little truth."

## THE QUESTION OF IMMIGRATION

"Immigration into America, in Dr. Evans' opinion, should be 'stopped absolutely,' at least pending extensive investigations. The investigations he proposes would require colossal state machinery and cost countless millions. They are impracticable. Besides some of the Imperial Wizard's tests of fitness for entry into America are foolish. He is against illiteracy, though many of the greatest men of the world have been illiterate-remember Abraham Lincoln's father-while Oscar Wilde, for instance, was only too literate. To bracket illiteracy with disease and insanity is ridiculous. And many a good man has been in jail. Christ was in jail. I am very doubtful, under Dr. Evans' dispensation, whether Christ would get through Ellis Island if He came to America today as a prospective American citizen, even if He succeeded in getting His visa from your Palestine consul, for, besides being in jail, He was an Asiatic."

"It is a cruel moment-the most cruel moment in history-for America to shut her gates against the immigrant. Europe's misery is unfathomable. Dr. Evans should remember the words of the founder of the religion on which he would base American institutions and American life. He should remember that Christ said, 'For as much as ye have not done it unto the least of these, ye have not done it unto me.' Humanitarianism bids America, not to close her gates, but to open them; and no charity of hers can suffice if she refuses this boon to the sore-stricken sections of mankind. Moreover, America needs European workers. Her industrial situation is calling for them. For every white immigrant she excludes, a black man will migrate from her cotton fields, and this means difficulty in the South and trouble in the North. America can take millions of Europeans to her own benefit, not less than to theirs. If she must shut her gates, let her do so when Europe is less naked and hungry than now. If Christ says anything to Dr. Evans and other exclusionists, I should think He would say this: I agree, anyhow with Dr. Evans that exclusions, when made, should be made in Europe to save the breakup of homes and the breaking of hearts."

## THE LUST FOR POWER

"Civilization is one and indivisible, says Dr. Evans. He is quite right. I am delighted to find this great truth in his mind. But his arrogance to himself and his followers of a position of pre-eminence, a supreme judgment seat, the power of command and of control this I cannot assimilate. True, he tells us his scheme and his organization are altruistic. Power is wanted only that good may be done. It is an old story. Dickens hit it all off in the Rev. Mr. Chadband. Greedy men, materialists industrial and commercial adventurers after oil and rubber and precious minerals-British and American and other imperialists-adore idealists like. Dr. Evans and Rudyard Kipling, who do the intellectual and moral work necessary to smooth the way for their masked and sheeted advance, for they too hide their faces. Dr. Evans gives us nothing looking to that unity and harmony of the world which he appears to desire."

"He objects to the Catholics and the papacy. But his argument amounts to a proposal to make a little pope of himself. I understand that the kloran contains a clause: 'I swear loyalty to the Imperial Wizard and the constitution of the United States,' thus putting the Imperial Wizard first. Catholics employ an elaborate ritualism; ritualism is an outstanding feature of the Ku Klux aggregation of absurdities. Dr. Evans seems to fear insoluble segregation in American society, yet he is endeavoring to segregate the so-called Nordics from the rest of the American people. Jews he regards as outside the American political pale, because of what he calls their separatism, yet his efforts are addressed to making that separatism real and conclusive."

## THE JEW IS A CITIZEN

"His assertion is that Jews are unassimilable by 'deliberate election.' If they are unassimilable at all, they are so, not by deliberate election, but by deliberate rejection. He declares that Jews reject intermarriage. It is not so. More Jews intermarry with gentiles than protestants with Catholics. In my play, 'The Moderns,' one of the best actors is the grandson or a famous American rabbi through a charming American lady. Dr. Evans' picture of the Jews as a close fellowship is utterly misleading. Jews have no unity except in suffering. The Diaspora-and even the so-called Jewish home in Palestine has become a part of the Diaspora -is remarkable for nothing more than for its leaderlessness and its disamalgamation. It will face any trial, any sacrifice, perform any prodigy of valor, but only under leaders or for countries not its own. To this day the Jews expelled from Spain in 1492 and the rest of Jewry have separate synagogues."

"Impugning Jewish character as material of American citizenship, Dr. Evans should know that the scattered Jewries of the world - what I term the Diaspora - are notoriously ultra-nationalistic. Were such a thing possible, American Jews would be, not 100 per cent, but 200 per cent American. I should like Dr. Evans to study the character of 'Baron Gripstein' in my play, 'The Cockpit' (Europe), designed as a pendant to 'The Melting Pot.' Gripstein is an international Jewish financier-the first, I venture to think, truly depicted in art - who, at the outbreak of war, at once became the greatest chauvinist in the country, and was made president of the man power board."

## A JEWISH PLEDGE

"I also would refer the Klan chieftain to a scene in the pendant play, 'The Melting Pot,' showing how Americanism, the love of the stars and stripes, is stamped into the hearts of Jewish children. 'David,' in this scene, describing in moving accents how he saw Jewish school children saluting the American flag, accurately reports them as saying:

'Flag of our great republic, guardian of our homes, whose stars and stripes stand for bravery, purity, truth, and union, we salute thee. We, the natives of distant lands, who find rest under thy folds, do pledge our hearts, our lives, our sacred honor, to love and protect thee, our country, and the liberty of the American people forever.'

"This to hearts, remember, at the most malleable stage. Has the 'Nordic' pledge or oath of the Ku Klux Klan anything better than this pledge of the Jew? Place, not race, I would tell Dr. Evans, forms nationality. Just a few persons on a ship, or in a railway car, traveling for some time together, strike up a camaraderie, a fellowship, a social loyalty, that is neither more nor less than the embryonic stuff of nationality. So wonderful is the attachment of the human affections to place, that I have known Jewish refugees, though prosperous in other lands, smitten with grief over the misfortunes of the very countries whence they had fled from persecution."

### NEGRO ABLE TO RISE

"Negroes, in Dr. Evans' *ipse dixit*, cannot attain the Anglo-Saxon level-cannot rise. In his view that the negro cannot rise, he is at odds with anthropological science. At the congress of races in London just before the war, it was urged by an eminent anthropologist and unanimously accepted that all races contain the raw materials of development-in other words, can rise. If this is so, the negro can rise, and if he can rise he ultimately can attain the Anglo-Saxon level. It is only a question of opportunity and time."

"Lincoln, writing from Springfield, Il., on Aug. 24, 1855, to Joshua F. Speed of Kentucky, said: 'I am not a Know-Nothing; that is certain. How could I be? How can anyone who abhors the oppression of negroes be in favor of degrading classes of white people? Our progress in degeneracy appears to me to be pretty rapid. As a nation we began by declaring that all men are created equal. We now practically read it that 'all men are created equal-except negroes.' When the Know-Nothings get control, it will read 'all men are created equal, except negroes and foreigners and Catholics.' When it comes to this, I shall prefer emigrating to some country where they make no pretense of loving liberty-to Russia, for instance, where despotism can be taken pure and without the base alloy of hypocrisy."

"Dr. Evans, if he is to be a good Lincolnian, must enlarge his conception of liberty until it has room not only for all white people, but for all negroes as well. Citizenship for the negro does not mean a premature assumption by him of the burdens of government. It was argued by some that enfranchisement of women would issue in political domination by women. Have we seen it? On the contrary, the majority of women elected to the British house of commons, from Lady Astor upward or downward, have simply their husbands' seats."

### THE MASK AND THE VOTE

"I am amused by Dr. Evans' argument touching the mask. He says it is an eliminator of vainglory and demagogy - a conservant of personal honesty and patriotism. Yet the supreme leader of the Klan, the imperial wizard, does not wear the mask! One is reminded of the Jewish story of the meekest man in Israel, who always walked last in the procession. Dr. Evans renounces the suggestion that the Klan is a political party. He says the members will vote how they like. I will tell him-though I ought not-that if he breaks up the mass strength of the organization he will reduce the organization to futility; it will have no effect whatever; it will be a sham. Either it will have mass strength and mass-action, like the Fascisti in Italy, and thus be a grave danger in America, or it will be nothing."

"I agree with Dr. Evans that what the world transcendently needs is peace. I also agree that American aloofness is no reliable barrier against a war, with America in it. This conclusion is overwhelmingly supported, both by reason and by history. Clear thinking and vigorous pleading we undoubtedly require -thank God for anyone who can supply them! But Dr. Evans has hardly stated his admirable thesis when he proceeds at a stroke to dash the possibility of its realization. Our independence, he avers, 'we shall keep inviolate.' If so, farewell to the hope of world peace."

"To independence inviolate belongs the maternity of war. So long as we have unlimited national sovereignties we can have no form of sovereignty insuring peace. The United States is the key. Lincolnize and federalize the world. Peace presupposes the abolition of passports, vises, frontiers, customs houses, and all other devices that make of the population of our planet a mutual irritation society instead of a co-operative civilization, just as in your separate states. Surrender of so-called sovereign rights is the price of peace, and no lesser price will purchase it. Mock prizes and all other shifts or contrivances will be vain so long as the fetichism of the political frontier restricts and distorts human psychology."

### AN APPEAL TO KLUXISM

"Let Dr. Evans and his followers give up their sectional chauvinism. Let them forego the vision of an American China of monotonous millions of one hundred per-centers. Let them, instead of drawing away from Catholics and Jews, unite with both in reasserting, not an American, nor a Nordic, but the Universal God; let them help to equate religion with life; there is too much politics in religion, too little religion in politics. All good Americans working together-Nordics, negroes, Catholics, Jews-will be none too many to save America from infidelity to her mission of salvation."

"Charitable, is she? Yes; assuredly, above all others. But mankind needs more than doles in aid: it needs ideas; it needs fellowship; it needs oneness and indivisibility of moral strength. America cannot stand out without incurring inexpungeable guilt. No amount of charity, in the sense of money-giving, will save her great name, if she fails in the opportunity and the duty of fellowship. Bryce, in his immortal work on America, likens her to Dante's lampbearer, shedding a radiance upon a path for others to follow. America's lamp has shone for a moment in our dark world; it threatens to go out, leaving a darkness that will be only the more tragically and tangibly felt."

## III

### TERRE HAUTE MAYOR TALKS

Ku Kluxism and anti-Ku Kluxism are aligned against each other frontally throughout Indiana. Politically there will be a pitched battle between them this year. One of the outstanding protagonists of the forces opposed to the klan will be Ora D. Davis, mayor of Terre Haute, lawyer, champion of good citizenship, a genial, rather bashful giant six feet three inches tall and weighing more than 200 pounds. Mayor Davis, a Republican, is the first man to declare his candidacy for the governorship in the approaching election, and he stands on a platform of uncompromising opposition to the klan.

"This organization, boasting all the time of its Americanism, seems strangely alien to me," said Mayor Davis, foe of red lighters and gamblers, speaking to the writer the other day in Terre Haute. What could be less American and less intelligible to American common sense than are the regalia, the insignia and the nomenclature of this order? What has Americanism to do with masked faces, cryptic mummeries and such terms as 'giants,' 'grand dragons,' 'night hawks,' 'wizards,' 'cyclops,' 'titans' and 'terrors'? Are the tar bucket, the whip, the rope and the boycott accepted paraphernalia of Americanism? They say they are Christian. Are these things not more pagan than Christian? Do they not date from a time before Christianity was known."

## STYLES KLAN AS ANTI-AMERICAN

"It will hardly do, in the light of the facts- this affirmation of a klan monopoly of Americanism and Christianity. I shall fight the klan, and I ask no quarter from it. In my opinion, far from being American, it is utterly and dangerously anti-American. It smacks of the primordial and the barbaric. Mind you, I am not quarreling with any individual klansman; thousands of upright citizens may have felt justified in joining the organization; many have joined it, to my certain knowledge, under a misapprehension of its purposes. I am not against the individuals in the klan; I am against the klan. I am against it as an institution, and especially as an institution that pretends to domineer over our politics. I am against it in its quality as an 'invisible empire."

"All the people, not part of the people, are the care of our federal constitution and of the constitutions of the states-at any rate, the constitution of the State of Indiana. Lincoln had it right in his ever-quoted description of our government as 'a government of the people, by the people, and for the people.' Religious tests always have been repugnant to American political conceptions. Our Indiana constitution says, 'All men shall be secured in their natural rights to worship Almighty God according to the dictates of their own consciences,' and 'No religious test shall be required as a qualification for any office of trust or profit,' and 'The courts shall be open,' and 'In all criminal prosecutions the accused shall have the right to a public trial by an impartial jury in the county in which the offense was committed, to be heard by himself or counsel, to demand the nature and cause of the accusation against him, and to have a copy thereof; to meet the witnesses face to face, and to have compulsory process for obtaining witnesses in his favor.' "

## DENOUNCES OATHS TO "EMPEROR"

"These constitutional provisions did not come into existence accidentally. They issued from history. They sprang from man's experience in society. They represent a freedom-loving people's effort to establish and fortify its freedom in law. Evils and tyrannies preceded them- see these things strewn all along the course of democratic evolution. Now the klan is striking at these fortifications. It is laying siege to the citadel of fundamental human rights. It is attacking democratic civilization as worked out by the great minds and by the valiant rank and file of the American people. If it could win, we should bid good-bye to Americanism as we have known it and as it has been known to the world."

"Ku Kluxism means an iron-clad oath. This oath is to an 'invisible empire' and its 'emperor.' This 'empire' and 'emperor' deny the accused the right to a public trial, the right to be heard by himself or counsel, the right to demand the nature of the accusation against him, and to have a copy thereof; the right to meet the witnesses face to face; and they also require a religious test as a qualification for office. They therefore deny the right of all men to be secured in their natural right to worship Almighty God according to the dictates of their own consciences. In its entirety, indeed, the klan moves squarely against the constitutional securities of the American commonwealth."

"One is deeply depressed by what plainly awaits us if we travel the path defined by the Ku Kluxers. It leads straight to strife. Strife means the flight of reason and justice and the advent of force. Force cures nothing in the complex structure of human relations. Force only breaks and destroys and smooths the way for passion, oppression and terrorism. Klansmen face backward, not forward. They would march toward the persecutions, the thralldoms, the outlawry, the anarchy and the sanguinary turmoil from which we have escaped. Foretastes of these we have in what klansmen already have done-in their terrorism, their mob violence, their whipping bees, kidnapings and murders."

### RIGHTS OF THE ALIEN

"Real Christian sentiment, not the Christian sentiment of exclusivism and privilege, is what we need in our American life, private and public. To put any section of mankind beyond the pale is not Christian. To monopolize political opportunity is not Christian. Catholicism, Judaism, African blood, so-called alienality of origin-none of these has forfeited by its teachings, still less by its acts, its right to what is symbolized by the American flag. Exponents of all these have played their part in the great constructive political and material achievement called America. Catholics and Jews and negroes and aliens have known how to die for our flag, and anyone who knows how to die for it ought to know how to live for it."

"Need for greater purity, more character, more courage, deeper wisdom in our leaders? Heavens, yes! But Ku Kluxism does not show us how to get these things. It does not show us how to mobilize the best there is in our citizenship. It shows us how to divide our citizenship and to set the divided elements at one another's throats. In order to make the best of our opportunities we want social harmony, not social conflict. If there are bad Catholics, Jews, negroes and aliens, so there are bad protestants, bad Christians, bad white men, bad old-stock Americans. We want all the good women and men together. Tags do not count. Character and ability are the acid and the only test."

### KLAN NOT DEMOCRATIC

"Looking over the klan's pretensions to a sort of quintessential democracy, one wavers between mirth and astonishment. Have these men no grasp of the meaning and the connotation of words, or have they no sense of humor, or do they put the intelligence of some of their followers in the plane of the ape? Democracy! Well, if it is democracy, where does 'His Majesty, William Joseph Simmons, imperial wizard,' get off? What does

'The Aulic of His Majesty' mean? What does 'Emperor of the Invisible Empire, Knights of the Ku Klux Klan, in the Imperial Palace in the Imperial City of Atlanta, Commonwealth of Georgia, United States of America'-what does this jargon signify, if Ku Kluxism is ready to be crucified for pure democracy?"

"I don't like the looks of it. I find nothing democratic in it. I feel its leaders either do not understand the word democracy or are deliberately misleading their people. Ku Kluxism is strong in Indiana, particularly in the rural districts, but I do not think it is strong enough to beat me, if I get the nomination for governor. Even if I did think it was, I hope I need not say I should fight it. It is the duty of every American, in my view, to fight it. This is what I shall urge in the campaign. Even if the plan were not, as I see it, an-un-American and un-Christian organization, there is no call for it in our politics. Secrecy was better kept out of politics. At best it breeds suspicion and is pregnant with evil. God's sunlight ought to be good enough and safe enough for all of us."

"Ku Kluxism has its vicious commercial side. It is a moneymaker for its officers. There is always the temptation for them to sell their nostrum to sufferers from all sorts of ills, real or imaginary. Consider the conditions in different communities. Few communities, indeed, are without their grievances. They are wronged by political cheapjacks and crooks. They are overtaxed. They feel public jobs are multiplied for no other purpose than to fleece the people and keep party machines in good repair and well oiled. Along comes our Ku Klux salesman, looking for $10 a throw. He can cure anything. Just get into the klan and get the klan into politics and you'll have the best possible of situations in the best possible of worlds. It's not a bad spiel, and it has separated many a man from a $10 bill. But these separations, in my opinion, will not be effected so easily in the future. And when the funds dry up the klan will dry up and we shall hear of it no more."

## IV

### PROMINENT KLANSMAN'S VIEWS

"Indiana Ku Kluxers of authority, unlike some of their Texas confreres, have not been giving interviews to the newspapers; their public appeals they have been confining to the platform and to their speeches as reproduced in the klan press. When, after a good deal of difficulty, a prominent Indiana klansman was induced to talk to me, he said:

"Some of us are in the position of Nehemiah building his great wall. You will remember he was asked to come down from the wall and talk things over with his enemies in the plain. He excused himself with these words: 'I am doing a great work. Why should the work cease while I come down to you?' And then Nehemiah's accosters made accusations against him, whereupon he replied: 'There are no such things done as thou sayest, but thou feignest them out of thine own heart.' One of my friends wanted me publicly to debate the question of the klan with him, and I gave him the answer of Nehemiah."

### SAYS KLAN IS FOR PEACE AND LAW

"But I do not object to stating my view of the klan to an impartial inquirer. We are not an aggressive organization. We are a law-loving, justice-loving, peace-loving organization. Our oath binds us to put the law above everything else. Our movement-a purely Christian movement-is looked upon by its members as holding out the hope of the perpetuity of American democracy through a well-informed and conscience-inspired public opinion."

"We have in this country too many laws and too many thoughtless and ignorant lawmakers. Of this fact any lawyer can cite incredible illustrations. When last in Washington I found 20,000 bills awaiting the statute book. These excesses and evils of legislation are destroying the law-loving sense of our people and threatening us with disaster. Federal, state and municipal laws want reduction and simplification. Ku Kluxism is against excessive, oppressive and ignorant legislation."

"Ability and purity in public life are our greatest objectives. Only ability and purity in public life, in our opinion, can save democracy. When we fight for these things, therefore, we are fighting for democracy. Some of my friends say to me, 'How are you going to control your vast organization?' One day, they seem to fear, our hundreds of thousands or millions of American citizens will run amuck. Strange apprehension! Firstly, as I have said, we solemnly bind ourselves to support the government and obey the law; and, secondly, we are a Christian organization, subject to all the moral inhibitions of Christianized mankind."

### A PROGRAM OF BATTLE

"Considering some of the anxieties aroused by the klan, one would think it the only secret organization this country has known. There are many others. They antedate the klan by scores of years. And let me say this: We are not fighting one of them. In the main, we are for things-not against things. As regards other organizations, we are on the defensive. Our sole offensive is for a better-educated, higher-minded, freer and happier people, with a local and national leadership worthy of them. It is not only ignorance and crime we shall fight in our so-called leaders; we also shall fight indifference, evasion, hypocrisy, cynicism, cowardice and lack of vision. These things we regard as peculiarly dangerous to our institutions-quite as dangerous as either ignorance or crime, and, as to most of them, more contemptible."

"You ask me what we are going to do with the Catholics, Jews and negroes. We are not going to do anything with them. We certainly are not going to harm them. Our idea is simply this: Primary responsibility for the preservation and betterment of our form of government rests upon native-born Americans who are white, who are protestants and who are gentiles. This implies no disparagement of other nationalities, races or religions; it is merely a claim for what we regard as the natural political precedence of this country-the precedence of those who mainly made the country. Ku Kluxism asserts the principle that the American political heritage-the heritage that is withstanding the shocks of history so well- must be safeguarded principally by native-born white protestant gentile Americans, who, nevertheless, contemplate no manner of unlawful attack upon the political, social or economic rights of other American citizens."

## WHY SOME ARE BARRED

"Why do we not take Catholics, Jews and negroes into the klan? For very much the same reason, I assume, that protestants are not taken into the Knights of Columbus, nor gentiles into B'nai B'rith, nor white men into Afro-American societies. We have the right, as they have the right, to choose a membership naturally in sympathy with our aims. Our principle of selection, like theirs, is that of natural affinity for the purposes in hand. This principle is universal m human life-in marriage in the family, in business, in professional and social relations and in politics."

"Now, as to newcomers to America. We used to be a melting pot; we are such no longer; melting pots, like other things, have their capacity, and ours has been overreached. Already a large a proportion of our population is foreign born that our country threatens to pass out of the hands of those who built it up and who understand it into the hands of those who had no part in building it up and who do not understand it. There is a great peril here-a great peril to all of us, native and foreign born. Ku Kluxism says the foreign flood must be checked. It says Americanism must be preserved for the good of both those to whom it primarily belongs and those who have sought or may seek its shelter from abroad."

## MASK AS A DEFENSE

"Why do klansmen wear masks? As devices of defense. As yet we are compelled to be on our guard against enemies, for we are misunderstood and maligned. Unprincipled persons are smuggled into the organization to steal its membership rolls. Anti-klan forces, subtle, shrouded in mystery, hitting out of the dark, stop at nothing from defamation of character to boycott and murder. Scores of thousands of our members live on farms without fire or police protection; we cannot expose these members and their families to the perils that would beset them if they were known. We authorize the wearing of masks only in lodge rooms, at funerals and when our members are holding celebrations of their own at specified places with the knowledge of the authorities. I have no doubt the day will come when the klan will be so thoroughly established in public confidence that the mask will be abolished. Meanwhile, within the limits defined, there is no reason of law or public policy why klansmen should not veil their faces if they like."

"Mark you, no sensible spokesman of our order pretends all klansmen are honorable or honest or without offense. As in every other body of men, hooded or un-hooded, disloyalty develops in the klan. Men violate their oaths and injure the organization. Even churches, as every one knows, sometimes fail to keep their communicants in the straight and narrow way. On the other hand, outrages and crimes with which no klansman has anything to do are deliberately committed and charged to the klan to discredit it. We are against bad men of every race and affiliation, and, indeed, especially against those who befoul the fraternity whose chief aim is to strengthen the foundations of democracy and whose principles they have sworn to uphold."

### ASSERTS KLAN OBEYS LAW

"It is asserted that we aspire to usurp the functions of government. We are called an 'invisible empire.' If there are invisible empires about we are not among them. If there are organizations in the United States with attachments or loyalties to ideas and institutions un-American, the Klan is not one. Remember, we swear unqualified allegiance to the constitution of the United States and to every law of the statute book, bad though it may be. Faith in law and obedience to law constitute the core of our creed. It follows that our weapons, whatever the problem, the menace, the fight, are the weapons of the constitution-ballots in the hands of an intelligent and uncoerced electorate. Instead of usurping the functions of government, we are exercising the interest and performing the duty enjoined upon every citizen in a government of the people, by the people and for the people."

"Two points: There are persons who are puzzled and repelled by our regalia and by certain other formal peculiarities of our order, and there are those who accuse us of violating the spirit of the constitution by what they conceive to be our attitude to certain races and religions. Concerning the first point, if we mask our faces, we do not mask our principles; any honest seeker may learn these. There are societies that show their faces, but hide their principles. We deem it of greater importance to the public to know men's principles than to know their names."

### DIFFERENCE NOT INFERIORITY

"Relative to the second point, it would seem to be suggested that our constitution as interpreted by our Supreme Court knows nothing of differences between races and nations. This is contrary to the fact. Our Supreme court has decided that a Japanese cannot be naturalized in the United States and that the so-called 'Jim Crow' law in Mississippi is constitutionally valid. In neither of these cases does the court imply inferiority on the part of the Japanese or the negro; it merely recognizes racial differences and accommodates its reasoning to these differences in the interests of the general welfare. Ku Kluxism adopts an attitude of precisely like nature; its implications are not those of inferiority, but those of difference; and it cherishes no hostility to Catholics, Jews, negroes or foreigners as such."

"To those who would measure our movement and understand our feeling I make this suggestion: Measure the evils from which our political society long has suffered. Measure the impudence of those responsible for these evils. Measure, if you can, the humiliation of the enlightened national conscience. Recall how these evils and this humiliation have been struggled against in vain. Remember the impotence of even the decent and fearless press to purge our public life of vulgarity and crime, not to mention defects on their face less disquieting. Make the measurements intimated and then say to yourself: 'It is against this wide front that the Ku Klux Klan is deploying and deploying with every purpose and hope to triumph.'"

## V

### FOR THE COLORED RACE

"All students of American life and of human relations generally are deeply interested in the grave and urgent problems discussed by Dr. H. W. Evans, imperial wizard of the Ku Klux Klan, and Israel Zangwill, great and high-minded Jew, in The Daily News last Saturday." said Edward H. Morris, distinguished colored lawyer of Chicago, and lifelong thinker on the status of his race among civilized men. Mr. Morris, as his legal confreres in Chicago know especially well, has a mind naturally keen, disciplined by rigorous use, and ripened by forty years of experience at the bar."

"One is pleased to note the good temper with which these controversialists present their respective points of view," continued Mr. Morris. "In what I have to say I trust I shall show myself equally free from heat. At the outset I wish to make it clear that I do not agree with Mr. Zangwill in regarding Dr. Evans as a naive man-an ingenuous man going wrong. On the contrary, I have great respect for Dr. Evans' understanding both of himself and of his movement. I also have a great respect for his power of expression. I should deem him a very formidable pleader upon a public platform."

## RACE, CREED, COLOR ONLY PAWNS

"Ku Kluxism, in my opinion, as apprehended by Dr. Evans and as we see it unfolding before our eyes-is a cold-blooded, deeply-calculated, able bid for political and social domination in this country. Dr. Evans and his friends want to run America. I believe that race, creed and color concern them only as pawns in a game. They think they know how to move these pawns to win the game. Dr. Evans' broad humanitarianism- I may misjudge him, I may be wrong, but I am giving you my honest opinion-seems to me but a smoke screen to hide his real intention. I think he is endeavoring to mass the hatreds of the many for the benefit of the few."

"These Ku Kluxers, as I view them, are men dreaming of lost things and planning to get these things back. They have lost domination. They have lost authority: They have lost power. These possessions have passed into other hands and lie behind almost impregnable defenses. Ku Kluxers want to breach these defenses and seize domination, authority, power. They are dreaming and scheming not only for themselves, but for their children and their children's children; they are taking the long view."

## FEAR TO SHARE VICTORY

"Let us try to analyze their strategy. They are expecting victory. What, they are asking themselves; 'do we want the position to be when we win?' Obviously, they do not want the Jews to be among the victors. The

Jews are the moneymen of the world, the masters of finance, hence powerful in the domain of business and, indeed, in every domain. If the Jews were among the victors, clearly they would be entitled to, and would claim, their share of the spoils of war. Thus the Ku Klux policy is to make them ineligible to membership in this power-seeking organization, with its masks and sheets and picturesque crypticisms. Ku Kluxers, when they win-if they win-desire to dictate to, not to be dictated to by, the Jews."

"If a Ku Klux victory, with the Jews in it, would be barren from the standpoint of the creators and controllers of the klan, so it would be comparatively barren if it succeeded with the Catholics in it. Catholics in this country include the Irish of this country, in the rough reckoning. Irishmen are politicians. They know how to get into and to hold the public offices of great municipalities like Boston, New York and Chicago. If the Kluxers marched to victory with Irish officers and men in their army, who doubts that the Irishmen would demand their share of the spoils? So it befalls that the Ku Klux dream and inclusion of the Irishman become incompatible, and the Irishman is barred from this converging movement upon the places of command over our political and social destinies."

### FOREIGN-BORN LACK GRIEVANCE

"Now as to the foreign-born man in the United States. Why would he not be a source of strength to the Kluxers? Because he has no grievance. Nobody here has done anything to him. He has not lost in America anything he is dreaming of, recovering. He wants to work, to make a living, to carve out a place for himself and for his descendants in his new home. So he is poor material for propagandist and political purposes. He dislikes agitation. He is immune against Ku Klux poison. Included in the klan he would be a constant source of weakness to it, and might prove its disintegration. There is such a thing, you know, as a bit of leaven leavening the whole lump. Hence foreign-born Americans are not wanted in the Ku Klux Klan."

"Finally, let us consider the negro, the colored man. Kluxers look upon the negro as an asset to them in their purposes. By ostracizing him they conceive they have everything to gain and nothing to lose. To be against the negro is to be popular in many circles and over large areas of our country. Ku Klux opposition to the negro means members for the klan. It means members not only in the south but in the north, where our race is beginning to abound. Antagonism to Jews and Catholics is also a member-getting influence for the klan. Exaggeration of the evil character of the immigrant has the same effect, for thousands of Americans fear the immigrant and think we should slam, bar and bolt the door against him."

## CALLS DESPOTISM REAL AIM

"Elimination of elements that would be embarrassing if co-victors, and the skillful play upon prejudice and antipathy in building up an obedient mass of citizens-these seem to me the outstanding features of Ku Klux leadership. If this leadership underlines nobility of sentiment, it is only in the hope that its actual aims will pass unnoticed. What it contemplates is despotism-a fact not left to inference, but avowed. Dr. Evans plainly tells us he prefigures an exclusive Nordic rule in this land, which our greatest minds always have thought of as a laboratory of democracy-a place where the humblest might attain the stature of a man. I say to Dr. Evans: We do not want your despotism, benevolent as you might wish it to be; we have no confidence in the power of even the strongest and wisest of human leaders to create and maintain despotisms really benevolent."

"Perhaps I may say a word more particularly about my own race. Dr. Evans avers it cannot attain the Anglo-Saxon level-cannot rise. Our English alphabet came from the Egyptian ancestors of the colored people; some intelligence must have been there. Pushkin, greatest of Russian poets, had hair curlier than mine, and so did the quadroon, Dumas, master of romantic fiction-both negroid, with the most pronounced negroid characteristics. St. Augustine, greatest of the Latin fathers, one of the most powerful minds the world has seen, the man who molded the spirit of the Christian church for centuries, the man to whom, in the Reformation, protestants and Catholics alike appealed-St. Augustine was the son of the saintly Monica, and today would be called colored."

### CITES EXAMPLE OF MOSES

"Moses did not think ill of the colored people; he married an Ethiopian woman. We find the story in the twelfth chapter of Numbers. Miriam and Aaron, Moses' sister and brother, did not like his choice of a wife; their sympathies were like those of Dr. Evans. They made complaint. Becoming seditious over the matter, they intimated that the Lord had spoken as certainly by them as by Moses. Thereupon the Lord, appearing in a cloud in the door of the tabernacle, gave emphatic sanction to Moses as his servant; his anger was kindled against Miriam and Aaron, and he departed."

"Josephine, wife of Napoleon, was a creole; intelligence and charm she must have had. Alexander Hamilton, our greatest master of public finance and a lawyer of primary eminence, was born in the West Indian island of Nevis, and today would be called a colored man. His mother was a Huguenot of colored blood. J. J. Wright, in the 1870s, was one of the three members of the Supreme Court of South Carolina, wrote a large number of its opinions, and established his legal learning and soundness of judgment in almost every Supreme court in the United States."

"Owassa Tanner, son of Bishop Tanner, is one of the great artists of the world, his masterpiece, Daniel in the Lions' Den, winning recognition in the celebrated galleries of home and foreign cities. Coleridge Taylor, an English black, is known throughout the musical world as a composer; and Roland Hayes, singer, is without a superior and with few peers. These and many other examples from ancient and modern life demonstrate the falsity of the assertion that colored blood incapacitates its possessor for distinction and for usefulness in the spheres of politics and art."

## SEES RELIGION RULE POLITICS

"I am with Mr. Zangwill and against Dr. Evans on the question of immigration. Immigration has built up this country, and we need more of it. To shut it out is to shut many of our factory doors. I am with Mr. Zangwill for the universal as against the Nordic God. Dr. Evans' assertion that the klan separates church and state I cannot grasp, for his whole idea seems to be that of a controlling political body inspired by an exclusive religious faith. If this is not, essentially, union of church and state, what is it?"

"I agree with both Dr. Evans and Mr. Zangwill in their conclusion that what the world transcendentally needs is peace. I agree with them that every great war is virtually certain to involve America, and that American statesmen, therefore, should support with vigor and pertinacity the world peace movement, even if we had no duty to others than ourselves. Isolation is a false light in the marsh; only foolish and dangerous public men will follow it-dangerous because they lead, if they lead at all, in the direction of calamity for the people."

"I am against Mr. Zangwill and with Dr. Evans on the point of our independence. I feel we cannot usefully impair our independence in the present state of human society. I would have America in world affairs, but would make the experiment gradually and with sagacity. We are too ignorant of other peoples and of the complexities of diplomacy to rush in. Yet our very ignorance, considering our interests and obligations, makes it our duty to learn, and we cannot learn while holding aloof-while, as it were, remaining away from school."

**CALLS ALL HUMANITY ONE**

"How I wish our people and every people might lay hold of the supreme political, social and economic fact that humanity is one! It is often on our lips, this saying, but it has slight, if any, lodgment in our minds. Sometimes my colored brethren say to me, 'Let us build a city of our own; let us withdraw somewhere into a corner, where we may be by ourselves and have peace.' Ah, I say to them, 'you are playing with fancies. We can have no such thing as a city of our own. In all the world there are no corners where any section of mankind may live in isolation. We are dependent upon the whites, the whites upon us, and all races and nationalities upon one another.' As expressive of the truth about all major human influences, as well as about freedom, I quote to my brethren these lines:

'When a deed is done for freedom.

Through the earth's broad, aching breast

Runs a thrill of joy prophetic.

Trembling on from east to west.' "

[Israel Zangwill was one of the most renowned Jewish writers and political activists of the early 20th century. Born on January 21, 1864 in London, he spent his earlier years on the East End of London, teaching at the Jewish Free School.

Zangwill graduated from the University of London in 1884, and began a career in journalism, eventually evolving into a writer and playwright of notable distinction. Numbered among his novels, Children of the Ghetto, two Ghetto Tragedies works, Dreamers of the Ghetto, Ghetto Comedies, and The King of Schnorrers were published between 1892 and 1907. His most memorable play was The Melting Pot, which was first brought to the theater in 1908.

Specific to Zangwill's concerns regarding the place of the Jewish people, he helped to form the Jewish Territorial Organization in 1905. The primary goal of this organization was to find a homeland for all Jews. Although he did not live to see his dream become a reality, his organization was credited with bringing thousands of Jewish immigrants to the United States in the early 1900's. Israel Zangwill died on August 1, 1926.]

Reprinted from THE OUTLOOK, March 7, 1928

# Afterword

Illustration TAKING TO THE WOODS by Kirby in the New York World

## THE KLAN UNMASKED

Kleagles, Kludds, and Kligraps must carry on bare-face hereafter for white supremacy, for Protestantism, and for "wholesome patriotism based upon the great fundamentals of Americanism." This is the order of Dr. Hiram Wesley Evans, of the Imperial Kingdom; it is to be "unlawful for any klansman to wear any mask or visor," and all the faithful are "forbidden to fraternize with or remain in Klannish fidelity to brethren who may still like to remain incognito."

At the time the Imperial Wizard revealed the formation of a new order or degree of Klannishness- the Knights of the Great Forrest. Dr. Evans said that the change had been under consideration for some time and that it was in preparation for "new and larger activities." Initiation fee is $1 a head. Membership is compulsory.

Reprinted from THE OUTLOOK, November 12, 1930

## Kollapse of the Klan

According to a recent news story in the Washington Post, the Ku Klux Klan is skidding dizzily toward oblivion. Its membership is estimated at 35,000, a figure which speaks volumes of the decline since the grand days of 1925 when the Kluxers were supposed to number about 9,000,000 and funds rolled into headquarters in freight cars.

Whether the Kluxers are really but 35,000 strong today we do not know. Nor do we know whether they numbered 9,000,000 in their heyday. If they did, if the order founded in Georgia eleven years ago by William Joseph Simmons and promoted by Edward Young Clarke attained this degree of success in five or six years, one can understand why Simmons is eager to imitate the Klan with his new organization, the Caucasian Crusade.

The crusade was launched a few months ago to "perpetuate the white man's distinctive ideals, social supremacy and economic interest - in all things." It began with an appeal to "sovereign, upright white men of true blood," to "real, red-blooded white Americans, inside and outside." We suppose that, by this time, thousands of real, sovereign, upright, white men of true red blood, white inside and outside, are on their way, purse in hand, into the new organization, and we suppose that that is nothing to run a temperature about. For, whatever has happened to the Ku Klux membership list, nothing has happened to the Ku Klux state of mind. It is still very much with us, and as long as it persists will find some means of organized expression. The ignorant and the bigoted might as well flock into the Caucasian Crusade as into anything else. Simmons always gave his Kluxers, and doubtless will give his Crusaders, a pretty good run for their money.

www.IDEAMENPRODUCTIONS.com

"When the police found him, even his mother couldn't identify the body."

"She stalked the bottle clubs and clip joints of Chicago and laughed as she bludgeoned her victims senseless with a flailing blackjack.

She was beautiful, she was brutal - and she was a Hellcat."

Meet Ellie Jarman, the FBI's "most wanted" dame of 1952 and just one of the female killers, hopheads, gun molls, and party girls in

# Hellcats, Vixens, & Vice Dolls

**Women, Crime, and Kink of the Fifties**

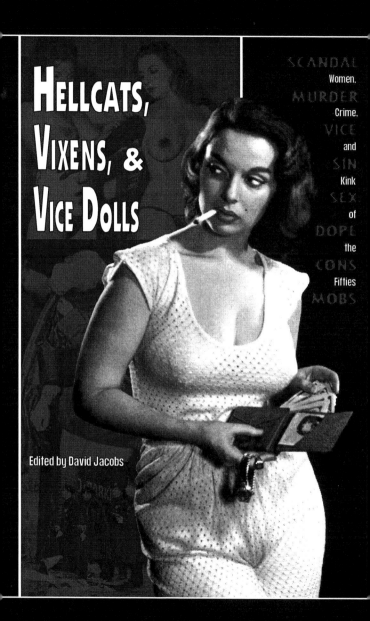

Made in the USA